Dr. Yocum
Teaches the
Epistles of Paul

Volume II

Other books by Dr. Dale Yocum include:

Armies of God
Ask the Animals
Conformed to Christ
Creeds in Contrast
Dr. Yocum Teaches the Epistles of Paul, Vol. I
Fruit Unto Holiness
God, the Master Scientist, Vols. I and II
Hijacker in the House
The Holy Way
Job: The Perfect Man
Study Notes From My Bible, Vols. I and II
This Present World
True and False Tongues

Dr. Yocum Teaches the Epistles of Paul

Volume II

Dr. Dale M. Yocum

ISBN 0-88019-297-6

Schmul Publishing Co., Inc.
Wesleyan Book Club   1992   Salem, Ohio

Dr. Yocum
Teaches the
Epistles of Paul

Volume I
Contents

Romans
I Corinthians
II Corinthians
Galatians

Dr. Yocum Teaches the Epistles of Paul. Copyright © 1992 by Ilene Yocum. All rights reserved. Printed in the United States of America. No part of this book may be used or reproduced in any manner whatsoever without written permission except in the case of brief quotations embodied in articles and reviews. For information address:
Schmul Publishing Co., Inc.,
Box 716, Salem, Ohio 44460-0716

Printed by
Old Paths Tract Society, Inc.
Shoals, Indiana 47581

DEDICATED
to

Andrea L. Marshall
Alyssa R. Marshall
Ashley J. Marshall
Deanna M. Russell

Granddaughters of the author
who dearly loved their Grandfather,
DR. DALE M. YOCUM

His influence on their lives
is greatly cherished

Table of Contents

Preface
Introduction

Ephesians 1

Philippians 49

Colossians 69

I Thessalonians 97

II Thessalonians 115

I Timothy 131

II Timothy 169

Titus 197

Philemon 217

Hebrews 229

Preface

Dr. Dale M. Yocum's teaching outlines on the Epistles of Paul give us new insights into the best thoughts of God's choice servant, the Apostle Paul.

Paul's depth of wisdom and contribution to the Christian church is probably greater than that of any other single human being. In his letters he dealt with many emergency situations that called forth challenge and correction. And he wrote letters in prison where he had long expanses of time to develop and articulate his vision of God's Good News.

In Volume I, under Dr. Yocum's skillful guidance, we are given the Gospel in Paul's most comprehensive and logical presentation (Romans). We learn abiding principles of church discipline, worship and doctrine (Corinthians). We examine the writings of Paul dealing with Christian liberty as it is compared and contrasted to lawlessness and legalism (Galatians).

In Volume II, we discover how human perfection can never be a result human techniques and efforts but can only be available through the all-sufficiency of Christ. We observe the church as it mounts up with Christ and joins in the unity of all things in Him (Ephesians). We are warmed by Christian fellowship (Philippians). We trace the manner in which solutions to problems are available to us as Christians (Thessalonians). We hear the wise counsel of a mature minister finishing his ministry to a young minister (Timothy). We are given insights into order in the Church (Titus). We enjoy a letter of charm, courtesy, and grace in regard to a transformed servant (Philemon). And we exult in the priesthood and sacrifice of Christ (Hebrews).

Dr. Yocum is well-known in numerous ways—as teacher, college and missionary administrator, preacher and writer. Yet there is a focus both to his life and the varied roles he lived. Whether living, speaking or writing, his keen mind always discerned the relevant biblical principles.

In bringing ancient truths to bear upon present needs, Dr. Yocum uses an organized and logical approach to show the relevance of Christ's message to all of us today. He does not proclaim a new teaching but gives fresh insight into the wisdom of the ages. Thus we are led to the living and eternal Word that nourishes all those who feed on it today.

R. Duane Thompson
Professor of Philosophy and Religion
Indiana Wesleyan University
Marion, Indiana

Introduction

Dr. Yocum's lifelong practice of keeping a daily diary began while he was a child in grade school. Bible study notes from the inspiration of his personal devotions are to be found among his papers from a very early age. These entries and notes have been an invaluable source for confirming points as books have been in the process of publication.

Dale Yocum was, first of all, a student. He loved learning and felt constrained to preserve any inspiration for future inspiration, refining, and sharing.

Secondly, he was a teacher. His love and aptitude for teaching doubtless came, in part, from his heritage: his maternal and paternal grandfathers were teachers as well as both parents and three sisters.

The teaching notes and outlines contained in these two volumes have needed almost no editing. They were prepared originally for the students of Jesus Korea Holiness Seminary in Seoul, Korea. Because he taught through an interpreter, it was all the more important that the ideas and concepts be clear and easily understood. Some of Dr. Yocum's colleagues believed he had a God-given ability to take profound and complex concepts and communicate them as inspiring and easy-to-understand truths.

If Dr. Yocum could write the introduction to these volumes, it would be his hope and prayer that these studies not only increase our knowledge but also increase our concept of the worthiness of Christ and the abundance of the provision He made for our learning and edification through the inspiration of the Apostle Paul.

Mrs. Ilene Yocum

The Epistle to the
EPHESIANS

Introduction

I. Author

There are some who deny Pauline authorship because the vocabulary and style differ from other epistles Paul wrote. However, the fact that he wrote this while in prison with plenty of time to formulate and phrase the letter can easily explain any differences. The letter is so exalted in matter and style that it is very doubtful that anybody other than Paul either would or could have written it. We may therefore safely assign it to his authorship.

II. Recipient

There is much doubt as to whom the recipient is; it is the consensus that it was not written specifically to the Church at Ephesus. It seems rather that it was written to Laodicea.

   A. Reasons for doubt

   1. There are no personal references to anyone at Ephesus, as there are in Paul's other epistles. This is strange, considering that Paul was at Ephesus for at least three years (Acts 20:31). He held the Ephesians in high regard, as is shown in his meeting with the elders at Melita (Acts 20:17-35). Yet, in this epistle there is no salutation in keeping with his feelings for the Ephesians.

   2. This seems to have been a circular letter, treating material he wanted all the churches to have. It is in substance an elaboration of the theme of Colossians, which was written at about the same time.

B. The Church to Whom it was Addressed
It seems likely that this letter was in reality addressed to the Laodiceans (see Col. 4:16 where it is plain that he wrote a letter to Laodicea). It is possible that he sent other copies with a blank in the place of address, and that the Ephesians filled in their name in one, thus linking their name with the letter.

III. Background

A. Time of Writing
The date is uncertain. What is known is that it was written from prison and probably from Rome, where Paul had time to write and even to preach (see 6:19, 20). Whether it was his first or second imprisonment is not known. Paul was martyred in 65 or 66 A.D., and it is believed he wrote this epistle between 61 and 65 A.D.

B. Occasion for Writing
In Colossians Paul wrote of the all-sufficiency of Christ. This epistle is similar and dwells on the unity of all things in Christ. A key passage is 1:9, 10. Paul was in a world of many divisions, particularly the separation of Jews and Gentiles. There were divisions within the churches with which he had to deal. In writing to Colossians it perhaps occurred to him how all things are united in Christ, so he elaborated on the theme here in this epistle. He seeks for Christian maturity.

The poet Samuel Coleridge, in speaking of this epistle, said that it is the "divinest composition of man." Others have called it "the queen of the epistles."

J.A. Stewart says the seven letters of Paul to the churches form a mountain range, and Ephesians is the highest peak. Romans and Ephesians are doctrinal, whereas the other five deal with problems in the churches. Galatians is the appendix to Romans, and Colossians is the appendix to Ephesians. Ephesians is a progression from Romans. In Romans we have the believer dead, buried and risen with Christ; in Ephesians the believer is ascended with Christ.

IV. Suggested Outlines

A. By J.A. Stewart ("The Alps of the New Testament," *Bible Study Handbook*, Christian Efficiency Course #5, p. 19)

   1. Introduction, 1:1-3

   2. The Heavenly Calling, 1:3-3:21

3. The Earthly Walk, 4:1-6:9
4. The Spiritual Conflict, 6:10-28
5. Conclusion, 6:21-24

B. By Graham Scroggie ("The Alps of the New Testament," p. 27)
   1. The Christian Age—Doctrinal (1:3-3:21)
      a. The Origin of the Church (1:3-14)
      b. The Glory of the Church (1:15-23)
      c. The Character of the Church (2:1-10)
      d. The Progress of the Church (2:11-22)
      e. The Function of the Church (3:1-13)
      f. The Fulness of the Church (3:14-21)
   2. The Christian Life—Practical (4:1-6:24)
      a. The Calling of the Christian (4:1-16)
      b. The Conduct of the Christian (4:17-6:9)
      c. The Conflict of the Christian (6:10-24)

The Study of the Epistle to the Ephesians

I. Introduction

A. Identification of Himself as an Apostle

1. Its Definition
   An apostle is one who has a special commission to fulfil on behalf of a higher authority. There were those who challenged Paul's apostleship, but it was an unalterable and undubitable fact in his own mind.

2. Its Source
   Paul was an apostle by the will of God. He could do no other than fulfil such a task. It amazed Paul that he was chosen for such a purpose, but he was absolutely positive it came from Christ; therefore he could say, "Woe is me if I preach not the Gospel."

B. Identification of the Receivers as "saints and faithful"

1. The word "saint" comes from the same root as "sanctify" and means to be set apart to a sacred purpose and to be made pure. Charles Hodge (*Systematic Theology*, Vol. 3, Grand Rapids: Wm. B. Eerdman's, p. 225) says, "The word signifies clean, pure morally, consecrated . . ." So it is evident that when God calls men out of sin, He calls them not only to deliverance but to spiritual advancement and maturity as well.

2. The word "faithful" refers to stability and perseverance. It is not enough to be delivered from sin; we must abide and grow. Such is the tenor of New Testament Scripture.

C. Benediction of Grace and Peace

The first aspect refers to the gift of spiritual beauty, and the second refers to the state of freedom from agitation that comes from sin. It includes security and prosperity.

II. The Destiny of the Church, Chapter I

Verse 3 to 14 is one single sentence in the Greek. It is difficult to analyze logically, for Paul is not following logical thought so much as he is soaring poetically from one height of inspiration to another. He allows himself to follow one thought, then another, as they are impressed upon his mind. It is a superb passage of inspiration and exalted thought.

A. The Source of the Destiny, vv. 3, 4

God the Father has planned for the future of the Church. Several terms are used to indicate His planning: chosen (v. 4), predestinated (v. 5), his good pleasure (v. 9) purpose (v. 9), the counsel of His own will (v. 11). All are related to the same idea and show how magnificent a thought it is.

The eternal God made His plan "before the foundation of the world." The term plainly means it was done before God created the world. It was settled from eternity. God's plan, which is so magnificent, so vast and glorious, was not conceived as a sudden afterthought because of an emergency situation. In the deliberateness of God's eternal abiding place, God worked on this plan. It is thus a perfect plan, with forethought having been given to its adequacy, perfection, and durability. Now such a plan embraces us. No wonder the writer is moved to bless God from the first utterance about such a plan!

B. The Blessings Included In the Destiny, vv. 3-14

Every heavenly, spiritual blessing is from God. We are here given an array of wondrous spiritual blessings that are heavenly in their origin and effect.

1. He has chosen us to holiness, v. 4. It is important to recognize who is meant by "us." It is repeated often in this passage and refers to the group who is predestinated, who is made accepted, who have made known to them the mystery of His will. Considering what all is said of "us," it is evident that it refers to all Christians. It refers to the corporate church; some Jews and some Gentiles are surely included.

    The purpose of our choosing was that we should be "holy and without blame before Him in love." This is a fine expression of the importance and meaning of holiness.

    "Holy" means to be separated, different, and pure from sin. It means to be set apart from ordinary use to a special purpose, and for that reason it cannot be that the holy one is just like others. It must be "meet for the Master's use" and thus cleansed from sin. Here at the beginning of the epistle there is the issue of our difference from the rest of the world. At a time when so much of so-called Christianity is just like the world, we should ask ourselves if we are ready to be truly different. In Paul's day the difference was such that Christians were hunted and killed by the world. They were to expect such treatment, and consecration to walk with God involved a willingness to be so persecuted. There is something within the natural moral disposition of man which shrinks from being different in this way; thus the necessity of purging.

"Blameless" is a sacrificial word which referred to the animals that were brought to God's altar. They were to have no defects such as lameness, scurvy, or sickness. They had to pass inspection before they could be offered. Just so, we must be examined before God and be acceptable to Him. This means that every part of our life must be acceptable and a fit offering to God. It applies to our human relations, our habits, our pleasures, our home life, our thoughts, our desires, our ambitions, etc. As Barclay says, "This word does not mean that the Christian must be respectable; it means that he must be perfect."

"In love." Love must be the motivation for all that is done. There will be areas in which men make mistakes and fall short of the absolute perfection of God, but it is interpreted through the love of the heart. "Love is the fulfilling of the law." Christian perfection then is basically perfection of love. If we love Him we will keep His commandments, and they are not grievous.

"Before Him." Fortunately, we are not judged by men as to our perfection but by God. He sees the motives, the love of the heart. Men *do* judge us, and they often do so improperly because they cannot see our hearts. "Man looketh on the outward appearance, but God looketh on the heart."

2. He has predestinated us to adoption, v. 5. "Predestination" is one of the doctrinal words which has been grossly misinterpreted by some. It has been taken to mean that some are determined to be saved and could not be lost, while others are determined to be lost and could never be saved, "all to the praise of His glorious justice." That would be a fearful doctrine indeed, which Paul surely does not have in mind when he bursts forth with such praise to God for His eternal purpose (v. 3). The word does not denote inevitability, however, but rather possibility and desirability. It is advance planning for a worthy human destiny. God has planned far in advance a scheme of salvation whereby all men may be recovered from sin and made heirs of eternal life. It embraces all men, but only those

who receive it will be moved as Paul to praise God for it. Cf. I Tim. 2:4, 5.

"Adoption" was a very important ceremony under Roman law. The father had absolute authority over the sons in his family, and when he died the rights went to the sons. When one was adopted, his old family relationships were gone forever, and he was considered a new person. Old debts were canceled and full rights in the new family were established. This is one of the aspects of our being saved from sin: the family relationship. Justification gives the right of sonship; regeneration the nature of sonship; and adoption the privilege of sonship. Justification removes guilt; regeneration changes our hearts; and adoption brings us into the family of God.

"According to the good pleasure of His will." Here is introduced an expression of measure. What God has done has been limited or measured only by what He desired to do. He was pleased with what He did in bringing sons into His family. There were no limits upon Him except His own will! He was not required to do what He did; there was no constraint upon Him whatsoever. His plan was out of the desire of His own heart. We humans are so limited in what we do, but God is not, except by His own will.

3. "He hath made us accepted," v. 6. It has already been mentioned that we must be blameless before the eye of God. This could never be of us in our natural state, and our state could never be changed by our own will. The marvel is that "He hath made us accepted." He has actually planned to make us so that we are acceptable before Him. There is much talk about men accepting Christ and yet going on in their sins. It is an erroneous concept, for God works to make us accepted and acceptable.

4. He hath redeemed us through the blood of Christ, v. 7. Here is the most basic yet the most profound truth of the Christian gospel.

Redemption means to be brought out of a situation where we are helpless and doomed. It applied both to prisoners or to condemned criminals. In the case of sinners, both senses were applicable, for we were both prisoners of our passions, and we were under sentence of death. It is the blood of Christ which availed and set us free!

Forgiveness of sins is not the whole of redemption, for the term also includes other aspects of salvation, even to our final glorification in heaven (Rom. 8:23). But this is the major initial part of redemption, one that should evoke the greatest wonder and praise. One who has known the burden of an accusing guilty conscience will appreciate the relief that comes with forgiveness. Shakespeare described the burden of guilt in these lines from *Richard the Third*:

"My conscience hath a thousand several tongues,
And every tongue brings in a several tale,
And every tale condemns me for a villain."

When guilt is forgiven, our tongues are free to praise the Lord!

"Riches of His grace" is the measure of forgiveness. He is not limited by the greatness of our sin but only by His ability to be gracious, which is rich indeed!

"Wisdom and prudence" were important words for the Greek thinkers. The first referred to knowledge of the most precious things, while the second referred to knowledge of practical things. In relation to God it refers to the wise plan He designed and to the foresight He had in ability to carry it to a perfect conclusion. Some can plan elaborately but execute poorly. He can both plan and execute, and He has done so. The problem requiring His great wisdom was the problem of how to uphold law and manifest love at the same time. If He enforced the law on sinners, His love would be thwarted; if He forgave without fulfilling the law, justice would be violated. He perfected a plan for upholding justice, manifesting love, and displaying mercy.

5. He hath revealed His wise purpose, vv. 9, 10. That purpose is to bring all things into unity in Christ. It has not been manifest before. There is in the world so much of conflict: between men and animals, between men and men, between men and God, even between the angels. History has been much marked by warfare, conflict, and senseless conduct, so much so that men deny any purpose in history. But Paul says that history has a plan, that God is bringing history to a grand climax when all divisions shall be removed. Animals will be at peace with men, who will be at peace with each other and with God.

"Dispensation" means literally "Household management." In those days there was a steward who planned household affairs so that everything was orderly and purposeful. So Paul declares that there is wise planning which is working toward a consummation in history—the fulness of times. Heaven and earth will be joined in perfect unity at that time. The time has not arrived yet, and so it is often hard to see the working of the plan. That is why Paul calls it a mystery, which means secret. Men do not see it yet, but we know by revelation that the plan is being worked out and that one day we will share in its glorious fulfillment.

Barclay says that vv. 9 and 10 are a summary of the entire epistle ("The Letters of the Galatians and Ephesians," *The Daily Study Bible*, Edinburgh: The St. Andrew Press, 1954, p. 96).

6. He hath given us an inheritance, vv. 11-14. Here Paul dwells on the first example of the unifying power of God through Christ. The Jews and Gentiles are united. In these verses the "we" refers to the Jews and the "ye" refers to the Gentiles.

    "Inheritance" refers to a spiritual inheritance. The inheritance in the land of promise was by lot, and the term means an appointment by lot. The Jews who first believed in Christ have their inheritance and are to the praise and glory of Christ, in that they are the means by which the news of salvation has been brought to the Gentiles. This fact is revealed in Isa. 43:21, "This people have I formed for myself; they shall show forth my praise." It was to the discredit of the Jews that most of them became proud and self-centered and wanted to keep religion to themselves, and so lost the revelation of Christ to them. Those who did receive Christ now have the glorious privilege of sharing Him with the Gentiles. The Gentiles also have an inheritance; the lot includes them as well as the Jews.

7. He hath sealed us with His Spirit, v. 13. A seal on a document or shipment is for the purpose of assuring the genuineness or authenticity of it and to preserve it from being taken away. It preserves the object intact. The Holy Spirit in our hearts shows that we are of God, and He keeps us in the will of God. He is the evidence to us of these facts, and His fruit is the evidence to others. It is the image of Christ which is impressed on our inward characters.

8. He hath given us the earnest of the Spirit, v. 14. "Earnest" was a down payment which gave assurance that the entire amount would be paid. (For the use of the pledge in the Old Testament, see Gen. 38:13-18.) In this passage it means that with the Holy Spirit dwelling within our heart and producing the character of Christ, there is: a) a little foretaste of the fulness of our inheritance in Heaven, and b) the assurance that we will be admitted to the fulness of our inheritance. The joy, peace,

assurance and love which we now have in our hearts through the Holy Ghost are an earnest of that which is ours through Christ, which we will realize in full some day. Without the Spirit there is no such right of entering our inheritance.

"Redemption" is used here in the full and final sense, as in Rom. 8:23. The initial purchase of the possession was for the purpose of the final redemption, to the praise of His glory.

C. The Means of Our Destiny, vv. 3-14

Christ is the means whereby the plan of God may be fulfilled. It will be noted that the Father, Son and Holy Spirit all have place in this portion of the epistle. Eleven times in these verses Paul uses the expression "in Christ" or a similar one. Every blessing we have contemplated centers in Christ as the means. It is in Christ that we are chosen to holiness, adopted as children, accepted of God, redeemed from sin, revealed His purpose, and given an inheritance. In Christ Jews and Gentiles may be brought together as one. This grand concept will be developed further in the rest of the epistle. Paul repeats the theme so often it might appear to be monotonous repetition, but it is not that with him; it is a glorious truth that sounds forth like a refrain after every truth presented.

D. The Revelation of Our Destiny, vv. 15-23. Here follows the first of Paul's great prayers for the church. Note that he prays to the Father for the church, first by giving thanks, and then by making request. He gives thanks that they have faith and love that demonstrate genuine saving grace in their lives, but now he prays earnestly that they shall advance in grace. It is characteristic of him, and shown in virtually all his epistles, that he is not satisfied to leave Christians at the level of infancy. He wants them to go on to perfection in quality and advance to maturity in quantity.

1. The Spirit of Revelation, v. 17. The Holy Spirit is the divine teacher, as Jesus told the disciples in John 14:26 and 16:13-15. He "opens the eyes of our understanding." This is a result of purity of heart. See Matt. 5:8. He gives "wisdom, revelation and knowledge." This is a progression from the general to the particular. Revelation is one kind of divine wisdom, and the "knowledge of Him" is one example of revelation. It is the knowledge of God for which Paul is praying. This is an area where the vast majority of professed Christians are woefully lacking today. They may know the creeds, the hymns and prayers of the church, but their eyes are blind to the wondrous beauty of God Himself. Paul knew it would require the inward

work of the Spirit to remove the blindness and increase the revelation of God, so he prayed always for it.

2. The hope of His calling, v. 18. In this phrase the saints seem to be the recipients: He has called us to a wonderful hope. Only by the divine revelation can we have any concept as to what is before us as Christians, and at best our idea is very faint and inadequate. We do see enough, however, to give up every other ambition to reach this goal. For the Christian this hope is not a nebulous uncertainty but solid reality. This hope has become a strong anchor to the soul, causing us to endure joyfully all that may befall us and to press forward with unaltering determination to achieve the prize. See Heb. 6:19.

3. The glory of His inheritance, v. 18. Many interpreters see in this another expression of our riches. However, it appears that Paul means Christ's inheritance—because of what He has done to bring about redemption He has a glorious and rich inheritance. This is mentioned in Psalm 2:8, "Ask of me and I will give thee the heathen [Gentile nations] for thy inheritance." Jesus referred to His desire for this inheritance in John 17:6. In Bible times the inheritance was a parcel of ground which could be used for production of fruit. God wants our lives to be open to His cultivation so that fruit can be borne for His praise. See John 15:8.

4. The exceeding greatness of His power, vv. 19-23

    a. Its demonstration: the resurrection and ascension of Jesus. This is the New Testament standard of God's power. Samuel Chadwick has said, "The biggest thing God has ever done was to bring again from the dead the Lord Jesus Christ. . . . It is the crowning act of God. . . . . He secured for all men the resources of His own inheritance, and made available for all the same power by which He himself had been raised from the dead." (*The Gospel of the Cross*, Kansas City: Beacon Hill Press, 1949, p. 76.) It is an even greater act than creation, for at the resurrection He was opposed by the hosts of Satan, and at creation there was no opposition.

    Jesus was raised from the hell of bearing our sins to the height of the throne of God. Satan had thought that Christ was within his power, but the demonstration of God's power is shown in this act of being elevated above all other powers.

b. Its service to the Church: it is to usward who believe. Through faith in Christ and His victorious work, this same power works in the Church and brings us to the same place of authority He has achieved. This is the concept that we must grasp if we are to have the victory that is ours. It is for this revelation that Paul prayed.

c. Its object: to make the Church effective as His body. He has reached a place of supreme authority where all contrary powers are under His feet.

   1) The right hand of God is a place of supreme authority. See Ex. 15:6, "Thy right hand, O Lord, hath become glorious in power; thy right hand, O Lord, hath dashed in pieces the enemy." (See also Ps. 118:14, 16; Ps. 98:1.)

   2) Under His feet is the place of complete subjection. See Rom. 16:20, "And the God of peace shall bruise Satan under your feet shortly." (See also Josh. 10:24.)

   3) The Church is His body. As a person is not complete with only a head, so the ministry of Christ is not complete unless the Church carries out His victory in the earth. He has the position of authority at the throne of God; He has the power, the wisdom, and victory. But His body is in the earth, carrying out the directive of the head. Just as the operation of the human brain is ineffective unless it can be executed through members of the body, so the position of Christ is made ineffective unless the Church fulfills His purpose. So His power is to usward who believe; His authority is for us; and we are the fullness or completeness of Him. It is His purpose to fill all things; He wants His power and redemption to reach and fill all the earth. But that cannot be unless the Church fulfills His mission for her. No wonder Paul prayed for the Church! How we should pray today that we might be the fullness of Christ in the earth! May we have the faith to appropriate it.

III. The Chronology of the Church, Chapter 2

This chapter is properly an extension of the thought with which the preceding one closed. It traces how the church is brought into the position of Christ through the power manifested in the resurrection—how it is brought out of a despairing past to a glorious and indescribable future.

A. The Past History, vv. 1-13, 11, 12

   1. Of the Gentiles, vv. 1, 2, 11, 12. The "ye" in this passage refers to Gentile Christians. A vivid and awesome description of their hopelessness is given.

      a. "In sin" they were dead. Paul uses the expression "in" frequently. It states our environment or situation. Death describes our condition in that environment. Death applies to our spiritual condition of separation from God. As a corpse is insensitive to voices, beauty, and the fragrance of flowers, so one dead in sin is entirely unmoved by the beauty of Christ, the loveliness of heaven, and the fellowship of the saints. Furthermore, he is totally helpless to do anything about it. He has no desire for God, no love for His Word, no apprehension of spiritual things.

      b. "In this world" they were controlled by the prince of the power of the air. As we advance in this study it will be apparent that Paul refers repeatedly to the organization of satanic powers. they are organized as principalities, powers, etc., but Satan is the prince of all the powers that operate in the heavenly places. Through his effective operation he controls the thinking and actions of men in large measure.

      One of Satan's chief devices in controlling men is "this present world." He has gained such control of the systems of the world and such control over the thinking of men that he keeps them blinded to the spiritual world of God and the world to come. It is in the "children of disobedience" that he works effectively. Just as naturally as human children resemble the traits of their earthly parents, so the men of this world resemble the disobedient spirit of Satan, their spiritual father.

      c. "In the flesh," (v. 11), the Gentiles, like the Jews, were controlled by sinful and depraved desires. They had no covenant promises in which to hope; they were strangers to the rights of Israel, and therefore had no reason to hope for deliverance in Christ, Who came of the stock of Israel.

2. Of the Jews, v. 3. Though they had so much in which to hope, they were also overcome by sin. They lived "in the flesh" although they were in the commonwealth of Israel by right. Living in the flesh, they were controlled by the desires of the flesh and mind. Here is shown to us the extent of human depravity. The mind is a higher faculty of man than the flesh and is to rule over the flesh and control physical activity in accordance with higher objectives. But the Jews were so depraved that not only the fleshly desires but the desires of the mind as well were taking them toward the wrath of God. This was so because of their inner nature, just as children are like their parents. It is clear then that Jews as well as the Gentiles were hopeless, and by nature were destined for wrath. "NO HOPE" can be written over the life of every sinner unless he looks to Jesus for deliverance!

B. The Present State, vv. 4-6, 8-10, 13-22

1. The source of the translation, v. 4. What a difference "But God . . ." makes! There was no hope for us, but God stepped in, not because of our merits or our rights or our works but because He is "rich in mercy." Mercy is that characteristic by which God withholds from us the penalty that is due us. He is *rich* in mercy—it is not a tiny relief that He has grudgingly given us but overflowing relief—the best and most costly gift that God could devise and Heaven could afford! His gift to poor, hopeless sinners is inconceivably great in what it cost Him and in what it brings us in eternal benefits. His great *love* is shown not only in what He spared us from but in what He gives us. It is by His *grace* that we are saved, and not by any works that we can do. The Jews were bent on working out their salvation, but it is shown that no amount of morally good works can save from the guilt of past sins. Salvation is strictly a *gift of God*. We must exercise faith in order to receive salvation, but faith will not operate unless our faculty of faith is quickened by the Spirit of God. Man has no merit to claim in his salvation. All is from God. Man left to himself is hopelessly lost forever.

2. The new position: "with Christ," (v. 5); "in Christ, (v. 6); "through Christ," (v. 7); "by the blood of Christ," (v. 13). All of the treasures from redemption are treasures in Jesus, and we must be living in Him to partake of them. We were in a position of death, and Christ came to that position to be with us (v. 5).

> a. He quickened us. That is regeneration, in which He shared His own life with us.
>
> b. He raised us up. That is the resurrection out of the place of death. Jesus did not regenerate us to leave us *in* sin but to lift us to a place of victory *over* sin. To be alive but still bound in grave clothes and fastened in a tomb would be helpless, but we have been given victory!
>
> c. He made us sit together "in heavenly places in Christ." In this we are identified with Christ in His throne and in His authority. Spiritually we are already there, sharing His victory with Him. Actually we will be raised to share His throne position in the resurrection (Rev. 3:21). The fact that the Church today is to execute the authority of Christ in its conflict with satanic powers is a tremendous contemplation. He sits above them in authority and power, and we share the privilege of His name and authority. May we learn to exercise that authority properly!

3. The purpose: good works, v. 10. We are not saved by our good works, but it is God's purpose in saving us that we should accomplish good works. If there are no good works, there is no evidence of our being regenerated. (See James 2:17-26.) As the body of Christ, we must perform good works in His name to fulfill His earthly ministry. (See John 14:12.)

4. The unity of Jews and Gentiles in Christ, vv. 13-22. There was deep animosity between the two groups, and the Jews considered the Gentiles as the "uncircumcised" and as dogs who were not worthy of salvation. There was a middle wall of partition at the temple between the court of the Gentiles and the inner court of the Jews, and the Gentiles could not pass the partition on pain of death.

   > a. Jesus is "our peace" or peace-maker. He showed His love and brought the two estranged parties together. Not only does He bring Jew and Gentile together, but every other warring segment of the world may be brought into true unity in Him.
   >
   > b. He makes *new men*, meaning new kind of men. He doesn't make Jews into Gentiles or vice versa, but He makes both into Christians.

> c. The cross removes the enmity, v. 16. The cross was completely an expression of love, proving to both Jews and Gentiles that they were hopeless without Christ's death. As a consequence, there is no room for one group to feel superior to the other. Both were lost before the cross, and both can be saved through it. Through the blood of Jesus both are introduced into Christ, and He is not divided. He removes the enmity and replaces it with love.
>
> In v. 18 we have all members of the trinity mentioned, and this theme is enlarged in Chapter 4.
>
> d. The unity is expressed in two figures.
>
>> 1) A household— "the household of God" (v. 19), meaning those who dwell together in one house. The Gentiles were considered foreigners with no rights in the kingdom. Through Christ, both have access. "Access" is a word which referred especially to the admission of a person to the presence of a king by an official at the royal court whose duty it was to introduce those who were to have audience. Christ has done this through the Spirit, Who brings us into His body and into His household. We are not merely introduced to the King but brought into His household.
>>
>> 2) A building (v. 21). God is building the Church as a building. Christ is the Chief Cornerstone who supports all and in Whom all is united. Apostles and prophets have been the foundation, and all of us—Jew and Gentile—are built into this building which God is indwelling.
>>
>> Paul shows how Christ brings unity where sin has brought division, and that unity is to be expressed by the Church. It is Christ's body; it is God's household; it is a holy temple of the Holy Ghost.

C. The Future Hope, v. 7

While the future of the Church is infinite, only a brief reference is made to what that future contains. There is no reference to what Heaven is to be like, but it is stated that in eternity those who have been saved from their sins will be a lasting proof of how boundless are the riches of God's grace in bringing us to Heaven. What a testimony it will be to the power of His love and grace when we see the vast throng of those who have been drunkards, adulterers, idolaters, blasphemers, murderers, etc. all transformed and cleansed by the power of His blood and made fit for a place in His holy kingdom! And it will be all because of His kindness, not for any claim we had on His redemptive power.

IV. Glory in the Church, Chapter 3

This chapter begins with a close connection to Chapter 2. However, at verse 2 Paul begins a digression which continues through verse 13. It is typical of His writing, particularly in this epistle, that he begins a thought, then at the suggestion of a word, he branches off to follow another thought at length before he comes back to his original topic. He is writing more from a majesty of inspiration than from a strict adherence to good grammar.

A. A Glorious Mystery, vv. 1-13

1. The ministry of the mystery, vv. 1-5, 7, 8. Paul himself is the minister. He was a prisoner of the Romans, but the majesty of his task had taken away from him all sense of shame or restlessness. The mission which had been entrusted him made him feel highly humbled and honored. He was a prisoner *of* Christ, *for* the Gentiles. Christ had placed him there for their benefit.

    This is a tremendous disclosure that came to Paul. In all past ages, it had been kept secret, and the Jews did not realize the truth that the Gentiles could ever share equally with them in divine religion. They had considered the Gentiles as fit for slaves at best, and fit for destruction at worst. But now they are shown that Jews and Gentiles are made one.

    Paul wants to make it clear that he did not discover this secret; it was not because of any merit in him that he was to convey this message, for he considers himself the least— less than the least— of all saints. Because of Paul's past, he always considered himself unworthy to be a special messenger of Christ. It was a gift of God's grace that such as he should have any position at all in the Kingdom of God, especially so in view of the highly responsible position that was his.

2. The content of the mystery, vv. 6, 8. The Gentiles are to be equally the recipients of grace, of the same body as the Jews. They are to receive the same gospel of salvation which is essential to the Gentiles. It was extremely hard for the Jews to accept this fact. In fact, many of them refused, and Paul was

put to death primarily for declaring such a thing. But this is the mystery that was purposed eternally in the plan of God. It did not come into being just because the Jews refused the message. That was the occasion for its announcement, but it was formed in the eternal counsel of God.

3. The revelation of the mystery, vv. 3, 5, 9-11. Paul repeats that this truth came by revelation. He did not devise it. He would not have understood such a remarkable truth unless it had been revealed to him. When he was apprehended on the Damascus road Christ said to him, "I have appeared unto thee for this purpose, to make thee a minister . . . delivering thee from the people, and from the Gentiles, unto whom now I send thee . . ." (Acts 26:16, 17).

One of the reasons for God's having kept the secret for so long was in order that the Church should make known the manifold wisdom of God. (The word "manifold" means "many-colored.") God's grace matches every circumstance. His wisdom is always new and inexhaustible. There will always be new revelations for those who live in His presence. This wisdom is revealed to principalities and powers—angelic beings which surround the throne of God. In the infinite wisdom of God there are secrets to be revealed which are inexhaustible and which will eternally demonstrate his excellency.

4. The benefits of the mystery, vv. 9-13

   a. Fellowship, v. 9. The dispensation of the mystery has enabled both Jews and Gentiles to be one in Christ. Where there was once enmity there is now loving fellowship. This fellowship is to be revealed also to the angelic beings who are also the creation of Christ. There is basis for Christian fellowship with them throughout the eternal ages, as we have a common Father and Creator with them. They are anxious to look into the things concerning our redemption. See I Pet. 1:12.

   In some of the Oriental religions there were mysteries into which only an elite group could be initiated. Others were forbidden the knowledge and participation in the secrets of the religion. There are no such prohibitions in Christianity. The inner riches are for all who will enter into them by faith.

      b. Boldness and access to God, v. 12. As shown in 2:18, "access" refers to the royal personage who brings an inquirer into the presence of a king. Now through Christ, not only the Jews but also the Gentiles have such privilege of coming into the immediate presence of God. The Holy of Holies is now open, and the walls of separation have been put away.

      "Boldness" particularly applies to the privilege of speaking in prayer. All—Gentiles and Jews—may now come in prayer boldly to a throne of grace. This was not known until this mystery was revealed. It is only through faith in Christ that this privilege is realized. Those outside of Christ are just as underprivileged as if He had never come.

      c. Glory for the Gentiles, v. 13. Paul mentions this here because he feared they would be depressed and discouraged because of all his sufferings for them. It is true that most of what he suffered in persecutions was because of his taking the Gospel freely to the Gentiles, but the advantages for them were so great that he was happy to suffer to complete the ministry of Christ. He wanted them to rejoice for these great benefits. He also expected to derive eternal benefits for himself, incidentally, for all he was suffering (II Cor. 4:17) so there should be no mournful depression because of it.

B. Glorious Riches, vv. 14-21

    Paul returns here to the thought of v. 1. In view of the wondrous mystery which is now made known concerning the destiny of the Church, Paul prays perhaps the most exalted prayer which was ever uttered by any other than Christ. Let us see some of the riches which come to the church in Christ through faith.

    1. Family membership, v. 15. It follows from the large concept of the Church that the *whole* family, not just the Jews, may call God their Father. The family in Heaven includes the saints who have triumphed before us. They are often called the Church triumphant. The family on earth is called the Church militant. All are in one family. How grand a thought this is! The family relationship is the closest possible one in human circles, and now this divine family is to include all those redeemed by the blood of Jesus. We are all one in Him, from every nation, race and age.

The Church is named after the Father; that is, it is properly called the "Church of God." He is the Father of all, and the Father delights to give good gifts to His children. These exalted requests are made to One who delights to give.

2. Inward strength by the Spirit, v. 16. He has just told them of his desire that they not faint. Here he gives the antidote for fainting: inner strength by the "dunamis," or the Spirit. Note how that strength operated in Paul's own life so that he never surrendered to his opposition, no matter how hellish it became. It can be so in the life of every one of us so that we never retreat from the devil's attacks or yield to the solicitations of this world or weaken through the avenues of the flesh.

   The inner man signified the intellect, the conscience, and the will. In every area of the inner life there is strength for perfect victory.

3. The indwelling of Christ, v. 17. The primary work of the Spirit in the inner man is the revelation of Christ. Jesus said, "He shall not speak of himself . . . He shall glorify me," (John 16:13, 14). To have Christ glorified within the heart is the glory of the Church! There is no higher experience on the earth than to have a revelation of Christ by the Spirit, and that not on a distant throne but within the inner man of the believer himself, manifesting the grace and beauty of His own character there. This is the aim of Christ, that His people should be conformed to Himself (Rom. 8:29), and this does not happen by pressure from without but from an inward revelation and transformation. See Paul's reference to this experience in his life (Gal. 1:15, 16).

   The word "dwell" indicates an intensive and permanent residing, not just a short visit. Christ comes with the purpose of staying.

4. Comprehension of divine love, vv. 17-19

   a. Establishment in love. "Rooted" refers to a plant deriving its very life from the element of love. This means that the roots of the nature are no longer in sin and lust but in love. Thus the inner life is possessed with love for God, for fellow Christians, and even for our enemies, as Christ loved His enemies! This theme Paul repeats often, for it is important in the full development of Christian character (see 1:4; 1:15; 4:15; 5:2; etc). This condition does not automatically prevail when one is first born of the Spirit. It is a condition of a higher life, to which Paul would have all Christians aspire. It is the life of holiness, as he makes clear in 1:4. "Grounded" speaks of a building being established.

    b. The taking hold of love. "Able to comprehend" is a very strong expression indicating to be fully able to grasp or take hold of. This condition of the love of Christ is not something merely to appreciate aesthetically in a detached way but something to grasp fully in one's own life. The reference to length, breadth, width, and height refers to the full scope of love or possibly to the full scope of redemption itself. Paul did not want these young Christians to remain mental, moral and spiritual dwarfs. He passionately desired them to take hold of this vast scheme of redemption and incorporate it into their lives. Such a prayer rules out forever a shallow, casual, second-hand Christianity. It was to become an inwrought, motivating principle in each life. May it be so with us!

    c. An experienced love. How can we know that which is beyond knowledge? The first knowledge probably refers to experience, while the second one refers to mental mastery. We can never understand or fully grasp the meaning of such love as God has shown to us, but we can experience it in our own lives. Let this prayer come to us as a personal request: individually we must know this overmastering, compelling, purifying love in our own lives. There is a tendency for some people to consider themselves Christians just because their parents were, or because they have gone to church for years, or because they have learned a creed or joined a denomination. The Christianity which Paul prayed for these Ephesians was a personal experience which transformed and motivated men to be Christlike and to lay down all in full surrender to Him forever. May it be so with each of us!

5. Filled with the fulness of God, v. 19. Here is surely the highest reach of this inspired prayer. This is a summary phrase that has awed and challenged me for many years. How vast are the contents of this request! It surely indicates that every Christian is to be brought to the highest level of grace which the indwelling God can bring him. There is to be no satisfaction with mediocre religion but an aspiration for the highest!

If one is to be filled with God, it must be that he is cleansed from all sin and carnality. It could not be otherwise. The Greek tense of the verb "filled" is aorist, showing that this is an instantaneous work. Just as the upper room was suddenly filled with the sound of a rushing mighty wind, so the inner man is suddenly to be filled with the fulness of God. After the initial fulness there is to be continuous enlargement, for God's fulness is an increasing fulness. Ephesians 5:18 shows this.

It will be noted in this passage that we are to be filled with all three persons of the Trinity. This is as Jesus said in John 14:17, 20, 23, "The Spirit of truth . . . dwelleth with you and shall be in you . . . . If a man love me, he will keep my words: and my Father will love him, and we will come unto him, and make our abode with him."

Since all the fulness of God dwells in Jesus (Col. 2:9), and He dwells in us, it is His purpose to reveal the fulness of God in us in a personal way.

Let us note the limitations on these glorious riches—the "according to" phrases. There are two of them. The first is "according to the riches of his glory." In v. 20 this is shown to be absolutely without restriction or lack on His part. His ability far exceeds our thought, imagination or desire. As if Paul thought his readers might think his requests were too high to be realistic, he gives emphatic assurance that God is able: that is the end of it! We too must know that He is able to do this work of cleansing the heart of sin and filling it with His presence.

The limitation on our part is "according to the power that worketh in us." In 1:19 Paul has shown the measure of that power that worketh in us. It was manifested in the resurrection and ascension of Christ. On our part the limitation is faith (1:19; 3:17). May we pray, "Lord, increase our faith!"

C. A Glorious Future, v. 21

We have been speaking of glorious things provided for us through Christ. Here we consider the glory that comes to Christ through the Church. It is when the church is made pure and filled with His fulness that He is glorified. It is this church which is to be the bride of Christ and bring Him glory eternally! Let us be sure we are in that throng.

V. The Unity of the Church, Chapter 4

In the first three chapters of this epistle, Paul has dealt with doctrinal matters. As is common in his writings, he moves from the doctrinal to the practical. Doctrine is sterile unless it applies in practice, so he consistently applies it there. The great messages of the doctrines of Christianity require that they be told to mankind. Now we see the character of the witness of the Church. What kind of people are required to bear this profound and precious message to the world?

A. A Threefold Unity, vv. 1-6, 13

   1. The unity of divine things, vv. 4-6. Paul puts this second, but since it is basic to the others, we put it logically first. A reason may sometimes precede a conclusion and sometimes follow it. It is because of divine unity that Christianity is possible and required.

      a. One body, v. 4. This refers of course to the Church which is the body of Christ in a real sense. With only one Head, there can only be one body. The unity is not that of human organization but of a divine organism infused with divine life. While it is not a unity of a mechanical or human organization, nevertheless it is true that schisms in many human organizations have injured the body of Christ and made it less effective. Christ has only one body, but that body has been injured because of the carnality of the members, which has shown itself in schism and divisiveness (I Cor. 3:1-5).

      b. One Spirit, v. 4. The Holy Spirit is the breath of life for the Church. It can have no life without Him. Since there is only one Spirit, there can be only one life. If we are members of God's Church at all we have His life which is through the Spirit.

      c. One hope of your calling v. 4. All members of the body of Christ have the same hope of eternal sharing in the victory of Christ. Therefore, it is only reasonable that they should be united here in pursuing that hope.

      d. One Lord, v. 5. Christ is the Lord and Master of all Christians. There is no reason then for Christians to be divided, since all are to obey their one Master. If all are servants of one Lord, then they will not pursue selfish and contradictory interests.

    e. One faith, v. 5. Objectively, this means the same system of doctrine. A doctrine which is true is true for all men. The race of men is one, and truth of God applies to all so far as the great doctrines are concerned. Subjectively, faith is an act of complete surrender and appropriation of God's grace and truth. All who have faith have it in the same way, by submission to God and to His truth. Since they are the same in all, there is no justification of division in the body of Christ.

    f. One baptism, v. 5. While not all endorse the same mode of baptism, it is agreed that baptism by water is the witness to faith in Christ. This was consistently adhered to in the days of the New Testament and generally so today. One witness to faith before the world should indicate unity of believers.

    g. One God and Father of all, v. 6. This means that there is only one family, begotten of the Father. What a powerful reason for unity among believers! Families are one in the source of their life, so let them be one in sharing together the fellowship of the family. God is above all; that is, He is in control of all things—in nature and in grace, including the Church. He is through all; in His providence He directs and upholds all things, in nature and in the Church. He is in all; His presence is everywhere—in nature and in the Church. Therefore let the Church be one!

2. The unity of the Spirit, vv. 1-3

    a. The fact of unity. It is not stated that we are to achieve a unity but to keep it, to guard and preserve it. When people are baptized into the body of Christ at the time of their new birth, they have this unity in the body (see I Cor. 12:12-14). The Spirit dispenses gifts or abilities for service, and He knows how to place people in the body of Christ for maximum benefit.

    b. The maintenance of unity. While the unity is given at the time of the new birth into the body, it is necessary for believers to "endeavor to keep the unity." Unity may be disturbed by carnal attitudes and actions, as Paul so clearly shows in I Cor. 3:3, 4. There may come schisms in the body disturbing the peace of the body and grieving the Spirit (see I Cor. 12:25). Here is a list of the heart attitudes which are essential to the maintenance of Christian unity.

1) Lowliness or humility. In the Greek world this was not considered a virtue but rather a sign of weakness. It was Christianity which raised it to a high virtue. Humility comes from seeing ourselves in comparison with the Person of Christ and the demands of God. As long as we compare ourselves with ourselves and measure ourselves by ourselves (II Cor. 10:12, 18), we will be able to exalt ourselves. But when we see ourselves in comparison with God's plan for us we will see the total impossibility of our attaining thereto in our own merits or efforts. We are nothing in comparison.

   It is this grace of humility that is the condition of receiving God's grace in other ways (James 4:6).

2) Meekness or gentleness. This word has two shades of meaning. First, it refers to a person who is angry at the proper things and not angry at the improper things. He is angry over the wrongs and sufferings that others have to endure, but not over those which he has to endure. Thus, meekness is not total passivity but a properly regulated indignation. Second, the word refers to the life of a person who has been totally surrendered to God and controlled by Him. The Greek word, *praus*, was the name of an animal which had been trained to respond fully to the command or the reins of his master. The Greek noun, *praotes*, comes from the same root and indicates total surrender to God's control. The meek person is not seeking to gain personal advantage.

3) Longsuffering or patience. It is the Christian spirit which never admits defeat in pursuit of the will of God. It is not broken by misfortune or stopped by discouragement, but persists until victory comes. In relation to other men, this spirit does not take revenge on its enemies, even though it may have the power to do so. It is the spirit which refuses to retaliate. Barclay pictures it as the attitude of a huge dog with a little dog barking and snapping at him. The big dog could eat him up in one bite, but the little dog maintains a

dignified reserve about him which refuses to retaliate for the little irritations. He is too big to bite back! This spirit bears insult and embarrassment without bitterness, and antagonism without becoming ungracious. It is a grace from God Himself to holy hearts.

4) Love. This is *agape*, the self-giving love which originates in the heart of God. It has been defined by Barclay as unconquerable benevolence. Agape is a matter of the will and not of the emotions. It is the will to seek the highest good of every person, no matter what is done, even at the cost of giving ourselves to bring that good to pass.

5) Peace, which issues from the presence of the foregoing graces. The bond of peace is that which holds people together in their mutual relations. Peace comes from right relations between men. When these right relations prevail, men can be held together in unity. When people are divided and rent asunder by strife, there is obviously no bond holding them in the unity of the Spirit. The unity of the Spirit is to show itself by a bond that holds people together. That bond should be obvious in the Church where such spirits prevail. When there is schism and peace is lost, it is because the foregoing graces are not in evidence. These graces obviously require holiness for their effective working.

3. The unity of faith and knowledge, v. 13. There are not two separate unities meant here but one. The reference is to a time when faith and knowledge will be one. We have said before that there is one faith—only one system of truth from God. It is evident, however, that there is more than one creed, more than one system of doctrine believed by men. Contradictory systems cannot both be true, yet men hold to such systems. Part of the reason is that knowledge is limited and men do not all see the truth alike. Another reason is that false teachers teach error in order to draw followers after them. It is God's purpose to bring His people to such perfection that the system of truth and their knowledge of that truth shall be united, that knowledge of truth shall be full and unmarked by error. He has given his gifts of apostles, prophets, evangelists, pastors and teachers to the church to bring men toward this goal of the perfect man. In this

portion, the faith and knowledge relate to the Son of God. We may never in this life agree on all incidental and minor details of belief, but we must agree on the Person and work of Christ. Such a state is expected to be reached in this life.

F. Unity in Diversity, vv. 7-16

1. Diversity of gifts, vv. 7-11. Christ gives gifts to the members of His body to equip them for varying functions and offices. These gifts are of grace and do not indicate merit due the holder of the gifts. The specific gifts are listed in v. 11, though a fuller list is in I Cor. 12:8-10, 28-30.

We should note, in contrast, the fact that gifts are given to Christ without measure (John 3:34). Men today have a measure of gifts; He had all of them in the fullest extent.

Paul quotes here from Ps. 68:18, using the figure of a triumphant military man drawing a procession of bound prisoners to demonstrate his victory. The winner expects to *receive* gifts in honor of his victory. As Paul uses the figure, Christ the Victor expects to *give* gifts in His ascension to a place of absolute victory. Then at the thought of the ascension Paul shows that the triumphant Christ is the same person as the lowly One Who came down from Heaven in the form of a babe. Now that He has ascended, it is not for the purpose of leaving the world but of filling the world with His power and presence! We are part of a Christ-filled Church, and we are in a Christ-filled world, though most men do not know it.

Following are the offices in the Church of that day.

a. Apostles. These were people who had seen Jesus and were witnesses of the resurrection, then sent as special messengers to the entire Church.

b. Prophets were forth-tellers of God's message. They usually had a special message for the churches, spoken from revelation from God. Their message was not so much the result of thought and meditation as direct burden or revelation from God. They went from place to place and from Church to Church, speaking God's message. It was easy for this office to be counterfeited, and from almost the beginning there were false prophets. So the office was early vacated and died out. In a sense any minister of God has this function in that he speaks forth the word of God.

      c. Evangelists also traveled from place to place, but their message was the "evangel" or good news of the Gospel. They were the missionaries of their day who took the message of salvation to various parts of the world.

      d. Pastors and teachers. Apparently the two terms apply to the same office. The pastor is to be a teacher, also. He is to explain and apply the truth of the Word of God so His people—old and young, mature and immature—will understand it and grow as a consequence of receiving it. The word *pastor* refers to a shepherd of the flock, one who guides, protects, feed and nurtures the flock. We have in John 10:11-13 a distinction between the true shepherd and the hireling. The true shepherd knows his sheep and is willing to give his life for them. The hireling is in the business for personal reasons; he will leave the flock in trouble to gain personal ends.

2. Unity of purpose, vv. 12-16. While the offices vary, the purpose is one. Here is stated in a most exalted way the goal of the church and the officers who have place in it.

      a. The perfection of the saints, v. 12. The word *perfecting* in this place has a meaning which is reasonable and attainable through grace for Christians in this life. It is used to mean the setting in place of a joint that has been dislocated or of putting something back in order so it becomes what it ought to be. In Mark 1:9 it is used of mending of nets. In Gal. 6:1 it refers to the disciplining of an offender until he takes his place in the church again. It does not mean the absolute perfection of God or the relative perfection of angels but the perfection which God means for Christians to have—a perfection of love and loyalty.

      b. The work of the ministry, v. 12. The man of God is a servant, a worker. He has more to do than just preach and teach. He is to build up, not tear down, the church of God. It involves real work—taxing, costly work. His life is to be poured out in such service.

      c. The edifying the body of Christ, v. 12, is included in the building up of the Church. The pastor must remember that he is dealing with Christ's body in a very real sense. To hurt or divide the Church is to mangle the body of Christ. It is a serious matter indeed!

The goal of this edifying is to reach the state where faith and knowledge of the Son of God are one.

Unto a perfect man refers to the person who has come to the "measure of the stature of the fulness of Christ." That is, he has matured until he truly represents Christ, not only with a pure heart but also with graces enlarged and developed until the very fragrance of Christ Himself shines forth from his life. It is the limit of maturity when we convey Christ by our talk, by our walk, and by the outflow of the Spirit through our lives.

    d. The growth into Christ, vv. 14, 15. There are many babes in the churches, and they must be helped to grow lest they be overcome with false teachers. There are many false doctrines today, and children in faith are easily persuaded by clever arguments of deceivers, now as then. They speak error with a covetous, self-seeking purpose. The man of God, on the other hand, speaks truth in love. He not only presents truth but he also does it in love, not for his own good but for the good of the members and for the glory of Christ. Let it be noted here that it is possible to speak truth in such a harsh or hurtful way as to do more harm than good. God's man loves others and wants to help them with the truth. He may have to rebuke and chasten, but he will do it with kindness and love. By this growth the members, and the Church as a whole, are to fill up the pattern given by the life of Christ. He is the Head, and the body is to be commensurate with the Head. It is to be a full-grown body, not a dwarfish, puny one.

3. The enlargement of the body of Christ, v. 16. The thought of v. 12 is expanded here. The Head, Christ, controls the action of the body. If every member fits into his proper place perfectly (see v. 12), and they all cooperate properly, then the body will grow upward (be edified) and outward (increase) at the same time and still have the nature of divine love about it! The ideal for the Church is beautifully expressed here. There are many congregations which are growing in size but not in holiness. The members are babes who make a nice nursery but hardly an army for God. There are other churches which concentrate on separation from the world but are always small. The ideal includes growth, upward and outward.

C. Unity in Conduct, vv. 17-32

It is not to be suggested that all Christians will act alike in every detail of life since there are differences of aptitude, education, opinion, and ability. However, there are certain Christian principles which apply equally to all believers, whatever their background or level of maturity. Some of them are shown in this passage.

1. A transformed character, vv. 17-24. All Christians are transformed individuals, made so by the power of God. God is working to bring every one of them to conform to the image of His Son.

   a. The old life and the old man. Paul's expression "the old man" is generally taken to represent the old nature under the influence of sin. In Col. 3:9 he says, "ye have put off the old man with his deeds." So "the old man" is something more than just sinful actions; it is the nature involved in those actions. In this passage, he emphasizes the same: we are to change our conduct and see that the old nature is removed as well.

      1) It is an empty life: "the vanity of their minds." There is no real satisfaction in the sinful life. It promises much but, like the Prodigal Son, the sinner is left with emptiness and disappointment.

      2) There is darkness and ignorance of spiritual things because of separation from God. The term "alienated" means an abhorrence of all that is pure and sacred. Their lusts drew them in the opposite direction from God.

      3) There is blindness of heart. The original word means to be petrified or hardened like the hardest stone. Once the conscience was tender in the commission of sin, but by repeated sinning against the light of conscience, there was hardening until there was no response in the conscience at all. This is an awful picture of the degenerating power of sin! This hardening of the conscience is at the bottom of the other conditions.

      4) There is greediness for all uncleanness. Having lost the checking power of conscience, all inner restraints are off, and they follow lusts without restraint. "Lasciviousness" is shameless wantonness, a greedy

seeking after sin openly where once there would have been shame. What a terrible picture this is of heathenism. The same could be applied to sin among the godless world today.

    b. The transformation

        1) They heard of Christ and learned the truth in Him. What power there is in truth from God! It is the sword the Spirit uses to penetrate to the inner man and lay it open before God.

        2) They were to put off the old man who was corrupt according to deceitful lusts. All the deceit and degradation of sin works through lusts, which pull a person away from God toward total and eternal ruin. This involves more than just forgiveness of sins; it also involves the removal of the old nature of sin with its inward deceitfulness and uncleanness.

        3) They were renewed in their minds; that is, they were regenerated.

    c. The call to holiness

        The end and aim of repentance is to turn to holiness. Putting away of the old man of sin is in order to put on the new man of holiness.

        1) The "new man" is the fully saved person which God aimed at in His redemption plan. It is the new creation. When man was first created, he was in the image of God. Now he is to be restored to that image, which essentially consists of righteousness and true holiness. Righteousness is right action—rightness before God and His holy law. Holiness is separation unto God and cleansing from all sin, within and without.

        2) "Holiness of truth" contrasts with the deceitful lusts of v. 22. If the heart is to be truthful it must be freed from sin, since sin is essentially deceitful. See Psalm 51:6, Rom. 7:11, and Heb. 3:13.

2. Outworking harmony from inner grace, vv. 25-32. Here are given some of the practical applications of this putting off of the old life and putting on of the new. (This figure obviously refers to a change of clothing. It should be remembered that in the Bible a person's clothes symbolized his character.)

a. The duty of truth, v. 25. If unity is to be maintained, there must be truthfulness. If our physical senses were not truthful—for example, if they signaled joy when they should signal pain—life could not long endure. So in the body of Christ there must be honesty. It is easy to slip into habits of distorting or misrepresenting the truth, so it is important to recognize that truthfulness is the basis of ongoing unity. The world of Paul's day justified lying in some cases, but the Bible does not.

b. The putting away of anger, v. 26. There is a time for righteous indignation, as was shown in the life of Christ. We should be indignant toward injustices against others.

   If there is ever an injury between members of the body of Christ or between a Christian and a non-Christian, there should be an immediate effort to find restoration. The longer people wait, the harder the adjustment becomes and the more likely it is that the difficulty will grow. Paul's rule is to deal with the problem at once. Not to do so is to leave a rift where the devil can get in and do his divisive work, and he is never slack in making the effort. We must leave him no such places to work.

c. Christian working and giving. Honesty in work is the rule for the Christian. If this rule of v. 28 had been carefully carried out, there wouldn't be much place for Communism today. This verse teaches private ownership, reward for labor, and Christian benevolence, which would alleviate in large measure the necessity of the government's sponsoring so many socialistic programs of welfare. God gives us strength to work and get money. When we get it, we must remember it is ours only in stewardship for the Lord. It is not really ours just to spend on our own pleasures. This sharing with others deepens the unity of the fellowship of believers.

d. The duty of edifying speech. We are stewards of our speech. What we say is to build others up, not tear them down. What a high standard this is! It is not possible except we have the Spirit of Christ enthroned within us. How often cruel and critical speech has injured the unity of the body of Christ! Again, it is possible to fulfill this command only if hearts are filled with love and we are conformed to

Christ. He had this kind of speech, and He can produce it in us.

    e. Grieve not the Spirit. Any of these violations of the unity of the body of Christ is a grief to the Spirit. It hurts Him at His heart. He seeks to preserve this unity, and if we violate it, we grieve Him. We have mentioned the sealing of the Spirit. His presence is the assurance that we belong to God and have citizenship in Heaven. If we grieve Him away, these benefits will be lost.

    f. Maintaining Christian relationships, vv. 31, 32. In these verses Paul exhorts them to put away all attitudes and forms of speech which would injure the relationships in the body of Christ. Instead, he urges them to manifest graces such as Christ has shown to us. If these two verses were faithfully carried out within the body of Christ, there would be no ruptures in fellowship, no ugly schisms. But this will not be where carnal men strive for their own way and show jealousy and enmity where they cannot have it.

VI. The Holiness of the Church, 5:1-6:9

    A. Holiness in Conduct, vv. 1-16

        1. The imitation of God, vv. 1, 2. In the Greek world those who studied oratory did so by imitating one of the experts. Imitation was a primary way of learning. Here Paul takes that word and applies it to God. We are to imitate God, and the way we are to do so is to imitate the love and forgiveness of Christ. This was a sacrifice which pleased God, as the sacrifices of the Old Testament pleased Him. Jesus always did that which pleased God through obedience, and we are to do the same.

        2. Separation from sin, vv. 3-5. In those days prostitution was so common that it was a part of heathen worship and used as a way of making gain for the building of heathen temples. Prostitution was so common that even the Roman Cicero said that to deny this action to young men might be ideal, but it was totally unrealistic. Yet Christianity introduced this virtue of chastity in such a world as that, and the power of Christ was such that the virtue was observed by the Christians. What a testimony to the transforming power of Christ!

          Not only are Christians to abstain from sexual sins, but they are to abstain from speaking lightly about such things. The filthy and foolish talk and jesting seem to be related to such matters. If the action is wrong, then light talk which would make the sin seem less horrible is wrong, also.

It may seem strange that covetousness is listed along with sexual impurity as one of the worst sins to be avoided, but this was the sin which the law located in Paul, as he related in Romans 7. He struggled to be free from it, but it showed him the horror of sin. Note the strong emphasis which Paul places on covetousness, calling it the same as idolatry.

Covetousness is the desire for and the pursuit of earthly things at the cost of spiritual things. It is excessive indulgence in that which, if used moderately, is lawful. It is the love of gain, and especially the desire for that which we do not really need for our best spiritual welfare. It may not seem as ugly as fornication, but its very subtlety adds to its danger.

Paul is bold to declare that people involved in these sins cannot have a part in the Kingdom of God. There are no Christian covetors, no Christian fornicators. Such men are lost and must repent to be saved.

3. Separation from false teachers, vv. 6-16

   a. The identity of the false teachers. It seems likely that these are Gnostics who taught that the body is essentially evil while the spirit is essentially good. Hence, what a person did with his body, according to some of the false teachers, was of no concern to the spiritual good of the individual. Paul contradicts this sharply. Such teaching is empty of any value. The fact is that God punishes men of such immoral conduct.

   b. The light versus the darkness. Here Paul is talking plainly about holiness in conduct. He states that the Christian lives in the light and is himself a light. This is in agreement with the teaching of Jesus. The heathen lived in the darkness and their lives were dark.

   Light reveals the distinction between right and wrong, v. 10. We can know what pleases God because the light of God makes manifest what is right, v. 13.

   Light makes the Christian fruitful, v. 9. It produces goodness (generosity of spirit), righteousness (the giving to men and God what is due), and truth. This truth is not just something for the mind; it lays claims and imposes responsibilities on the will. We are not just to contemplate the light but to walk in it, v. 8. When God's light shines on us and we walk in it, fruit is certain to follow.

Walking in the light breaks all fellowship with evil. It gives us fellowship with God (I John 1:7) and exposes the inconsistency and ugliness of sin. When walking in the light, we will have discernment as to evil and a hatred for it (v. 11).

The light comes from Christ, v. 14. This verse seems to be part of an early Christian hymn and is a call to men to respond to the light. Those who do will have more light and will have life from the dead. To give the call to those in darkness is our duty today.

Light enables us to see where we are going, v. 15. We are to walk circumspectly (looking about us) in order to see possible sources of temptation. Paul has been emphasizing the necessity of avoiding that which is dark and unfruitful; now he stresses the avoidance of that which would be wasteful of our time in an evil world. Our time is a gift from God; we are to redeem or buy it back from this world that has brought corruption. Men in sin waste their entire lives and are fools. We will be so, also, unless we live in the Spirit and put our time to good use, not being led into pursuits which are wasteful and degrading.

B. Holiness in Attitudes, vv. 17-21

1. The fulness of the Spirit as the sources of our attitudes, v. 18

    a. Contrast with drunkenness. The heathen world was given to wine. The Christian world should be as fully given to the fulness of the Spirit. There are some noteworthy similarities between drunkenness and the Spirit's fulness.

        1) Not all who drink get drunk with wine; likewise, not all who have the Spirit of Christ are filled with the Spirit.

        2) Those who take a little wine have a thirst for more; likewise, the presence of the Spirit in our lives give us thirst for more until we are filled.

        3) Fulness of wine brings a person totally under its control until he is dead to all else; so does the fulness of the Spirit.

4) As one continues drinking, his tongue is loosed and he speaks without any inhibitions. This characteristic marked the feasts of the heathen, even feasts to their heathen gods. Likewise, those who are filled with the Spirit have a liberty of speech for Christ; this was most notable in the New Testament. People who were filled with the Spirit began to speak with boldness (see the Book of Acts); they could not go on quietly as if nothing had happened.

5) Those under the influence of alcohol become liberal; so do Spirit-filled people.

Paul strictly forbids drunkenness. "Excess" means that which is unsafe, lost beyond recovery, and abandoned to sensuality, lust and debauchery. The drunkard is in a dreadful condition; his only hope is in Christ.

b. A continuing fulness. The Greek tense is progressive. The meaning is "Keep on being filled with the Spirit." Just as the drunkard continues going back for wine, those who are filled with the Spirit must keep being filled. This filling is not a once-for-all experience. It must continue, as a river continually is filled with water from the spring from which it flows. In Acts the statement that they were filled with the Spirit is often made of Christian leaders. We should note that the Ephesian church had a beginning in the fulness of the Spirit (see Acts 19:1-6), but it is the continuous life that is urged upon them here. Even those who have been filled with the Spirit can fall if they do not look to the continuous life in the Spirit.

2. The attitudes which are produced.

a. Joy and singing, v. 19. The heathen worshipers who were drunken had noisy songs of evil and were riotous. Christians had another kind of song, spiritual songs, that expressed the joy of the heart and brought praise to God. Note that the songs of joy did not depend on outer circumstances; they depended on the fulness of the Spirit. Those early Christians sang in prisons, while being beaten, at the stake, and in every other circumstance. By this means they spread abroad the power of the Christian faith.

b. Thankfulness, v. 20. Because all things work together for good to those who love God and are called according to His purpose (Romans 8:28), we can, by faith, thank God for everything that comes if we love and follow His purpose. Often our circumstances do not seem good, but it is our faith in God that enables us to praise Him for hard things. By such praise we allow God to bring blessing out of what otherwise would be harmful. This is a high requirement; let us be sure we follow it.

c. Submissiveness, v. 21. Christianity does not disorganize the relationships of life. It brings them into proper focus and enforces that which is proper. Sin disorders; Christian grace makes human relationships easier where they are proper and removes those that are improper; thus Christianity is truly good for society. One day God will remove all from this earth which will not submit to such a society.

The fear of God is primary. Those relationships which can not be in submission to God are removed, while others are strengthened. The next section will apply this truth in various situations.

C. Holiness in Human Relationships, 5:22-6:9

1. Husband and wife, vv. 22, 23

   a. The situation concerning marriage in that day. In the Jewish world, a woman was considered of almost no value except as a servant. The man had rights of easy divorce, but the woman had no such rights except in extreme cases. Hence, the very marriage bond was endangered, and many Jewish girls were refusing to marry because they had such little security.

   In the Greek world, things were almost as bad, and perhaps even worse. Prostitution was common, and most men had women besides their wives. Marriage and true family life were in danger of disappearing. Into such a world Christianity came with a beautiful and exalted view of marriage.

   A similar breakdown in marriage is occurring today in many places. More and more people live together without marriage and separate easily, even if married, because of greater economic freedom for women, loss of Christian influence, the removal of laws against sexual sin, and increasing secularization. This message of Paul is much needed!

   b. The submission of the wife, vv. 22-24

      1) The reason: the husband is the head of the wife. Paul explains this elsewhere by saying that the man was created first and the woman sinned first. The woman was made as a helpmeet for man. However, in Paul's world, the woman was far too much degraded. While he shows that the woman is under the headship of man, he lifts this relationship to a noble and sacred position.

      2) The comparison: Christ is head of the Church. Male headship is not a tyrannical, domineering headship but a headship of love, loyalty, sacrifice, and provision. The head works in the interest of the body, not just to make the body subservient to the head.

         This very comparison between the husband-wife relationship and the Christ-Church relationship lifts the concept of marriage far above what was held in that day and what is popularly held today. In the Christian family, the husband is head. His authority is respected, and his counsel is sought. The modern women's liberation movement is at variance with the position of Scripture.

   c. The love of the husband, vv. 25-33. This immediately places the relationship in a far different perspective than it was seen in Paul's day. In that day a Jew's morning prayer consisted of thanksgiving to God Who had not made him "a Gentile, a slave, or a woman." Every woman ought to thank God for giving her a place of respect and love and honor. Often, even in this age, a woman is considered just a thing to be exploited than a real person to be respected and honored. Today women are often debased as mere sexual symbols rather than symbols of virtue, beauty and purity.

      1) The example of Christ and His Church. Let it again be said that marriage is lifted to a very high plane indeed by being compared with the relation between Christ and His Church. The love of Christ for the Church is a sacrificial love (He gave Himself), a purifying love (He cleansed the Church), a caring love, and an enduring

love. The husband is to cleave to his wife and consider her as his own body. He would not mistreat his own body, and neither should he mistreat his wife.

2) The lesson about Christ and the Church.

    a) The Church is here symbolized as a bride of Christ. She is in a very special love relationship to Christ.

    b) Christ gave Himself to sanctify the Church. This is the counterpart of John 3:16, where God loved the world and gave His Son for it. There is in this passage a clear portrayal of entire sanctification as a second grace from God. The proper reading is "That he might sanctify it, having cleansed it with the washing of water by the word . . . ." It is evident then that the cleansing of regeneration by the Word and signified by baptism is first, and this is followed by the sanctifying work which makes the Church pure and blameless and holy. The aorist tense is used for both the word "cleansed" and the word "sanctify." These are two instantaneous graces which prepare the Church for marriage to Christ.

    There is perhaps an allusion to the Oriental marriage custom of first bathing and then putting on the marriage garment, which Paul says is to be without spot or wrinkle. The marriage garment in Rev. 19:8 is a type of the righteousness of the saints, the bride of Christ.

    If we are truly looking forward to the presentation at His coming, we will pursue with all eagerness and faith the work of entire sanctification in our hearts, and we will not be ashamed to let it be known that we are His sanctified people—a bride ready for her Bridegroom.

    c) The presentation at His coming. The preparation is here and now (see Rev. 19:7: "the bride hath made herself ready"). We must be ready for this glorious presentation. The parable of Mat. 22:1-14 suggests that those who despise and neglect this grace will not be allowed to enjoy the wedding feast with the King, the union with Christ.

The phrase "without spot or wrinkle" means to be free from the corruption of sin or the blemish of decay. There must be no deterioration of this grace in our lives.

In conclusion, Paul restates and reemphasizes the importance of the marriage bond, quoting from Gen. 2:24.

2. Children and parents, 6:1-4

   a. The children's duty: obedience. The reason is that it is right; the limit is "in the Lord." This means that if there is a conflict between what God commands and what a parent commands, the Lord must be obeyed. This would be a rare circumstance in a normal, and especially in a Christian, home.

   The fifth commandment (Ex. 20:12) commands honor to parents with the promise of long days in the land.

   In the days of Paul the plight of children was, in many instances, horrible beyond words. Parents had absolute control, even to the execution of their own children. Weak or sickly children were commonly drowned by their own parents, and girl children were often abandoned at birth. Often, unwanted children were abandoned in the Roman Forum, where they were picked up by whoever wanted them and made into slaves or prostitutes. Christianity changed all this! Never let it be said that Christianity and the Gospel have not changed the world!

   b. The parents' duty: to train them in the nurture and admonition of the Lord. Children are not to be too severely treated lest they sense injustice and develop antagonism. They are to be trained. The word *nurture* is essentially the same as our word "educate" and includes all the means whereby moral and spiritual training are accomplished. This is particularly placed as a responsibility of the fathers, who are the head of the house and therefore ultimately responsible for the training of children. The mother has an important place to fill, also.

   Admonition is a more particular means of nurture, and refers primarily to word-of-mouth teaching.

   Not only teaching in general but also teaching "in the Lord" is referred to here. We owe it to our children to give them the truth of the Gospel and apply it to their lives consistently. It is not enough just to give facts; the child is to be disciplined in the way of Christian living. Just as the law was to bring men to Christ, so the teaching of the parent should do the same for the child.

   3. Masters and slaves, 6:5-9

      a. The slaves' duty: obedience, as unto the Lord. The plight of slaves was often extremely difficult. They could be put to death simply on the will of their masters. They could be cast out to die when old or infirm; they could be beaten for the slightest pretext. Christianity prevailed to a large extent among the slaves. They were taught not to fight for their lot but to prevail as Christians and show the nature and victory of Christianity under pressure. When situations are the most adverse, the challenge to show the power of Christ is the greatest.

        All workmen are to work as if the eye of God were the primary evaluation of their work. They are to seek to please Him first of all, regardless of the character of the human employer.

      b. The masters' duty: to remember he is the servant of God and to act as pleasing God. This means that all action which debases the servant will be stopped. Masters today need to remember this; they are to act in keeping with God's kindness and love toward them if they would be approved of God.

VII. The Warfare of the Church, 6:10-20

  A. The Enemy Faced, v. 12

    Here we have one of the most impressive descriptions of our spiritual foe. This is not just figurative language but also language which expresses an important and impressive truth about the organization of forces in the realm of evil. Our battle as soldiers of Christ is not with men but with the spiritual forces which control the minds and actions of men. The terms used refer to different orders and functions of evil spirits, all of which act under the dominion of Satan. These beings fell from heaven and are in perpetual revolt against God. The Bible tells us that they blind the minds of men by directing them against God and His cause. Daniel 10 gives us the account of how some of these spirits worked in the days of Daniel's praying and how they influenced rulers among men.

1. Principalities. These were the highest order of spirit beings, being princes in the kingdom of evil and serving directly under the devil himself. They are related to nations, kings, civil officers, etc. One of them is called "the prince of Persia" in Dan. 10:20. They seek to influence the courses of nations and the decisions of legislators to oppose the work of God. The story of Daniel shows how important prayer can be in countering their evil influences.

2. Powers. They are under the principalities and probably are greater in number, having their realm of action the opposition of Christians and the attack of individual persons of importance. They doubtless work as accusers of the brethren, stimulating division and promoting tale-bearing, scandal, gossip, etc.

3. Rulers of the darkness of this age. The darkness here includes all of the realm of sin, superstition, ignorance, rebellion, and willfulness against God. It is stirred by these evil forces, and we must recognize this fact as we work with people. Wherever there is fortune telling, witchcraft, soothsaying, palm reading, or any other kind of heathenism; where there is rejection of the truth and willful continuance in sin; there these dark forces hold sway, seeking to control the minds of men and keep them arrayed against God.

4. Wicked spirits in high places. This perhaps refers to the fact that they have their location in the heavenlies, not being confined to any particular place on earth. It may also mean that they attack in the realm of religion, thought, and philosophy, not only on the level of the physical realm. It is certain that they appear under the guise of religion, persuading men to error and false doctrine. They oppose the true Word of God, taking it from the minds of men and often appearing as "angels of light". They may oppress the mind with evil thoughts, suspicions, tormenting fears, etc. They must be recognized and opposed.

B. The Armor of God, vv. 10, 11, 13, 17

We can thank God that we do not have to face these sinister forces alone or merely in the strength of the flesh. In the Lord we are assured of strength against them. Christ in His victory of resurrection has achieved final and total triumph over them. Our position of authority is at the right hand of the Father with Him.

See also Col. 2:14, 15. All the hosts of Satan are now deprived of their authority. The only way they can succeed against Christians is for those Christians to fail to recognize the victory of Christ and to fail in faith in the victory purchased for them. We are meant always to be victors over the enemy!

1. The girdle of truth. The girdle bound the armour together about the loins. Now Satan is first of all a liar and deceiver; he is devoid of truth and is the father of liars. It is reasonable that the first piece of armour with which to resist him is the truth, because it shows up his errors. If we are to be on God's side, we must be wholly committed to the truth and have it implanted in our minds and consciences. "God desireth truth in the inward parts." This truth is found in the Word of God, is interpreted to us by the Spirit of God, and is expressed in the Gospel.

2. The breastplate of righteousness. This covered the front and back of the chest area and was a protection against injury. Righteousness in life is a strong preventive against injury from the assaults of the enemy. It is not self-righteousness but the righteousness of Christ in the fullest extent intended by our God. The best way to defeat the lies of the enemy is to live a transparent life of holiness and righteousness.

3. Preparation of the Gospel of Peace on the feet. There is readiness in this image, both to obey and to publish the Gospel of Peace. We must be ready to move always in the will of God. A barefooted soldier would be of little use in warfare; likewise, a Christian who knew not the Gospel and was not ready to go at God's command would be of little use to God in His warfare. Note that this is a Gospel of *Peace*; it brings men into the peace of God.

4. The shield of faith. A shield was a large rectangular piece made of wood and used to protect the entire body from flying arrows which were often tipped with tar and set aflame when shot. The shield absorbed the tips and quenched the flame. Our faith, or total and intimate reliance on God, will keep the fiery darts of temptation and accusation from injuring. Living close to God in faith will deprive temptation of its power. Faith is not only objective truthfulness of doctrine but subjective reliance on God as well.

5. The helmet of salvation. We have pointed out that the enemy attacks through the mind. He does not always have access to our bodies, but he has access to our minds, bringing suggestions, accusations, and temptations to us. The helmet of salvation is for protection of the head and the mind. The full salvation from Christ involves a renewing of the mind, a purifying of the mind, and an illumining of the mind through the Spirit until we are enabled to recognize the approach of the enemy and to resist him by faith. If the mind be not thus strengthened and illuminated by salvation, we will be open to error and deception.

6. The sword of the Spirit. This is the offensive weapon. (The girdle was defensive.) Again, it is the Truth, or the Word of God. There is no power in mere human arguments to defeat the devil, but he must yield before the Word of God (see Rev. 12:11). Jesus resisted the devil and drove him away by using the Word of God. We will be able to do the same if we know the Word and use it. It has power!

C. The Engagement, vv. 18-20

Prayer is not the weapon or the armour; it is the battle, the place of wrestling and victory. It is here where the enemy most firmly opposes. In prayer Daniel came to grips with the enemy's force, and he won. Jesus wrestled in prayer in Gethsemane, and He won, being strengthened by an angel visitor. We also can win if we pray effectively. Note the *alls*:

1. Always. there is never a time when we should take a vacation from prayer. The enemy never rests, so our prayer battle can never cease.

2. All prayer. There are a number of kinds of prayer, as Paul shows in I Tim. 2. Supplication involves a continuance in prayer until the answer comes. We should have private prayer, family prayer, group prayer, etc.

3. All perseverance. This means to pray with intense concern and concentration, never giving up until the desire is reached. Of course, it is assumed that our praying is *in the Spirit*. That means that He inspires the desire and energizes the praying. We may be assured of an answer when we pray in this way.

4. All saints. There is a prayer fellowship that is vital. None of us can get along without help from the prayers of others. Paul

begged for the prayers of saints so that his preaching might be with power and effectiveness. There is value in praying for others and their praying for us. Such agreement in prayer gives it special force to overcome the enemy. Paul did have mighty force as he preached before kings, governors, and men of lower stations. The penetration of the truth was supernatural; he knew the necessity of such and so pleaded that God would provide the necessary force to his preaching. How blessed it would be if every minister of the Gospel today had such anointing and utterance until it penetrated the hearts of the hearers, laying them open to the gaze of God and revealing eternal truth to the hearers! This requires much prayer by the preacher and by those who are supporting him. This is how we ought to speak! Nothing less than this will suffice for the magnitude of our task, not brilliant display of intellect or flashy use of oratory or logical persuasion alone can succeed in the weighty task that is ours to bring men to God. We must have utterance, and this requires prayer.

VIII Conclusion, vv. 21-24

This letter was probably an encyclical letter, as we have seen. It was thus to be carried from church to church by Tychicus. This brother is described in very warm terms of confidence and respect by Paul. It appears Tychicus was one of Paul's most trusted friends. He is mentioned in a number of places, always with respect. Tychicus would tell the brethren of Paul's state in prison and thus comfort their hearts as to his condition.

In closing, Paul brings together again the great words which he loved so much: peace, love, faith and grace.

Sincerity of love is an expression which essentially means love out of a pure heart. Sincerity is freedom from flaw; their love was shown by incorruptibility of life. This is really the goal of the Gospel: to have love in the heart and to show it by an undefiled life of sincerity. Thus Paul ends with the note he knew so well and loved so much: holiness.

Review Questions
EPHESIANS

1. To whom was the epistle written?
2. For what reason do some critics deny Paul as author?
3. What is the central theme of this epistle?
4. Where was Paul when he wrote this epistle?
5. State four different purposes for which God has chosen or predestinated us.
6. Which of the Persons of the Trinity is said to predestinate us?
7. What is the meaning of the word "predestinate?"
8. Explain how the term "adoption" applies to our spiritual life.
9. There are two different meanings of the word "redemption" in Chapter 1. What are they?
10. Explain the difference between "wisdom and prudence."
11. Give a figure of the church which is used in each chapter.
12. Explain the meaning of the "sealing of the Spirit," and the "earnest" of the Spirit.
13. What measure does Paul use to measure the exceeding greatness of God's power to usward who believe?
14. What demonstration of resurrection power has already been seen in the lives of believers?
15. Quote Ephesians 2:8-9 and explain what is meant by the gift of God.
16. For what does Paul pray in his first prayer? In his second prayer?
17. What is the purpose of God's power operating in the Church?
18. What terms does Paul use in this epistle in referring to Satan and his demons?
19. How does Paul describe the past life of the Gentiles? of the Jews?
20. For what purpose does Paul say that God saves us? (2:10)
21. How did Christ bring unity between Jews and Gentiles?
22. How are we brought nigh to God when we were once far away?
23. What great mystery does Paul describe in Chapter 3?
24. When did God make the plan involved in this mystery?
25. When was the mystery revealed to men?
26. What is the "one new man" of 2:15?
27. What comparisons does Paul make between a temple and the Church?
28. How did Paul find out the mystery of the church?
29. When Paul prays that we may "know the love of Christ that passeth knowledge," what does he mean by "know" and "knowledge?"

Ephesians 47

30. In his second prayer, Paul prays for some special benefit from each Person of the Trinity. What are they?
31. What are the two limitations on the benefits in Paul's second prayer?
32. What are the seven divine unities in Chapter 4?
33. What is meant by the "unity of the Spirit?"
34. What heart attitudes are necessary in maintaining unity of the Spirit?
35. Explain the meaning of the word "meekness."
36. In speaking of the unity of faith and knowledge, what particular knowledge does Paul mean?
37. Although believers are to be made one in Christ, how are they still different?
38. What special gifts has God given the church, according to Chapter 4?
39. What is the purpose of these gifts?
40. What is meant by the "perfect man" in Chapter 4:4?
41. When Paul speaks of the old man and the new man, what figure does he use to represent the change?
42. Describe the condition of the old man.
43. What specific duties does Paul present for the new man?
44. What are the characteristics of light as Paul discusses it?
45. How does he define "light?"
46. What contrast does Paul make to the fulness of the Spirit?
47. What three special attitudes are produced by the fulness of the Spirit?
48. How does Paul compare husband and wife with the church?

49. What are the articles of the soldier's armour?
50. In what ways is the Spirit involved in our warfare?

The First Epistle to the
PHILIPPIANS

Introduction

I. Author

Paul was its author. About this there is almost no question.

II. Background

    A. Time of Writing

        About 63 A.D., which was some 12 years after Paul's first visit there.

    B. The Occasion for the Letter

        Paul was in a Roman prison—his first imprisonment there. Benevolences had been received from the church at Philippi, especially through Epaphroditus. Now Epaphroditus needs to return, and Paul wants the people at Philippi to know that he is not a quitter but a faithful man who has fallen ill in the path of service.

        The letter gives thanks for gifts sent, warns against division (4:2), and also warns against false teachers (3:2). Finally, it encourages the Christians in the face of suffering for Christ (1:28-30).

    C. The Establishment of the Church at Philippi.

        The record is found in Acts 16 and illustrates the guidance of the Spirit and the victory of faith. This was Paul's second missionary journey.

III. Recipient

The Church at Philippi. Philippi was a Roman colony and very proud of it. They had been settled by Roman people who maintained Roman culture although they were surrounded by people who were not Roman citizens but Greeks. The citizens were pagans who had established a reputation for military feats under Philip of Macedon and

Alexander. Philip was the father of Alexander the Great, and the city was named after him. There was no synagogue in the city but much witchcraft and demon possession.

IV. Outline

Instead of analyzing the book verse by verse, we will choose a central theme and relate the major points to that theme. There are several possible topics such as Christian joy, excellent things, the mind of the Christian, etc.; however, we will be studying the theme of fellowship.

A. Introduction

B. Fellowship in the Gospel

C. Fellowship of the Spirit

D. Fellowship of His Sufferings

E. Fellowship of Giving and Receiving

F. Conclusion

The Study of the Epistle to the Philippians

I. Introduction to the Epistle, 1:1, 2

   A. The Senders

      Paul and Timothy are the senders of this epistle. In Paul's first imprisonment he was allowed to have visitors, and Timothy was permitted to be with him although Timothy was not himself a prisoner. Here Paul introduces himself as a slave, showing that there was no need to display his authority in dealing with the Philippian Church and also showing the absolute control of Christ over Paul's life.

   B. The Recipients

      "All the Saints in Christ Jesus." Here the tone of friendship and fellowship is set. Paul and Timothy are two dear friends, and they are writing to friends. Note the references to "you all" in the following verses: 1:1, 4, 7, 8, 25; 2:17, etc. The *saint* is one who is "holy." The term means to be set apart and to be purified. God's people are all set apart from the world, and all are called to purity.

II. Fellowship in the Gospel, 1:3-30

Fellowship means the association of people of the same *kind* or in the same *position* for the promotion of a common *interest*. In our present study, the kind of people were *saints*; they were *in Christ*, and the interest was the *Gospel of Christ*. We should emphasize that there is no Christian fellowship with those who are not saints, who are not in Christ, or who do not endorse the gospel of Christ. See Paul's strong position on this expressed in Gal. 1:8, 9; also II Cor. 6:14. Fellowship is not an end in itself. We can not have real fellowship by emphasizing it; it is a by-product of our position in Christ Jesus and our common interest in the Gospel.

   A. Confirmation of the Gospel Produces the Joy of This Fellowship, v. 7

      1. The prevalence of joy in this epistle. Although Paul was in prison when he wrote this epistle, each chapter starts with notes of joy: 1:4, 18; 2:2; 3:1; 4:1, 4, etc. Joy is defined as the emotion stimulated by well-being, success or good fortune or by the prospect of possessing what one desires. None could

have higher well-being, success or prospect of possession than the saint of God. Christian joy does not come from circumstances but from inward assurance and well-being. In the present case, it comes from the fact that the Gospel is confirmed.

2. The grace brought to Philippi. From the study of Acts 16 we learn of the mighty power of the Gospel to bring change into a city and into individual lives. It was not a man who upset Philippi but the power of the Gospel borne by a man of God (see Acts 1:8 and Phil. 3:10). What power there was in the healing of the demon-possessed girl, the opening of the prison, and the conversion of the jailer! That is sensational indeed. But there is power also in the ability of men in Christ to sing in jail at midnight, in Paul's willingness to change plans by the leading of the Spirit, and in his willingness to proceed with the work of the Gospel when there is such affliction connected with it.

Not only is the Gospel confirmed in Philippi; it is in Rome, also.

B. The Defense of the Gospel Shows the Cost of This Fellowship, vv. 7, 17

1. The meaning of the term. Does the Gospel need our defense, or is it our defense? Both are true. The Gospel has power, and it protects us from the errors of the devil, but in this passage the primary meaning is that we are to defend the Gospel before men who oppose it. This defense is not just an intellectual one. We don't need to rationalize and justify it before carnal intellectuals—it will always be foolishness to them. It is power to the believers.

In v. 17 Paul says he was *set* for the defense of the Gospel. The word means to lie outstretched and prostrated and appointed thereto. God has constructed His defense out of "set" individuals, against demonic hosts and godless men. As sandbags are laid to hold back flood waters, so men of God are laid out in defense of the Gospel. The Gospel is always in conflict, and God's men are expendable!

Under Alexander the early Philippians were exposed to great danger in conflict. At the age of twenty Alexander assumed command of the army when his father died. They massed to cross the Granicus River to meet the forces of Medo-Persia under Darius. Crossing the river and climbing the opposite bank, they were exposed to withering fire of arrows, but they prevailed on raw courage. The campaign through Persia and into India was long and hard. The men longed to return home, and once or twice they refused to fight further. Alexander pleaded with them personally, and they would not fail him. In his honor men spent their entire lives in his regiment, some of them outliving Alexander. Such an attitude of sacrifice intensifies fellowship.

2. Defense is associated with confirmation. As long as the Gospel demanded the literal laying down of life, it was confirmed with power. Wherever there has been a reduction to mere words and wishes or a tendency to remove the line of conflict, the confirmation has suffered. The beginning at Philippi illustrates this fact. The Gospel cost suffering there, but out of the suffering came victory. In Korea the strength of the Gospel has never been greater than in the days when men laid down their lives for the truth. The greatest danger today comes from materialism and ease creeping in among us.

3. Defense of the Gospel involves self-giving. Paul was not set to defend himself but the Gospel. This explains his attitude toward the contentious preachers (see vv. 15-18). He did not stoop to fighting back but rejoiced for what good was coming from the situation and for the fact that the Gospel was being preached. It was the welfare of the Gospel and not his personal welfare which was at the basis of his motivation and joy.

C. The Furtherance of the Gospel Means the Enlargement of This Fellowship, v. 12

Fellowship follows naturally from the enlargement. Note the twofold furtherance.

1. Furtherance in breadth, v. 12

   a. The passion of Paul for preaching it (see Rom. 15:15-21; I Cor. 9:16-22). He would gladly spend years in jail, as he did again and again, if thereby the Gospel could be advanced. Here he sees the results he delights in: the spread of the Gospel.

   b. The victory of Paul in spreading it, vv. 12-14. He can see that the years of misrepresentation, shipwreck, and imprisonment have yielded enlargement. These were designed to halt the spread of the Gospel, but they "fell out" to its advancement. "Fell out" is a gambling term. The soldiers who guarded Paul were probably given to gambling with dice; the outcome depended on how the dice "fell out" by chance. In the service of the Gospel, the results are not a matter of chance (see v. 19). Events which appear to others to be disadvantageous will "turn to salvation" through these helps.

A church was started right there in Rome, and some of the members of Caesar's household were members. He paid the fare and provided quarters, and the Gospel grew in its effects.

  c. The confidence of Paul for the future, v. 19. Note three necessary things.

    1) Prayers of the saints. Paul always emphasized this (see Rom. 15:30, 31; II Thes. 3:1, 2). Prayers were necessary if he was to be delivered from unbelief and the Word was to move freely.

    2) Supply of the Spirit. The Spirit will supply whatever is needed in abundance. He keeps the ammunition and sends wisdom, strength, etc. "Supply" is a term which often was used concerning a banquet spread by a wealthy citizen.

    3) Paul's own faith. "My earnest hope and expectation." He doesn't aim at saving himself but at magnifying Christ in his body. If more glory should come to Christ in death, Paul would have it so.

2. Furtherance in depth in Christian character, vv. 6, 24. Paul had a passion for this, also. Since the Philippians needed him for this purpose, he concluded he would remain. How unselfish! His purpose is expressed in 1:6, the desire that grace should increase in the formation of character. Note the prayer of vv. 9-11.

  a. Love abounding in discernment. We sometimes hear it said that "love is blind." Beginning love is strong but often quite undiscerning. Babes don't have very sensitive tastes (Heb. 5:14). What hinders the growth of love must be counted as wrong. John Wesley's mother said to him that whatever should decrease his love for God, his relish for the Word, or his peace in Christ should be counted sin for him.

      b. Approval of the excellent. The choice here is not between good and bad, as borderline Christians would choose. They often ask, "Is this wrong?" and if not, they feel free to participate. Mature Christians, on the other hand, ask, "Is it less than the best?" and if so, they reject it. This is a real basis for choice today. The wrong is being reasoned out of jewelry, mixed bathing, movies, immodest dress, formalism, barrenness, etc. It is evidence of dull sense. It is possible for worldly people to so have the taste of the world in their minds that they do not discern what is best for them. The wandering Israelites loathed the manna God provided and refused Canaan because they had the taste of Egypt too much in their mouths.

      c. Sincerity until He comes. Sincerity is equivalent to holiness. The Greek can be interpreted "sun-judged." Cloth was tested in the sun. In Latin the word means "without wax." Potters and sculptors sometimes used wax as patchwork for defective pottery or sculpture. Holiness is freedom from the defects of sin. The sanctified person can stand the light of the sun. He can stand before God.

D. Becoming the Gospel is the Duty of Fellowship, v. 27. (Compare Titus 2:10)

    Nothing short of what has been described here will suffice to do credit to the Gospel. Shoddy lives rob it of its power, but Christ-like lives give it power to prevail and bring conviction to lives in sin.

    1. **Unity in spirit, mind and faith, v. 27.** Division within the body of Christ always brings reproach to the Gospel of Christ. The unity of the Spirit gives us one spirit of fellowship in this Gospel. The one mind is a controlling purpose to do what glorifies Christ. The faith brings us into the same army to battle against the enemies of Christ.

    2. **Suffering for His sake, v. 29.** One of the facts which always has given greatest impetus to the work of Christ is the willingness of His followers to suffer for Him.

II. Fellowship of the Spirit, 2:1-30

The whole emphasis of the chapter, as well as of the appeals of v. 1, is centered in fellowship and its condition. Note that it is the fellowship *of* and not *with* the Spirit which is mentioned. This may refer to two things: Christian fellowship which is made possible by the Spirit or the Spirit's fellowship with us. (In this last instance, note that the Spirit is said to have fellowship with us but we are never said to have fellowship with the Spirit, as with the Father and the Son.) In either case, the conditions are the same. Each is indispensable to the other.

The context indicates rather the Spirit's conditions for Christian fellowship.

A. The Basis for the Fellowship: "Likemindedness"

Note the multiplied appeals: 1:27; 2:2, 20; 4:2. In 2:2 the sense is "Have the same sentiment, opinion, or interest of mind, being equal-souled." Verse 20 indicates "equal-souled." Verse 4:2 means to have the same attitude. The "mind" here is not a faculty but an attitude.

1. The source of such a "like-mind"

   a. It is not human. A common aim of the natural man is to produce self-centered like-thinking: he wants others to think as he himself does about matters. Pride makes general unanimity impossible or at least difficult to attain. One who has a fixed opinion hates to renounce it because it is a blow to pride and causes loss of face. Arguing about facts soon involves the honor of the person espousing those "facts." "Likemindedness" is impossible to the natural man (see I Cor. 2:14-16).

   b. It is a divine-centered mind. "Likeminded" means to be like Him; if all are like Him, all will be like each other. The mind cannot be carnal and "likeminded" at the same time. This is a manifestation of humility, which is supremely illustrated in Christ. Note His humility and exaltation.

      1) In the form of God. He shared the light, glory, crowns and throne. He was the very expression of God, worshiped by angels—the Creator and Upholder of all things. If we had visited Heaven, we would have seen Him as the brightest Person of all and the center of all.

2) Of no reputation. He had a reputation, the highest of all: as Creator, Sustainer, the Logos or Expression of God. Men cherish their reputations more than many other things, but some think more of reputation than of character. He had both, but He emptied Himself of glory, honor, position; He laid aside His royalty to serve.

3) A man. He became true man that He might enter into the entire range of human experience. He wanted to know and feel the needs of men that He might be fully fitted as Captain of our salvation.

4) A servant man, made lower than the angels, His own creatures. He might have insisted that some lesser one should go to earth to be the Redeemer, but He took a lower place than the servant angels. He became a servant to His parents, to his disciples, to children, to the poor. He said, "I come to do thy will, O God."

5) A humble man of obedience. He could have ruled men (Matt. 26:53). He could have called legions of angels to His bidding, but rather He learned obedience by the things that He suffered (Heb. 3:8). He washed the disciples' feet, not as an act but by His nature of humility and service. Fenelon said that the real test of a man's character is how he acts under pressure. Jesus was a perfect man under pressure.

6) The accursed death. He *died*, in the fullest sense of the term. Others slept, in the New Testament way of speaking, but He died. He made the greatest possible descent. At the bottom He put His spirit into God's hands and poured out His soul in death.

7) The exaltation. God exalted Him. This is the secret for us: "He that humbleth himself shall be exalted." Christ was exalted higher than ever before. Only Heaven praised Him before; now He is praised in Heaven, in earth, and under the earth (Rev. 5:11-14).

3. The characteristics of likemindedness

   a. It is peaceful, without strife, v. 3. "Only by pride cometh contention," (Prov. 13:10). "Where there is no talebearer, the strife ceaseth," (Prov. 26:20). Jesus did not kick and spit at His tormentors; He was gentle and forgiving. The Roman Centurion said, "Truly this was the Son of God. The soft answer turneth away wrath (Prov. 15:1), but grievous words stir up anger. This mind would rather win a soul to Christ than to win an argument for self. This mind is firm without being hard; it clings to the right without seeming to be dogmatic and bigoted. We must watch our attitude that in standing for right we do not show a wrong spirit.

Note that in 1:27 we are told to "strive together." The command not to strive refers to division among saints; the other refers to the uniting of the saints against a common foe. Even there we must show a right spirit at all times. Our honor is not above that of Christ!

    b. It is humble and lowly, preferring others, v. 3. This mind delights to see others exalted. There is no jealousy over the promotion of others. It does not seek a position of eminence but of service. Many are tempted to seek position, even in the Church, but there is only one rule for the followers of Christ in this area: we are to seek to serve. If promotion comes, let it be from the Lord, not from our ambition for self-exaltation (Ps. 75:6, 7). In the wilderness Christ rejected the temptation to seek exaltation. There is no sin in the temptation, but we must reject the temptation as Jesus did.

This mind is quick to see its own faults but dwells on the fine points of others in the body of Christ. If of necessity it sees some fault in others, it corrects in love and helpfulness, with carefulness and a warning to self. It doesn't advertise the fault before the public.

    c. A sympathetic mind, v. 4. It enters into the situation of others. Ezekiel said, "I sat where they sat," (Ez. 3:15). Christ entered into our position, and we ought to do the same for others. This is the demand of the golden rule. The proud mind won't do it, but the humble must. The mind works this way when it is a mind of love (see v. 1).

4. The attainment of a like-mind, vv. 12-18.

    a. God works it in us. He gives the will or attitude; none can produce it within himself. He makes His commands possible. He produces an attitude of love and Christ-likeness when He transforms us by His grace.

       b. We must work it out. Salvation here is not pardon (v. 12). Rather, it is the evidencing the Christ-like life, not for reputation's sake, but to please God. This is the highest motive of the individual.

          This mind works in secret just as consistently as in public (v. 12). The results will be undimmed lights leading others to Jesus. (The figure here is that of a lighthouse which directs mariners into harbor through the storms at sea and through the darkness.) Paul was willing to die (v. 17) if thereby he might help to bring men to such a place of consistency and service.

B. Examples of Likemindedness, vv. 19-30

  1. Timothy

     a. Declared to be like-minded, v. 20. That is, he had the mind of Christ, and others might well imitate his example.

     b. He was the only likeminded person with Paul. It is surprising that so early in the Church it should be said that all sought their own rather than Christ's things. How subtle this is, that the early Church should be so beset! Demas was an example. How persistent the tendency to put self first and still claim to be putting Christ first! Even preachers can fall prey to the snare of putting their comfort first. It is a marvel the church has so long survived with so much of materialism and self-seeking.

     c. Timothy had a nature to care for others rather than to seek self first. He was physically weak. He was the type that might stay at home and lean on parents for support, but he became a soldier for Christ, an example for others to follow.

     d. He served as a son with his father. Paul must have been thinking of the Son of God and His obedience to the Father as already given (v. 5-10). He left home and comforts, with no guaranteed wage or security, in order to serve *in the Gospel*.

  2. Epaphroditus. Note the endearing terms (v. 25). He had come from Philippi, had been sick, and was now to return home with the epistle. It is evident that he was highly respected by Paul. The term "messenger" could be rendered "apostle." The man had such qualities. The term "minister" may refer to priests or even to angels. Epaphroditus is a man who poured out his life

for others. The mutual love between Paul and Epaphroditus deepened through severe pressures.

- a. The mind of sympathy, v. 26. He was full of heaviness for his own people, not for his sickness, but because they had heard of it.
- b. The lowliness and sacrifice, v. 30. He followed in the apostolic train of "regarding not his own life" to carry out his commission. "He served others; himself he could not save."
- c. The true reputation attained, v. 29. Such people should be exalted, not to their own selfish honor, but to the glory of God Who is working in them! If we want a reputation, here is a way to get it. Give your life in service for others and in devotion to God and in His service.

    In conclusion, this is all the work of the Spirit, and it intensifies our fellowship with each other as well as His with us. The natural man may lay down his life; he may give much; he may be devoted. But in each case, self is prevalent. The like-minded does so for God's glory and the good of other people. The life is laid down for Jesus' sake.

III. Fellowship of His Sufferings, 3:1-21

We are treading on most sacred ground in this passage. Unhallowed feet dare not, and ungoverned feet care not, to tread here. Beginners want to have others share their sufferings; mature souls want to share the sufferings of others. Paul never tried to enter the manger experience of Christ's birth or into the wilderness experience of His temptation, but he did desire to enter into the passion of His death and the power of His resurrection. There is no other place we can get so close to Christ as at His cross. This is generally true: people will let us draw close to them in their sorrows. So while the Apostle wanted the power of Christ's resurrection, it was the cross he chose as the pattern for living, being made conformable to His death.

A. The Context of This Fellowship, v. 10

1. The knowledge of Christ, first of all. This does not mean to know *about* Him but to know *Him*. Paul wanted supremely to know Him personally. This use of the word "know" involves communion and entering into the very life of Christ. None can know Him after the natural man but only by spiritual revelation.

2. The power of His resurrection (cf. Eph. 1:18-20). This does not mean just that one has been resurrected himself but that such power marks his ministry (see Rom. 15:19; I Cor. 2:4; I Thes. 1:5). There is intensity and weight to this desire of Paul.

3. The fellowship of His suffering, being made conformable to His death. Samuel Chadwick says the order is essential. The resurrection works only where the cross is applied, so our lives must always be marked with the cross if we are to exercise the power of the resurrection. If one has a cure for a dreaded disease, then he must go where the disease is to apply the cure. The power of the resurrection works in the region of death, so we share the death anguish of Christ in order to apply the power of the resurrection. Note some expressions of the suffering of Christ.

   a. "He began to be very heavy," (Matt 26:37). This means "distracted, separate from mankind."

   b. "My soul is exceeding sorrowful," (Matt. 26:38). This means "encompassed, overwhelmed, encircled." "He was plunged head and ears in sorrow, and had no breathing hole," says Godwin.

   c. "He began to be sore amazed," (Mark 14:33). This means such extremity of amazement that one quakes and trembles. These all refer to His experience in the garden when He began His awful sorrow for the sins of the world. It was not so much physical sorrow immediately as it was mental and soul sorrow which reacted so upon His physical frame as to force blood as sweat through the pores of His body!

B. The Content of This Suffering

1. The suffering of consecration, vv. 3-9. Paul is parallel to Christ in giving absolutely all to do the will of God (cf. Col. 1:24).

   a. A cutting away (circumcision) of fleshly attachments to live in the Spirit. We are not dealing with sins here but with the flesh, all those natural assets which are the basis of human self-confidence. Paul was a supremely confident person in facing life. Many think he was already a member of the Jewish Sanhedrin at a young age.

1) Ancestry: like a man born now in the president's family.

2) Religion: of the largest and strictest religious sect.

3) Ability, education, morality, position: When this is all gone, there is nothing left for him to depend on in the flesh or natural man.

b. A loss suffered. There are two words for "loss" in the New Testament. One means something rejected as of little or no value. The use here is to something taken by a superior power (see Acts 27:21). There was a struggle involved. Compare the wrestling of Jacob.

The issue was not settled by feeling but by the constraint of the Lord. Anything which would keep us from Him is to be considered the vilest of refuse, though to the natural man it seems desirable.

This consecration is permanent: "I counted" and "I count." It should begin in one's youth and last through all of one's life.

c. The joy attained: the knowledge of Christ. This one single asset more than compensated for all the loss and suffering. See II Tim. 1:11, 12. It is the joy of having everything in life related to Him and having His approval of our life. A person may say he is consecrated, but if he does things, says things, buys things, etc., without reference to whether it is for God's glory and the promotion of His cause, the said consecration is spurious. When we are truly consecrated, God's will and work are our highest passion. Such consecration will touch our time, talents, and all, because it touches us first.

Paul was sure that his knowledge of Christ would safely get him past all the devil's obstacles here, past the judgment, and into the eternal presence of Christ. He had committed his all to Jesus, and he was sure it would be kept for him.

2. The suffering of delayed desire, vv. 11-17

a. The strong desire for the glory of Christ. Compare the request of Christ in John 17 for the glory with the Father. It pervades Paul's thoughts. He said, "If in this life only we have hope, we are of all men most miserable." He suffered too much to feel at home in this world. He had been to the cross, and he longed for the glory to follow.

b. The keen awareness of his imperfections. Any brand of "holiness" which makes a person "cocksure" and gives a pious pride is specious. The revelation of the glory of Christ exposes much that is inglorious about us: inefficiency, dullness, backwardness—physical and mental limitations. What a glad day it will be when we are no longer hindered by infirmities, personality weaknesses, etc.

c. The pain of intense concentration

1) The possibility of failure yet. No presumption of attainment should appear in the sanctified so as to cause him to relax his watchfulness. See v. 12, 13. "By any means" (v. 11) denotes that it will take everything he has to make it.

2) The concentration needed, v. 14. No half-interest will do. If Paul had to give everything to make it, so will we. He strained until it hurt! We are in a race to win!

d. The joy in suffering

1) A perfection already attained. Something buoyed him up, right in prison. In a most gracious way Paul testified to a perfection already wrought in him. In this chapter we find a perfect concentration of aim, a perfect strength, a perfect example, as well as a perfect consecration.

2) Concentration of aim. He hadn't attained the goal, but his aim was perfect. Jesus spoke of those who had a "single eye." Soren Kierkegaard said that "perfection of character is to will one thing." Paul did this.

3) Sensitiveness to divine revelation. An attitude ready always to receive light, admit faults, and take the remedy is a perfection. Those who assume they are the ultimate in perfection, who gloss over their faults and criticize others, are far from perfection.

4) A governed, harmonious walk. It is a walk by rule; that is, a disciplined walk. Everything else is brought under the government of the supreme aim of life. It is

governed by Christ's mind within. This is not a spasmodic life but a disciplined one.

5) Exemplary conduct, v. 17. There was no duplicity in Paul's walk. He could say, "Follow me, and you will be following Jesus." Such a man is either a supreme egotist or he is completely lost in Another who shows through his life and gets the honor. Compare I Cor. 11:1 and Gal. 3:1. When Paul appeared in Galatia they saw Christ crucified. They had the example they needed.

6) Anticipated glory, vv. 20, 21. He looks forward to the glory of Heaven and a new body. The word "vile" in v. 21 does not mean sinful but earthly and mortal.

3. For enemies of the cross—intercession

   a. This is Jesus' present intercession, in part. He entered into the death of all men, yet sees them dying. How He must suffer over it! Those who reject the greatest outpouring of love are enemies of the cross. They are not people who never heard of it but those who have heard and oppose submission to the claims of Christ. The greatest suffering is over those who have come the nearest and yet have rejected the cross.

   b. The saints share this suffering. Paul is moved to weeping because these enemies of the cross are lost. Note the piercing contrasts.

      1) Destruction vs. Heaven's glory. We see both: "knowing the terror of the Lord, we persuade men" (II Cor. 5:11). When we saw our doom in sin, we turned our wills about and turned to serve God. Now we see others going onward to destruction, and we would change them about if we could. Some do turn, but the majority do not. This is the greatest suffering of Gospel workers: not sickness, physical trial and loneliness, but the fact that those whom we seek to influence toward God will not turn from sin and hell to be saved.

      2) Fleshly vs. spiritual. Men give more respect to that which appeals to the flesh than to the spirit. Delights in a full table of food and social company are counted higher than delight in God's presence. Earthly gain is felt higher than Heaven's glory.

3) Glory vs. shame. Many are so twisted in nature that the thing that is really shame and eternal loss is their greatest glory and appeal. Social popularity at the cost of sinful and sensual living is counted the high goal, when actually it will add to eternal shame and loss.

4) Earthly things fill the mind. This is in contrast to the Christ-mind. They are short-sighted and lost—blinded to eternal reality. We are to intercede for such people, bringing them and God together.

c. Joy in seeing some saved. It is worth all the effort if some are recovered from the snare of this world and brought to honor the Lord.

IV. Fellowship of Giving and Receiving

In verses 14 and 15 the word "communication" is the same as "fellowship." Paul ends on a practical note (all preaching must be practical). This is a fellowship in which each provides something for the other. See I Cor. 9:11, 14.

A. The Giving of the Philippians (cf. II Cor. 8:1-5)

1. A spontaneous grace. They began at once when Paul went away (see v. 15). The spirit of giving is a grace, a blessing from God. "It is more blessed to give than to receive," said Jesus. When Moses asked for material for the tabernacle, God gave the people the spirit of giving, and they had to be restrained. After Pentecost the disciples counted nothing their own. There was great grace upon them all.

   We are told that when a baby is born his grasping muscles are his strongest ones. The natural man seeks to get for himself; when touched by God's grace, men want to give.

2. Out of deep poverty and great trial of affliction. Every one should give. The greatest giving is out of poverty. The widow's mite was honored by Christ. The giving was so deeply sacrificial that Paul was reluctant to accept so much.

3. In sacrificial measure. A tithe isn't even mentioned. They gave "beyond their power," Paul said (4:18). They took the very necessities for their own life and gave them. We don't really sacrifice when we just give up luxuries; we sacrifice by giving what really costs us. A sacrifice is that which is given to be consumed. They gave themselves first (living sacrifices), then

made a sacrifice of their possessions, v. 18. This produced a sweet fragrance before God, as the animal sacrifices did.

4. It was continual. They gave once and again, v. 10. They gave whenever the opportunity presented itself. This was not just a single impulse with them: to give sacrificially became a pattern of life. How precious it appeared to Paul.

B. The Receiving of the Philippians, see v. 19

They had already received many blessings before, but note some benefits in this chapter.

1. Joy and rejoicing, v. 4. They were a rejoicing people, and Paul rejoiced with them.

   a. It is rejoicing in the Lord, not in things. Do we rejoice in position (in Christ) or in possessions (of the earth)? Those who depend on things are wretched. Paul gave up everything to be found in Christ.

   b. It may be a rejoicing in the absence of things. Paul had learned how to be full and how to be empty (vv. 11-13), and yet to be satisfied and rejoice. Most people learn only the first half of this. Paul liked to be full, as he suggests in v. 18, but since his position was in Christ, he would accept joyfully what came to him as being designed by the Lord. He was not puffed up when in good circumstances nor let down when in poor circumstances. He gave up everything to get in this place. He is a prisoner of the Lord, not of circumstances.

2. The immediate presence of the Lord, v. 5. The Lord was right with them. He is with all of those who call upon Him in truth.

3. Freedom from care. Note the trick of words in vv. 6 and 10. Verse 6 means "distracted;" v. 10 means "interested." Paul wanted them to be interested but not distracted. We should never let things "pull us apart" from Him. When things pull us away from God, we must pull toward Him the more carefully. Worry is useless and sinful. It is called "a high rate of interest on borrowed trouble."

   We can request God's provisions for all our needs. We have an account with Him (v. 17).

4. Peace in the soul. The peace of God (v. 7) and the God of peace (v. 9) are with them. This is higher than the peace with God.

God doesn't worry nor is He terrified. We are garrisoned by this peace and fortified at our weak points.

Paul sets his own life as an example in vv. 9 and 11. "Not that I desire a gift." Not to ask for money although it was due him was his rule. "I have all" was his attitude. Thus he could be content in any state.

Review Questions
PHILIPPIANS

1. Why did Paul write this epistle?
2. State the general theme of each chapter.
3. What is the meaning of the word "fellowship," and what are the elements of it?
4. Paul said he was "set for the defense of the Gospel." What did he mean by that expression?
5. What is meant by the furtherance in the breadth of the Gospel? What is meant by furtherance in depth of the Gospel?
6. Explain the meaning of the term "sincerity" in 1:10.
7. What is the source of "likemindedness?"
8. Paul illustrated the basis of likemindedness in Christ. Give the steps of His condescension by which His humble mind was displayed.
9. Contrast the human way with the divine way by which a person is to be exalted. Show how this was true in Christ's exaltation.
10. Give three characteristics of the Christ-like mind.
11. How may we attain a Christ-like mind?
12. In addition to Christ, Paul gave two examples of "likemindedness." What were they? How did each one compare with Christ?
13. What sufferings of Paul could be called the fellowship of Christ's suffering?
14. Describe the consecration of Paul as set forth in Chapter 3.
15. What did Paul expect to win as a result of the loss of all things?
16. What perfection did Paul deny in Chapter 3? What perfection did he affirm in the same chapter?
17. What perfection will come to us at the appearing of Christ?
18. Who were the "enemies of the cross of Christ," and how did Paul describe them?
19. Give three characteristics of the giving of the Philippian Christians.
20. What special kind of rejoicing marked Paul and the Philippians?
21. What difference is there between "peace with God" and the "peace of God?"
22. What promise did Paul make about the supply of their need?
23. What did Paul say that he had learned through his many experiences?
24. What was the source of Paul's great confidence when he said, "I can do all things?"

The Epistle to the
COLOSSIANS

Introduction

I. Author

There are some who deny Pauline authorship because of the difference in style between this and his other epistles. However, there is no good reason to deny his writing it; a man does not need to use exactly the same style in all of his letters.

II. The Time of Writing

A. It seems apparent that it was written while Paul was in prison (4:18).

B. It is also apparent that it was sent at about the time the letter to the Ephesians and Philemon was sent. This letter was sent by Tychicus and Onesimus (4:7, 9). [The letter to Ephesians was written from prison in Rome and was sent by Tychicus (Eph. 6:21); Philemon was sent by Onesimus (v. 12).] Hence, it would seem that they were delivered at about the same time.

Later we will see that the contents of this letter are very similar to that of Ephesians. Hence, it probably was written about the same time, 61-65 A.D, and more particularly about 62 or 53 A.D.

III. The Historical Background

A. The Establishment of the Church at Colosse

1. We are not positive who started the church there. There are those who do not believe Paul had been there, because he said in 2:1 that there were some who had not seen his face in the

flesh. If Paul did not start it, perhaps Epaphras did so (see 1:7; 4:12, 13).

    2. There are those who strongly feel that Paul did start the work there. The statement of 2:1 could easily mean that Paul was concerned for those at Colosse and Laodicea and for others who had not seen his face.

       It is said in Acts 16:6, 7 and Acts 18:22, 23 that Paul went over all the area of Phrygia. It is doubtful that he would have covered the area and missed the main cities since Paul usually went to the centers of population.

       Further, Paul in effect says in Col. 1:24, 25 that he was the minister to Colosse. It seems a safe conclusion that he did preach there, though it is not conclusive.

B. The City of Colosse

The three cities of Colosse, Hierapolis, and Laodicea were located very close together. They were in a rich agricultural area. Laodicea was important for its textiles and dyes, and Colosse had also been important as a city of some wealth, although it had begun to decline. Today there is not a trace of it left. At the time of this writing, it is said that this was the least important city to which Paul ever wrote.

IV. The Reason for Writing

A. He Gives Thanks for Them

Paul has heard through Epaphras of their faith and love (1:4), fruitfulness (1:60, and stedfastness (2:5).

B. He Counters an Error at Colosse

We are not told just what that error is, but from studying Paul's response, it seems obvious that it was Gnosticism combined with Jewish ceremonialism.

    1. According to Gnosticism, the world, being evil, was not created by God but by an emanation far removed from God. Consequently, Paul insists on the creative work of Christ (1:16, 17).

    2. Since matter is totally evil, the Gnostics taught that Christ did not come in the flesh. Consequently, Paul insists on the bodily reality of Christ (2:9).

3. In emphasizing the essential evil of matter, they concluded that we must sometimes oppress the body with rigid regulations of many kinds. Paul refers to this in 2:20-23.

   On the other hand there were those who said it did not matter what we do with the body since it is evil anyway. Paul appears to write against this danger in 3:5-8.

4. Some emphasized the importance of angels as mediators between God and man and were inclined to give them reverence. Paul attacks such an error in 2:18.

5. As the Jews modified Gnosticism there was much emphasis on holy days, new moons, etc. Paul refers to this in 2:16.

6. The high knowledge of Gnosticism was considered to be so exclusive that only a small elite could obtain it. Paul attacks such an exclusive philosophical element in 2:8. Also, in 1:28 he shows that *every man* is involved in the Gospel appeal.

C. He Gives Practical Christian Instructions, Chapters 3 and 4

V. The Theme of the Study: Perfection in Christ (1:28) (The term "in Christ" appears 164 times in Paul's letters)

A. Paul's Introduction, 1:1, 2

B. Saints in Christ, Chapter 1

C. Stedfastness in Christ, Chapter 2

D. Submission in Christ, Chapter 3

E. Servants in Christ, Chapter 4

F. Conclusion, 4:18

The Study of the Epistle to the Colossians

I. Introduction to the Epistle, 1:1, 2

    A. The Emphasis on Brethren, 1, 2

        It is interesting that in Paul's early epistles he addresses the churches: I and II Thessalonians, I and II Corinthians, and Galatians. His later epistles, however, show a contrast: he addresses the individuals more than the collective body: Romans, Colossians, Philippians, and Ephesians. There seems to be a growing appreciation of the worth of the individual in the constitution and strength of the church.

    B. The Two Environments, v. 2

        1. In Christ

        2. At Colosse. The Christian always has these two environments: the world and Christ. Physically, he is in the world with its necessity for food clothing, shelter, etc. There are temptations that come from this environment.

           The Christian is also in Christ. His source of life and strength in the Spirit come from such a source. While he has these two environments, the Christian cannot isolate one from the other. He must show His spiritual life within the world. He is called to bear witness to the life within.

II. Saints in Christ

    We can tell which of the Christian's environments is more real and meaningful to him by how great the measure of his sainthood. The worldling is shallow in sainthood, if he has any grace at all.

    A. The Supremacy of Christ

        There was error in Colosse which said that Christ was good but not sufficient. He was downgraded to a lower order of emanation from God.

        1. His supremacy in creation, 1:16, 17

            a. Visible. We can get a bit of an idea of the greatness of Christ when we consider the starry heavens. Antares, the largest single star we know, is 365 light years away from the earth and 400,000,000 miles (5,640,000,000 kilometers) in diameter. If it were placed where our sun is, it would swallow up the sun, Mercury, Venus, Earth, Mars and extend 50,000,000 miles (85,000,000 km.) beyond Mars! Einstein said there are 10^{28} stars in the universe. Astronomers are now receiving radio signals from near 9 billion light years in space and have no idea how vast the universe really is.

Christ brought it all into being with the word of His power. There was nothing at all—no speck of dust, no ray of light or breath of life—before He spoke the command of creation. "Through faith we understand that the worlds were framed by the word [command] of God" (Heb. 11:3). He is also "upholding all things by the word of his power . . . ." (Heb. 1:3).

b. The invisible creation, v. 15, 16. The primary realities are invisible, contrary to what worldly-minded men believe. In II Cor. 4:18, Paul said, "While we look not at the things which are seen, but at the things which are not seen: for the things which are seen are temporal; but the things which are not seen are eternal."

Even in the physical world, there are marvelous things which are not visible, and they are the basis of all things temporal. The atom is invisible; it is so tiny that 5 million of them could be lined up across a pinhead, yet it is a complex realm of whirling electrons and protons and forces which bind them all together. No man understands the forces operating within the atom, but Christ created it. It is by His power that these things stick together (v. 17).

Another example of the invisible is gravity, a mysterious force acting between all the bodies in the universe. This force between the earth and sun is so strong that if replaced by a steel cable, it would have to be 5,000 miles (8,500 kilometers) in diameter.

Angels are His creation. There are tens of millions of them, created to be ministering servants of those who are heirs of salvation (Heb. 1:14). Christ is before all of them. They are not creating beings, as the Gnostics claimed, but created beings. And they worship Christ.

It is well to recognize that even fallen angles, including their leader, Satan himself, are all created by Christ. He is supreme over all of them. They can go no farther than He permits them to go.

2. His supremacy in the Church, v. 18

   a. He is the head of the Church. What the head is to the body, Christ is to the Church. The head gives life to the body. We can live without a leg, an arm, or even a stomach, but without there head there is no life. Christ is our life.

   The head controls the actions of the body, and Christ is to control the actions of His body. The head is the seat of wisdom. The brain has connections with every cell in the body and is equipped to govern the action of them. It responds to pain in any one of them. It also coordinates the actions of all parts. So Christ is the wisdom of the body, the Church. He desires to coordinate and control the church to the Glory of the Father.

   b. He is the Firstborn from the dead, vv. 15, 18. In this section (vv. 15-23) Paul presents a superbly written portrayal of the supremacy of Christ. We must remember that this is written against the background of the Gnostic belittlement of Christ.

   The term "firstborn" was used by the Jews to express the idea of superiority. The firstborn Son was the highest and most honored son. Jesus is the firstborn Son of God, so He has the highest honor of all beings in the universe. Not only in His original being is He first, but He is also first from the dead. Because He rose from the dead, it is possible for all to come forth from the dead.

   When Paul says Christ is the *image* of God, he used a richly meaningful word meaning that Christ shows us what god is like; He is the perfect manifestation. Inasmuch as man was made in the image of God and then fell, Jesus shows us what man was meant to be from the beginning. An image in that day was often a portrait of another. So Christ is a kind of portrait of God. However, all the fulness of God dwells in Him (v. 19) so the portrait of God is not dead and helpless; rather, He is all that God is yet is truly man.

   Christ truly died in the fullest sense of the word—he was more than just physically dead. He knew what it meant to be separated from God, under the weight of sin.

Yet He came forth and opened the way for others to find victory over death, sin and hell.

    c. He is the Beginning of the Church, v. 18. Not only is He the beginning of the physical universe by creation; He is also the beginning of the Church by a new creation. The word "beginning" means not only the first in point of time but also the source from which the Church comes. It is His death and resurrection that makes the life of the Church possible.

        These things being true, it is obvious that Jesus is not just another of the emanations of God as the Gnostics said. He is the *first*, and He is *all* to the Church.

B. The Sufficiency of Christ

Note how many times the word "all" is used in this epistle—some 25 times. Paul hits hard at the idea of the limited littleness of Christ.

1. Initial grace. This is mentioned, but it is not the primary emphasis of the epistle. Note the terms which apply to the work of grace whereby men are forgiven of their sins.

    a. Redemption, v. 14. This properly includes all that is involved in recovery from sin and being brought to eternal salvation: justification, sanctification, and glorification. It means a buying back from bondage. Some manuscripts include "through his blood." Whether it is properly included or not, it is true that the purchase was at the price of His blood.

    b. Deliverance from the power of darkness and translation into Christ's kingdom. Darkness is in opposition to the light of v. 12. It symbolizes the kingdom of Satan, the kingdom of this world under his sway from which he designs to keep out all truth of God and eternity.

        In the ancient world, when one nation defeated another in battle, the people of the defeated country were taken over into the victor country. It was so with the Jews going into Babylon. Now Paul uses this figure and declares that Christ has taken us out of the kingdom of darkness into the kingdom of light and truth. It is a transference from bondage to liberty, from sinfulness to righteousness, and from the power of Satan unto God.

c. Peace and reconciliation, v. 20. Sin is fundamentally disharmony between men and God. Men were to blame, but God has taken the initiative to bring reconciliation. The cross shows how much God wanted to bring peace. He paid the infinite price to show His love of men and His hatred of the sin that separated.

It should be noted that God did not reconcile Himself to men but men to Himself. There is nothing in Him that needed to be changed. Some Calvinists have taught that the death of Christ satisfied something of wrath and hatred in God so He could now accept men, but it is not God that is reconciled, it is men.

Verse 21 shows what we once were. Through his death, however, He has made it possible for our total adjustment to God's will. We should praise God for this always. Note that not only men but all of creation can be reconciled. There fell a curse on the physical and animal universe which will one day be lifted so that all of nature will bring praise to God when it is recovered from the effects of the fall and the curse.

d. Faith, hope and love (vv. 4, 5) came as a consequence of redemption.

2. Fulness of grace, vv. 9-11. There is clearly shown that the initial grace has a preparatory aspect. It prepares persons for a fulness of grace. Paul prayed for their perfection, as he did for all young believers, v. 9.

a. Fulness of the knowledge of His will (v. 9). This is a supernatural impartation of knowledge. It is not just an academic knowledge but also an experimental one. It is perfect knowledge by revelation, leaving no nagging doubt or uncertainty. This is a part of the revelation of the Spirit. It is known in experience and is part of the sanctifying work of the Spirit.

It is assumed in this verse that the persons are already made wiling to do God's will. When they are made willing, they can know. If they are not willing, they are not able to discern.

Wisdom and spiritual understanding are important qualities. *Wisdom* refers to knowledge of first principles. *Spiritual understanding* refers to the ability to apply principles to situations. Taken together, they refer to theology and to practical living. We all need this combination.

    b. Fulness of fruitfulness, v. 10. The walk of the Christian is to be brought to the place where it pleases God fully in all things. Every work is to be fruitful. The inward grace is to be shown by outward fruitfulness. There can be no true religion in only one of these aspects without the other.

       The Christian is sensitive to what please God, especially when he is filled with the Spirit. Christ did always the things that pleased His Father, and we will have the same character when we have His Spirit. Some children do only what their parents command them to do, then do it grudgingly. Others love their parents so much that they look for ways to please their parents, doing more than what is required. When a child does what is pleasing to the parent, the parent will be satisfied, even if there is not full maturity expressed in the action. The motive to please is the quality that is approved.

    c. Fulness of strength for the journey, v. 11. The dynamic of energy from God is not just to erupt in spectacular displays but is also to give us strength to go on. It would seem in this verse that the author is building up to some spectacular achievement, but it is unto all patience and longsuffering with joyfulness. The testings in life are to increase our endurance. We are to hold under the strain.

       The terms *patience* and *longsuffering* refer generally to endurance of *situations* and endurance of *people*, respectively. Sanctified believers have grace that gives them patience with both people and things. In both they have joy from the indwelling God.

3. Increasing grace. This was always a burden of Paul. It was not enough to be filled with the Spirit; there must be continued growth. Sanctification is preparation for maximum growth, but the growth does not come mechanically. There must be attention to the means of growth.

    a. Increase in knowledge, v. 10. There is nothing meant to be static in our Christian life. Holiness is not a condition but a relationship, and it must be growing if it is alive. God will put us into situations to bring us into a better knowledge of Himself. The person who is sanctified wants to do God's will, but He may not always clearly know that will. He is willing, but he is ignorant. As he knows God better, he will also know His will better. There will be an increasing sensitivity to the will and pleasure of God.

  b. Increasing possession of our inheritance, v. 12. When the children of Israel went into Canaan, the land belonged to them but it was their task to possess it. Some of the tribes never did claim all that was theirs. The sanctified child of God is in possession of an inheritance in the kingdom of light. (See Acts 20:32; 26:18).

   Before the Children of Israel had a right to their inheritance, they had to be circumcised. Without this the covenant was nullified. Even though a person was born to Israelite parents, without circumcision he forfeited his birthright to an inheritance (see Gen. 17:6-14). Now circumcision is a type of the sanctification of the soul (Deut. 30:6; Col. 2:11). This grace makes us meet to inheritance, but we must diligently possess.

4. Ultimate grace

  a. Presentation by Christ, v. 22. The word means to "stand by and exhibit." Christ will be proud to show His bride to the Father. Heb. 2:13 says, ". . . Behold I and the children which God hath given me."

   Notice that Christ wants to present a holy and blameless people to God. His death on the cross for us was for the purpose of making His people holy. This truth is so clearly revealed in the Word that none should misunderstand it. See Eph. 5:25-27; Rev. 19:7, 8.

   It should further be seen that the grace of entire sanctification must be accompanied by establishment—grounding and settling—if one is to reach that day of glorious presentation. There is nothing here of an automatic eternal security. Even sanctified people must be careful to abide in grace. See also I Thess. 3:13. Holiness is the establishing grace.

  b. Presentation by the preacher, vv. 24-29. Paul wanted to share the glory of that day by presenting the fruit of his labors to Christ, v. 28. What an incentive this is to diligent labor!

   He was willing to suffer some of Christ's own sufferings to bring this to pass. This is a daring thought, that a man can "fill up what is behind of the afflictions of Christ." This does not mean that Christ's sufferings were insufficient but that man's sufferings are in doing the work of Christ to fulfill the ministry He has given to us. We suffer for a similar purpose—to bring people to His glory.

Paul again shows how his special ministry was to bring Gentiles as well as Jews into the kingdom of God.

In this section Paul opposes again the Gnostic error that only a few could come to know God. Paul shows that every an must be warned, that every man may have the invitation to come and be made perfect in Christ.

Note finally that Paul wanted men to be perfect for their presentation to Christ as His bride. It is Christ within them that makes this possible and thus becomes their hope of glory. This hope is so great and wonderful that Paul strove mightily for it. The indwelling Christ produced not only the hope but also the energy which made the labor effective. May we all have this mighty in working of the Lord's power that we may present some treasures to Him in that day!

III. Stedfastness in Christ, A Masterful Portrayal of His All-Sufficiency

A. The Opponents of Stability

There were those (v. 8) who would try to "spoil" these believers. That is, they would strip them of their possessions and carry them away captives. In the use of the word "spoil," Paul refers to the military practice of taking away the possessions of conquered peoples. In reality, Paul shows that Christ has "spoiled" the hosts of the devil (v. 15) through His cross and proven His all-sufficiency and absolute supremacy.

Robbers sometimes come to a bank window displaying a toy gun and frightening clerks into handing money over to them. The gun has no power, but it is used as a bluff. Believers may also be persuaded of the power of these false forces through ignorance. Therefore, Paul wants to show that Christ is the Supreme One, and these false forces have been robbed.

1. Vain philosophy, v. 8. This evidently refers to the Gnosticism that had been united to Judaism. The teaching was that Christ was good but not sufficient. He was of God only in the sense that other "principalities and powers" and other mediators were of God. Christ was just one of several such intermediates.

We should note here that Oriental religions such as Hinduism and Buddhism teach the same thing: Jesus is good, but only in the sense that many others are good. Even in liberal "Christian" circles today, there is much emphasis on tolerance which would allow other religions as much basis as Christianity. The Bible becomes a good book only in the same sense that other books are good books. Christ is only a good man like other good men.

Many modern educators teach that all truth is relative. Therefore they say that we should not be dogmatic about any position; since we cannot know the truth for sure, we should be tolerant of any position. We should be committed to some position, but never as if it were the final truth. As we shall see, Paul had no place for such relativism that places Christ on par with other teachers and doctrines. We must not, either.

2. Traditions of men, v. 8. The Gnostics denied the final authority of Scriptures. They held that there was special truth that had come to them, some of it by word-of-mouth from Christ through Mary, Matthew, and Peter. Today, there is great emphasis placed on tradition by the Roman Catholics. At the Council of Trent they said that the traditions of the Church are equal in importance to the Old and New Testaments. There are many ministers in liberal churches today who are clearly leading the people contrary to the Word, placing their interpretations against the plain sense of the Scriptures. Many people are following the leaders instead of the Word.

3. Elements of the World, v. 8. There are two possible meanings to this term. First, it may mean the basic teachings of the Jews relating to earthly things such as altars, sacrifices, and external rituals. The Jews were trying to bring the Christians back under the system of externals. Today there is sch a trend in liberal Christian circles, a trend back to robes, ritual, prayer books, incense, and form without power. When God's presence and power wanes, there is always a tendency to substitute satisfying rituals in His place.

Second, it may refer to the supposed influence of heavenly bodies on the lives of the people. There was great superstition that the location of stars and planets had influence over the lives of the people. Even noted men like Julius Caesar, Alexander the Great, and Tiberius believed they must consult the stars before undertaking any expedition or mission. The Gnostics taught that if a person knew the right password, he could escape the influence of the stars over him. Their type of knowledge was eagerly sought by those brought into bondage to the stars.

4. Legalism, vv. 20, 21. The Jewish Gnostics were given to minute legalistic requirements. They taught that Christianity was too simple and that the superior knowledge was in the details of legalism. The Jews in that day had 248 positive commandments and 365 negative ones for a total of 613 commandments. They were ceaselessly arguing about the relative order of these.

   a. There was an imposition of minute details in the same way on all followers of religion. For example, concerning the laws of the Sabbath, it was a rule that people could not have nails in their shoes because that would be bearing a burden on the Sabbath.

   b. There is a Spirit-given conviction in the details of life. There are some who would make our religion consist primarily of minute regulations, but we don't become spiritual by observing a list of such regulations or by imposing them on others. There are details for each of us to obey, but the first reality is Christ within.

   We need to distinguish between the moral law which Christ reinforces and enables us to keep and the ceremonial law which has been nailed to the cross (v. 24). Those who say they are followers of Jesus will keep His commandments, which are not grievous; they do not have to keep the ceremonial law.

5. False worship, v. 18. The error of that day made Jesus just one link in a long chain of personalities. Paul says He is the only link, and He effectively unites us to God. He took hold of our flesh, an din Him we have access to God. The hymn "Arise My Soul, Arise" expresses this truth.

B. Opportunities of Stability

Note in v. 1 how great an agony of struggle Paul was experiencing for these people who were in combat with serious error. He would have liked to be there to shield them from evil, but that was impossible since he was in prison. Hence, he was laboring in intense prayer that these Christians would not be overcome. He points to the true source of stability in Christ.

1. The bond of love in the body of Christ, v. 2. Saints are to be bound together. It is interesting that the word "saint" never

occurs in the singular in the New Testament; it is always plural. Saints belong together in fellowship. One can be a saint alone, but saints are meant for fellowship.

- a. Divine love is the bond of perfectness. See Eph. 4:3 and Col. 3:14. Peter says that above all things we should have fervent charity among ourselves (see I Pet. 4:8).

- b. There is a knitting together in love. This does not refer to a mechanical process but to one of growth. A bone which breaks can not be forced back together. If force is used, there will be further injury. Rather, there must be time for healing, and then the broken place when healed can be the strongest part of the entire bone. Likewise the healing of love will strengthen the fellowship of the body.

- c. Love gives us earnest care for each other (3:16). This will hold us steady in times of test. Wesley and Whitefield once had a sharp theological difference, and Wesley wrote a very strong letter to Whitefield. The latter answered in a spirit of great love as follows: **SOURCE?**

  My Honoured Friend and Brother:

  For once hearken to a child, who is willing to wash your feet. I beseech you by the mercies of God in Christ Jesus our Lord, if you would have my love confirmed towards you, write no more about the misrepresentations wherein we differ . . . . Will it not in the end destroy brotherly love, and insensibly take from us that cordial sweetness of soul, which I pray God may always subsist between us? How glad would the enemies of the Lord be to see us divided? Honoured sir, let us offer salvation freely to all by the blood of Jesus, and whatever light God has communicated to us, let us freely communicate to others.

  While the enemy tries to bring division in the body, this spirit of love can produce strength in the body.

- d. The divine increase, v. 19. This is not mechanical enlargement but growth. An organism grows from within, not just by addition from without. See Acts 9:31.

2. The stedfastness of faith in Christ, v. 5. The words "order" and "stedfastness" here both refer to military formations. "Order" means an arrangement in ranks. "Stedfastness" means a solid bulwark and immovable arrangement and speaks of strength

that comes from disciplined cooperation. The church should have this character "in Christ." It is to be rooted in Him as the source of life, and its members are to be built up in Him as the pattern and end of all their activity. This is an absolute and final truth. The church is nothing of worth at all if it be not in Christ, deriving everything from Him and doing all things for Him. I was once in a storm at sea. The ship pulled into the lee of an island and cast anchor. It was good to know that the anchor was fixed and immovable, although I could not see it. Likewise, faith can be immovable when anchored in Him. We do not see now all that we believe in, but our faith holds us from moving in the storms that come against us.

3. The full assurance of understanding, v. 2. This is to be added to the "full assurance of faith" (Heb. 10:22; 6:11). There are three words for "wisdom" used here. The *full assurance of understanding* really means the ability to apply first principles to real situations, the ability to make right decisions in practical problems. *Wisdom* (v. 3) means the power to support and defend the truth with intelligence presentation, while *knowledge* is the power to apprehend the truth.

The Gnostics declared that they had the secrets of knowledge, but Paul says all of the hidden wisdom is in Christ. In Him are revealed all the Persons of the Trinity. His reason for declaring this is to combat the false teachers, he says.

Note that the knowledge in Christ is a true treasure. There are unfathomable riches to be found in an increasing knowledge of Him. One who diligently studies the Word will find that all through it there are truths pointing to Christ; He is the fulfillment of the Old Testament types and ceremonies. Rites and ceremonies in ages past were lessons pointing to the dispensation of Christ. Noah in the Ark, the law in the ark, the ark in the Holy of Holies, Jonah in the whale—all these were figures of Christ and of us in Him.

4. Hidden treasures in Christ, v. 3

　a. Their all-sufficiency. All the fulness of the Godhead dwells in Him bodily. Everything that God is and has is available through Christ. We do not need Jesus *plus* something else, as the Gnostics taught (Rom. 7:32).

　　There is a two-fold inwardness: Christ in us (1:27) and we in Christ (1:28, 2:6). With our lives in Him, we have all we need even though the world does not understand it.

b. The hidden nature of His riches

1) We are to search for this treasure. The greatest riches of the world are hidden where men must seek after them. Gold, silver, uranium, diamonds etc. do not lie on the surface like clay. David spoke of his love for the hidden things in God's Word (Ps. 119:72, 162).

2) We are to be rooted for nourishment and anchorage, v. 7. We must go down into Christ before we can go upward in strength and fruitfulness. Some never become fruitful because they do not send downward the roots of faith and diligent study. In large trees, the root system is as extensive as the top. The resources of the earth are constantly drawn upon in the production of leaves and fruit. We may be always victorious in Christ if we have our roots in the riches of Christ. The tree does not struggle to produce or to withstand the winds that blow. It has its strength and source of life in the soil. We have it in Him. This is an essential secret to learn for joy and victory.

3) Baptism into Christ, vv. 10-13. In this section Paul gives a powerful blow to the claims of the false teachers. He declares that we are complete in Christ and that Christ is above all other orders of beings. He takes up two of the ceremonies and shows how the truth of them points to Christ and what He has done for us.

The real meaning of baptism is the entering into the death and resurrection of Christ. When early Christians were baptized, it really meant that they were dead to their past and their human attachments and were alive in Christ. To this day, when a Jew is baptized as a Christian, his family counts him as dead and refuses to recognize him further. Rising from the water symbolizes resurrection victory of life in Christ.

The true meaning of circumcision is putting off the old sinful nature so that we can love God with all our heart. Being born into a Jewish family was a type of the new birth, while circumcision was a type of sanctification (cf. Deut. 30:6).

IV. Submission in Christ

Whereas Chapter 2 contained expressions of passive action, this one contains active commands.

A. Submission of Our Members to Death, v. 5

This brings us to the age-old question of whether a person may be pure and holy while in the body. Gnostics said the body was sinful. They taught that we should abase and mortify the body. There is a modern view of suppression which is similar, the teaching that sin is inextricably interwoven with the body and cannot be removed from it in this life. Hence the best we can do, according to this view, is to suppress sinful tendencies and desires.

1. The crisis "putting off" of the "body of the flesh" (2:11). (Most versions omit the words "of the sins.") Just as in circumcision there is a putting off a source of fleshly uncleanness, so in this spiritual circumcision there is a crisis putting off of the body of flesh—the sinful nature.

    a. The body of the flesh is the same as the body of death or the body of sin to which Paul refers in Romans 6:6; 7:24. His figure is to the Roman method of punishing a murderer by fastening to him the corpse of his victim. In reality, there is an opposing force seeking to control the body of the unsanctified. It is carnality. It is to be putt off by Christ through spiritual circumcision. We are to have one Master only. David prayed "Unite my heart to fear thy name" (Ps. 86:11).

    b. There is a death with Christ, 3:3; Gal. 2:20. There is also a resurrection with Him. We are in Him in His death and resurrection. The Gnostics spoke of the wisdom that was hidden in their books and philosophy; Paul says the true hiding is in Christ—we are in Him and hidden from the world. Our life in Him is not dependent on earthly things. It would actually be enlarged into the immortal realm if we were suddenly cut off from all earthly things. Food and drink hold us in the grasp of the physical and earthly.

    We derive our true rights and support from the throne at the right hand of the Father. Jesus, our High Priest, is there, and we are in Him.

2. The application of this death in detail.

   a. We are still on earth and still in the body.

   b. There is still temptation through the appetites of the body. In the former sinful life there were habits and practices which were unclean. These are to be left completely. The word "mortify" does not mean suppression but total removal. There is to be no more participation in unclean practices whatsoever.

   The application begins in outward sins of the flesh, but Paul then moves inward to the attitudes of the heart. Here he mentions covetousness, the attitude the law found in him and by which he was brought under condemnation (see Rom. 7:7). Covetousness is a desire for that which is not necessary, a desire to have more and to have what we do not need and have no right to have. This desire, Paul says, is essentially idolatry, for it puts some other desire before our desire for God.

   Paul then proceeds to such attitudes as wrath, malice, anger, etc., from which come wrong speech and wrong conduct. These are to be put to death utterly. This is true crucifixion that brings inordinate affections and attitudes to total end.

   Through such a death a real victory is won. It is as when a victorious army possesses the land of the defeated and maintains authority. Jesus Christ bring us victory, then lives within us to enforce the victory. The conflict is not prolonged, but the victory is continually enforced.

3. The exercise of a single affection, vv. 22, 23

   a. Our affections are purified and made single in the work of entire sanctification. Jesus said, "If therefore thine eye be single, thy whole body shall be full of light" (Matt. 6:22). The Psalmist said, "Unite my heart to fear thy name" (Ps. 86:11). The single heart is one of the greatest blessings of holiness.

   b. The affection is to be exercised, v. 23. If we express our affection in action, it will grow. Otherwise it will shrivel as an unused member.

B. Submission of Our Life to His Adornment, vv. 8-17

1. Putting off the "old man." The words "put off" in v. 9 are from the same original as "spoiled" in 2:15. It means to be robbed or deprived of power. Literally it refers to the taking off and putting away of clothing. Note it is the "old man" and his deeds which are to be put away.

   Here the resurrection victory of Christ over all opposing powers comes into practical demonstration as we are lifted to a place of victory and authority over the nature of sin. It is utterly spoiled and put away. The "old man" refers to the nature of sin, and "his deeds" are the acts. What Christ did to Satan and his hosts when He was on the cross, we are to do to the sinful nature in actual experience! That is victory.

   This victory is to be exercised against the temptation to all past sins such as wrath, filthy communication, lying, etc. The will is to be exercised in faith against the workings of sin in every form. Through Christ we have the victory!

2. Putting on the "new man." The words "put on" come from the same root as "endued" in Luke 24:47. It means to "sink into" our clothes and to be covered thereby. There are numerous similarities between Ephesians and Colossians. One of them is between verses 8-13 and Eph. 4:22-26. Here in v. 10 the new man is said to be renewed in knowledge after the image of the Creator. In Eph. 4:24 the new man is after "righteousness and true holiness." Adam Clarke wisely points out in his comment on Gen. 1:26 that the image of God "consisted in righteousness, true holiness, and knowledge. Hence man was wise in his mind, holy in his heart, and righteous in his actions." The knowledge is that clear illumination by the Spirit which gives us perception of spiritual things. The natural man can not possibly have such knowledge.

   The graces here listed all refer to our relations to others. The Christian life is designed to be lived in a community of Christians. While we have a vital individual relationship to Christ, we are also vitally related to fellowship of Christians. The terms in v. 12 originally referred to the Jews, but here Paul applies them to Gentiles. None need be excluded from the wondrous Christian fellowship. Christ is our example in these traits, showing us how we are to manifested this grace. Many of these graces, such as pity (mercy), humility, and meekness were quite unknown and unemphasized in the ancient world, but Christianity introduced and effectively implants these Christ-like graces.

Charity (or love) is to be placed above all else. Barclay says, "The tendency of any body of people is sooner or later to fly apart; and love is the one bond which will hold them together in unbreakable fellowship." If we have God's love within us, it must show toward our brethren.

The peace of God within us is the arbitrator of questions which we cannot readily decide by principle. Whatever disturbs our peace must be considered the wrong decision. When we can find no principle of the Word by which to decide an issue, and when we have honestly prayed for guidance, we may choose that which brings us undisturbed peace from God. This is often His way of showing approval. Note that this is the action of a sensitive conscience and not the self-deceiving rationalization of one who has a strong self-will operating.

We are to do all in the name of, or according to, the character of Christ. We are to act always as if acting in His stead. He gets all the praise.

C. Submission of Our Relationships to His Pleasure, vv. 18-25

This Christian life works right at home under the most commonplace of circumstances. There is sharp contrast here between Christian principles and the practices of those days. Wives, children and servants had virtually no rights. The husband, father and owner could treat them with the utmost severity and suffer no punishment. The privileges and rights all belonged to the husband, father and master, while the duties all rested on the wife, child and slave. But Christianity changed all this. It applied mutual duties and responsibilities.

1. Husband and wife. Some may think that since we are subject to Christ, we are not subject to others. This is not true; we show our subjection to Christ through our subjection to others.

   a. The husband is head of the wife, and the wife is to submit to him as fit in the Lord. Here is a test of the "in the Lord" relationship in a very meaningful way. If this doesn't work at home, it is not a true relation to Christ. The heavenly relationship must work in an earthly setting. Even if the husband is unsaved, there is to be a recognition of his place, though it costs longsuffering. It was practically difficult in that day, as it is now, but the grace of God makes it possible.

    b. The husband is to love his wife. Authority is not to produce tyranny, although some cruel husbands seem to think they should be tyrants. The husband is to see that no bitterness is introduced into the relationship.

2. Children and parents. Again, "unto the Lord" applies.

    a. Obedience in all things. The emphasis in much of modern education is to let the child choose for himself. The first thing, though, is for the child to respect proper authority and the limits within which he may properly choose. This must be done if the child is ever to respect the will of God and his responsibility to choose under the watchful eye of God.

    b. The father is not to over punish the child to the point of inducing frustrations and hatred. The child is to be taught the principles on which his own choices are to be made. These principles must be incorporated into the lives of the parents so the child can see them. The only way a child can ever become self-disciplined is to learn the principles which govern, and to learn to make choices accordingly. If he sees them in his parents and loves his parents enough to want to be like them, he will easily adopt the principles of his parents into his own life.

3. Servants and masters, 3:22, 4:1. The rule "as to the Lord" applies again. Servants are not just serving time as "clock watchers" but are seeking to please God as if He were the Paymaster. Real rewards and punishments come from Him.

    Masters are to be just and fair to servants. God has no pets, and the master should not. "Just" means to treat the man fairly as an individual; "equal" means to treat him fairly within the group. The maser must remember that he also has a Master to whom he must answer for his stewardship.

    About 130 A.D. the Athenian philosopher Aristides wrote a letter about the early Christians. In it he remarked about the outstanding lives lived by the Christians. He said they refrained from the sins of the day; "they honour father and mother; their wives are pure as virgins, and their daughters modest; and their men abstain from all unlawful wedlock and from all impurity, in hope of the recompense that is to come in another world. But as for their servants or handmaids, or their children, if any of them have any, they persuade them to become Christians, for the love they have towards them; and when they become so, they call them without distinction brethren. They walk in all humility and kindness, and falsehood is not found among them; and they love one another."

"And because they acknowledge the goodnesses of God towards them, lo, on account of them there flows forth the beauty that is in the world."

V. Servants in Christ, Chapter 4

As in other letters, Paul moves to the entirely practical areas of living.

A. Essentials of Service, vv. 2-6

1. The proper aim of Christian service, vv. 3, 4. Every church must have a clear vision of the aim of its service if it is to be effective. Paul presents the aim here: to make manifest the mystery of Christ. In 1:27 it is expressed as "Christ in you, the hope of glory." To know the indwelling Christ and to bring that knowledge to others was the supreme passion of Paul. The burden here is expressed for those that are without (v. 4) as well as those in the body of Christ.

    Note in 1:24 the suffering Paul was willing to endure to fulfill this purpose of Christ which was also his own purpose. He had a missionary heart. He yearned to go to Rome and on to Spain to make manifest what otherwise was a mystery to the multitudes of earth. Today we must have the same passion if we would really be effective workers and servants of the Gospel of Christ.

2. The method. We must have this supreme aim before us and utilize the methods necessary to accomplish it. We need to utilize the proper Biblical methods which are shown here instead of developing new methods. Let us all measure ourselves as to whether we are accomplishing this purpose and whether or not we are utilizing the methods prescribed.

    a. Prayer, vv. 2, 3. In Eph. 6:18-20, Paul presents this as the battle in which the Christian soldier is engaged. The aim set forth before us cannot be met by merely human methods. We must secure divine aid through prayer.

        1) Continuous, v. 2. This is a repeated New Testament concept. It means more than just putting in time through vain and repetitious means; it means to pursue

a goal and persevere until it is achieved, no matter how fervently the praying must be.

Before the Holy Spirit came, the disciples continued in prayer (Acts 1:14). After Pentecost they continued in prayer and doctrine (Acts 2:42). The apostles determined to continue in prayer and the ministry of the Word (Acts 6:4). As they did so, the Word multiplied greatly. My God inspire us to continue in prayer, pressing toward the goal of true praying—revealing the mystery of Christ. Many are prone to grow faint in praying. They should take a lesson from the church in Acts 12:5.

2) Watchful, v. 2. It means to be awake and alert in prayer, seeing the need and possibility. It is easy to make resolutions about prayer and fall in them, because men do not easily see the quality of our secret praying. Teachers and officers would not easily miss their appointments with men, and neither should they miss their appointments with god in prayer!

3) Thankful, v. 2. Because we have confidence in God and His faithfulness, we do not come begging to a stingy giver. We approach One who delights to give when conditions are met, and therefore we pray with gratitude. We may be assured that when we pray in the Spirit Gd intends to give an answer if we faint not. James says some ask and receive not because they ask amiss. There is no lack on God's part, so we can thank Him in advance for answered prayer.

4) For the minister, v. 3. He must have prayer that God will open the door before him, that God will give utterance (power in speech) and that men will hear attentively and submissively.

At one time a Canadian missionary society maintained a mission in India which had only one missionary. They could not send more because they were low on funds. Consequently, the board decided to close the mission. But the one missionary there said he would let his bones bleach in India as a witness that he would not give up in his effort for revival. The board resolved to make one more attempt, sending another

laborer. The two joined in earnest prayer for revival. It came, and 2, 222 converts were baptized at once.
- b. Witness, 3:3-6
  1) Preaching. How great a work it is! See 1:28, 29. It involves warning (negative) and teaching (positive). It embraces every man. By the indwelling Christ Paul labored with earnest striving. It is costly. For this purpose Paul was in prison but still an ambassador even in bonds. May the Lord work in us in the same mighty way to make Christ known.
  2) A wise walk, v. 5. We are to buy up opportunities. As a salesman is ever looking for sales prospects, we should be always looking for opportunities to represent Christ. We must live so that even when we are not conscious of our influence, it will still count for Christ.
  3) A seasoned talk, v. 6. Salt is used in Scripture often to represent wisdom, terseness, elegance and usefulness. We should study to speak effectively of our faith so we can answer any man. What higher goal of study is there than to represent Christ effectively?

B. Examples of Service, vv. 7-18

This study will show what diversity there was among the men, and yet how many possibilities of service there were among them.

1. Tychicus (Fortuitous). An unpredictable person, he became dependable, being sent as a messenger. Probably in Acts 20:4 he was sent to bear an offering. He must have been a close associate of Paul. He was "in the Lord," Paul said. Nothing is said of his faults, for he is seen in the Lord. Paul said he determined not to know men after the flesh. He wanted to know them and see them as Christ did. May we do likewise. Tychicus was a deacon who would run errands and comfort hears while doing so.

2. Aristarchus (Best ruler). Now he is a prisoner. He is an example of dedication. Converted in Thessalonica during Paul's short stay there, he went to Jerusalem, Rome, and on to prison with Paul (see Acts 20:4). He was with Paul often in a hard situation and could be depended on to be true. Evidently he saw so much of devotion in Paul that his own fire of dedication was ignited, and he was wiling to go to prison himself to be with

Paul. What an example Paul was to follow! May we likewise inspire others by our lives to follow Jesus, even to prison and death!

3. Epaphras (Devoted to Aphrodite). Now he is a slave, devoted to Christ. Some worthy things are said of him. He was a servant, or a slave, or Christ. This means that he counted nothing for himself but all for Jesus. He agonized in prayer for the brethren at Colosse. He shared the same passion that Paul did that the church might go on to perfection, doing all the will of God. There was no satisfaction with a merely formal or nominal Christianity, with many members having shallow spiritual lives. They wanted perfection in all the will of God.

   Finally, he was zealous. His spirit was boiling hot. We might compare Demas who evidently was cooling off even at this point. No good thing is here said of him.

4. Archippus (Horse trainer). Tradition says he was the pastor of Laodicea, the same who receive the message of Christ in Revelation. If so, he should be a warning to us. he was warned to take his ministry seriously, but he may have slipped into a cold professionalism. What a danger this is now, even among us.

   a. His ministry was in the Lord, both as to its source, its aim and its strength. The others illustrate how a ministry may be fulfilled, but possibly his illustrates how a ministry may fail.

   b. Laodicea means "people justice or right." It represents a kind of church where the ministry follows the desires of the people instead of faithfully standing for the highest against popular and easy ways. Fervency was too disturbing to the Laodiceans. They were attached, involved, flourishing. Should the minister labor to disturb them and stir them up or settle down with them? This is a pressing question for many preachers. It is easier to settle down. George Whitefield in old age prayed that God would stir him up if he ever began to settle down, to put thorns in his nest if he began to sleep on the job.

   We should ask ourselves: Are we fulfilling our ministry, in warning, teaching, and agonizing in prayer? Is Christ working mightily in us?

Review Questions
COLOSSIANS

1. Under what circumstances did Paul write Colossians?
2. What was his reason for writing this letter?
3. What aspects of Gnostic error does Paul combat in the letter?
4. Give the general theme and the subject of each chapter.
5. In what two great areas does Paul declare the supremacy of Christ, and in what way does Paul say this supremacy is declared?
6. Give the meaning of the term "image."
7. Analyze the four aspects of grace in which the sufficiency of Christ is demonstrated.
8. In Chapter 1:9 Paul speaks of the "knowledge of his will." State the characteristics of this kind of knowledge.
9. What is the mystery that has been hidden from "ages and generations?'
10. Paul spoke of presenting men perfect in Christ. What figure does he employ in this expression?
11. At the end of Chapter 1, Paul shows that preaching consists of a positive and a negative aspect. What are these?
12. Name several enemies of Christian stability that Paul mentions.
13. Name the possible meanings of the expression "elements of the world."
14. What is the distinction between the moral and ceremonial law? How does each affect us today?
15. Explain the meaning of the figure "kit together in love."
16. Explain the spiritual significance of baptism and circumcision.
17. In this epistle several things are spoken of as "hid." What are they?
18. What is meant by "putting off the body of the flesh?'
19. What figure is used in the expressions "put off" and "put on?"
20. In the sanctified life there is a singleness of affection. In what way does Paul present this truth?
21. Of what does the image of God consist?
22. Analyze the expression, "Let the peace of God rule in your hearts."
23. State the difference between the peace of God and peace with God.
24. What grace is considered to be above all others?
25. What is meant by "doing all in the name of the Lord Jesus?"
26. Show how the matter of Christian submission works in the various relationships of life.
27. How did Christianity change the lot of wives, children, servants?
28. What is the supreme aim of Christian service according to Paul?
29. Why was it called a "mystery?"

30. What two methods did Paul present for accomplishing the purpose?
31. Explain what is meant by "continuing in prayer."
32. In what ways is Christian witness to be effected?
33. Give the characteristics of each of the servants whom Paul describes in Chapter 4.
34. What does the term "Laodicea" mean, and what does it represent?
35. For what was Epaphras praying earnestly?

The First Epistle to the THESSALONIANS

Introduction

I. Author

There is very little debate about the authorship of this epistle. Paul is the author, and this is the first of his recorded epistles. There is no sign of immaturity, however, in the writing.

II. Background

A. Chronology and Date (See Acts 17:1-9)

Paul was in Thessalonica on his second missionary journey for at least three weeks—some think he may have been there longer. He was forced out of the city because of persecution, and naturally had a deep concern for the young Christians. From there he went to Berea and then to Athens, from where he sent Timothy to Thessalonica to find out about the welfare of the church. Paul went on to Corinth, where he stayed for about eighteen months. Timothy and Silas came to him there and brought the news of Thessalonica. From there he wrote both of his epistles to the church, the first one during the early part of his stay in Corinth.

Thessalonians was probably written during 51 or 52 A.D.

B. The City

1. Modern Salonica, with nearly 250,000 people, is located on the Gulf of Salonica, a thriving port city. Its location on the international Egnatian Road brought much traffic through the city.

    Thessalonia was made a free city by Augustus of Rome because it had sided with him in his struggle for power. The people therefore selected their own magistrates. It was named after Thessalonica, who was a daughter of Philip of Macedon and a half sister of Alexander the Great.

2. Thessalonia was a populous city of cosmopolitan people made up of idol worshiping pagans, Jews, proselytes, and Greeks. It was also a prosperous city, involving much commerce. We may recall that Demas returned to Thessalonica when he departed from Paul because he loved this present world. Thus we may judge that Thessalonica was the typical city "of this world."

3. Thessalonica became a stronghold of Christianity for that part of the world and was called "The Orthodox City."

D. The Crusade There

1. Paul went to Thessalonica from Philippi when he was asked to depart from there, and stayed at least three weeks. A "great multitude" believed, including many Greeks and "not a few" of the notable women.

2. Paul taught a wide range of doctrinal truth: Christology, deliverance from the wrath to come, turning from idols, sanctification of heart and life, the Christian walk, and the return of Christ. He was driven out by the envy of unbelieving Jews.

III. The Occasion for the Letter

Paul wrote Thessalonians for the following reasons:

A. To deal with a whispering campaign against him, his motives, and his work (2:3-10).

B. To express joy for the good news about them (3:6-9).

C. To deal with questions about the second coming (4:13-18). Some had the idea that Christ's coming was imminent, and they were inclined to cease the normal activities of life and wait. There was also the question about what would happen to deceased Christians at the coming of Christ.

D. To give instructions about some unruliness, probably concerning some lazy spongers on the charity of the Church (5:14).

E. To encourage advancement in grace (Chapters 3, 5).

IV. Outline of the Book (Themed "The Coming of Christ")

A. Waiting for His Coming (Chapter 1)

B. Joy at His Coming (Chapter 2)

C. Holy at His Coming (Chapter 3)

D. Reunion at His Coming (Chapter 4)

E. Kept Till His Coming (Chapter 5)

VI. Method of Treatment

The study will not treat Thessalonians section by section but will rather be a topical study of special subjects important in this epistle.

The Study of the First Epistle to the Thessalonians

I. The Personality of Paul

In this first of his epistles, Paul reveals his inner character and shows his love and tenderness for the believers at Thessalonica in response to some of the occasions back of the letter.

A. The Man

Here Paul stands, as one has said, "in all the charm of his rich and varied personality." See 2:1-12; 3:1-10; 5:12-25.

To understand this revelation of Paul's heart and life, we must understand that evidently there had been some in Thessalonica who had started a whispering campaign against him. He had left Thessalonica because of envy among the Jews. Doubtless they started an effort to discredit him after he left.

1. The following charges appear to be back of Paul's statement of defense.

   a. That he was deceived or possibly mad (2:3). Those who are as different from the standards and conduct of the world as Paul was are very likely to be charged with fanaticism, if not madness.

   b. That he had impure motives (2:3). The pagans and other enemies of Christianity eagerly seized on such things as the "love feast" and the "kiss of peace" and charged Christians with impurity.

   c. That he was willfully deceiving others for some personal interest (2:3).

   d. That he was trying to please men rather than God (2:6).

   e. That he was teaching for money (2:5, 9).

   f. That he was seeking personal prestige (2:6).

   g. That he was acting like a dictator (2:7).

2. The characteristics which Paul displays.

   a. Faithfulness (2:8). He never let opposition cause him to weaken. It is typical of him to declare the whole counsel of

I Thessalonians

God, regardless of the stern opposition to such things as the resurrection, Messiahship of Christ, and other doctrines.

    b. Goodness (2:3, 5, 10). He had been charged with ulterior motives, of preaching for gain (2:9). Weymouth translates v. 3 as follows: "For our preaching was not grounded on a delusion, nor prompted by mingled motives, nor was there fraud in it." Paul declares his innocence.

    c. Meekness (2:6), not self-seeking. Paul didn't inquire whether his message would please people, increase his reputation, or make money for him.

    d. Gentleness (2: 7, 11). Weymouth says, "We showed ourselves as gentle as a mother is when she tenderly nurses her own children." He was not a hireling. Verse 8 says Paul was "affectionately desirous," continuing the figure of a mother. Faithfulness is balanced by gentleness.

    e. Thoroughness (2:11). Paul pleaded with each one personally. He didn't have a passing professional interest in the Thessalonicans; he had a concern for each person in need.

    f. Love (2:8; 2:17). Paul had an earnest-hearted love for them, willing to spend and be spent (2:8). This is a good example of divine love which he claimed restrained him. The care of all the churches rested on him, causing him to pray night and day exceedingly for them.

    g. Joy (2:19), 20). Paul's source of joy in all his tribulation was the knowledge of all his converts. This would also be his joy as he stood before God. If we could feel this as he did, we would count this joy above all else on earth except our own joy in Christ. No wonder Paul could say, "Ye became followers of us, and of the Lord"(1:6), for surely Paul followed the Lord.

B. The Theologian

Paul's theological emphases have been mentioned and will be seen in a review of those doctrines of election, Christology, conversion, sanctification, advent of Christ, resurrection, judgment, mutual concern in the Church of God, and practical living.

II. An Example of New Testament Evangelism

    A. The Human Entrance, 2:1

1. A human entrance was necessary; God has ordained that the Gospel be carried by men and not by angels. "How shall they hear without a preacher?" Paul asked in Rom. 10:14.

2. Paul was willing to work to pay his own way since there was no board or church guaranteeing his support. See 2:9.

3. He was a faithful bearer and exhibitor of the Gospel. He not only proclaimed it; he lived it also. See Gal. 3:1: "Who hath bewitched you that ye should not obey the truth, before whose eyes Jesus Christ hath been evidently set forth, crucified among you?" Paul exhibited Christ. He states that he was put *in trust* with the Gospel (2:3-6).

4. Paul paid a great personal price to bring them the Gospel. He suffered at Philippi and was "shamefully treated." In spite of such treatment, he went on with the proclaiming the Gospel. This was his supreme task. He was not free to stop, for the interest of Christ and the Gospel, not his own, was preeminent.

B. The Divine Entrance, 1:5

If a man uses the Gospel to elevate his own self, he forfeits the power of God. Here is an excellent example of the respective parts of human and divine participation.

1. There was the human spokesman of the Word.

2. There was power in the Holy Ghost and much assurance. The assurance is evidently first his own, while he preached. Paul fully believed the Gospel, and this conviction was apparent in his preaching. If a man does not fully believe the Word, there will be no conviction in his preaching. Paul had such devotion to the message and to the people hearing him that his commitment was evident to them. He was among them for their sake, not his own.

3. There were mighty results. They became followers of him and of the Lord. They had the joy of the Holy Ghost even in their affliction. This is a certain work of the Spirit, to give joy in those conditions where the world has no joy to offer. It is what certifies as genuine the work of the Gospel. They turned from idols to serving the living God. What a conversion!

C. The Formation of the Church, 1:1-10; 2:13, 14

1. Their election of God, 1:4. This could be better translated, "Knowing, beloved of God, your election." It should be pointed

out again what this term "election" means. Some have taught it means an irrevocable choice of some to personal salvation and others to damnation. But such is clearly not the case. As Vincent says, election is "the act of God's holy will in selecting His own methods, instruments, and times for carrying out His own purposes—is a fact of history and of daily observation." God first elected the Jews as a special people to be His witnesses to the Gentile nations. The Jews failed as a people, and God chose the Church for this purpose. So the Church, collectively, is chosen for the purpose of witnessing for Christ in the world. This does not mean at all that certain individuals are chosen unalterably to either salvation or damnation personally. Individual salvation is always tied to personal faith, and that is not predetermined but individually free. This passage shows the personal responsibility plainly (1:7; 2:13).

God has chosen to save all who will believe rather than to condemn them (see 5:9).

2. Their conviction, 1:5; 2:13. If we can visualize those simple services, we will see an example of divine power in the midst of simplicity and even crudeness of surroundings. Paul must have appeared as a rather simply attired man, with features that some did not find attractive. But the message of the speaker had power to reach the hearts of the people. A multitude believed in the synagogue.

3. Their affliction, 1:6. They had outward affliction but inward joy. Compare John 16:33: "In the world ye shall have tribulation," Jesus said, "but be of good cheer; I have overcome the world" (John 16:33). No wonder the church grew.

4. Their separation, 1:9. They turned from idols to Christ. The change was genuine, and they were empowered to live a new life. The meaning of the term "church" is "the called out ones." Separation from the world is essential to the very idea of the church. If it isn't separated, it isn't really the church.

5. Their waiting for Christ to come, 1:10. Perhaps there is no better example in history of people who eagerly looked for the return of Christ while going on about the work of winning others to Christ. Their common word of greeting was "Maranatha," meaning "The Lord cometh."

6. Their witness, 1:7, 8, 9

a. "Ensample" (v. 7) comes from the language of printing and means type, print, image, pattern or mold. The idea is that their lives were formed by the mold of the Gospel, as a stylus made an imprint on a sheet of papyrus.

   b. "Sounded forth" (v. 8) means to sound as a trumpet or to thunder forth. Theirs were not muted voices. The receivers became transmitters. The Gospel had a sounding board in them. It should be so today if the churches had the power of the Holy Spirit for witnessing.

   c. "Spread abroad" means to go forth like fire spreading. The fame of that church spread in just such a manner. Paul got the news back from others. The Gospel was "news", and it spread like waves of fire. May God give us such examples here of the spread of His Gospel.

III. The Doctrine Presented

A. Holiness

   1. Chapter references: each chapter treats some aspect.

      a. Chapter 1:5: The Holy Ghost, the Producer

      b. Chapter 2:10: Holy behavior, Paul's witness.

      c. Chapter 3:13: Holy hearts, establishment in holiness

      d. Chapter 4:7: Holy conduct, the life of holiness.

      e. Chapter 5:27: Holy brethren, the fellowship.

   2. The prerequisites. We have already seen the change in their lives.

      a. Transformed lives, 1:9.

      b. The fruits of the Spirit in a measure, 4:1.

   3. The necessity of holiness

      a. The will of God, 4:3, 7, 8. That God has willed our holiness is reason enough to emphasize the subject constantly. All our lives are to be governed by His will.

      b. The weakness of the flesh, 4:3-7. They had just come out of a background in which there was no emphasis on the evil of sexual sins. Immorality was common even in pagan religious practices. Consequently, there was a strong pull

I Thessalonians   105

back to such loose practices. The work of sanctification was not necessary to stop the practices, for they were already stopped, but sanctification would strengthen them against the temptation and thus lessen the likelihood of their returning to sin.

    c. Imperfections in their character, 3:10-12 (cf. Heb. 13:20, 21). Their faith particularly needed perfecting. It is noteworthy that their faith was unusually strong and effective already (see 3:6, 7). Yet Paul was deeply concerned that it be perfected. It was not just that he feared they might fail under temptation; he knew something was basically lacking.

        Faith is partly mental, and they needed information about holiness.

        Faith is partly volitional, and they needed to do God's will.

        Faith is, finally, confidential trust in the faithfulness of God, and Paul certifies that God is faithful, 5:24. He is the God of peace Who gives His own peace to those who trust His faithfulness.

    d. The demands of His coming, 3:13; 5:23. A bride is being prepared for Christ at His coming, and holiness is the wedding garment which is provided for those who look for His coming (see Eph. 5:27; Heb. 2:11, 12; Rev. 19:7, 8; Isa. 35:8; I John 3:2, 3). Heaven is a holy place prepared for a holy people, and a holy people is prepared for the highest glories of that place.

4. The nature of holiness.

    a. Of God, by His Holy Spirit, 4:7; 5:23. The word "given" is in the aorist tense, showing an instantaneous, completed action.

    b. Instantaneous, 5:23. The word "sanctify" is in the aorist tense.

    c. Complete, 5:23. There are many places in scripture where the word "sanctify" refers to a work which begins in regeneration, but in this passage, the completion of the sanctifying work is indicated. It is not a process which goes on indefinitely but an act which is perfected in this work of God's grace. The whole of man's personality is included: body, soul and spirit. Those who teach that the body is inseparable from the sinful nature have their theory contradicted by this passage. This does not mean that a person is instantaneously mature but instantaneously pure.

    d. Cleansing of the heart, 3:13. This is so wrought that a person is made unblameable before God. God sees all the impure attitudes of the heart: pride, jealousy, laziness, self-pity, etc. He cleanses so perfectly that there is nothing left that He condemns.

    e. By faith in His promise. Such a promise is given in 5:24. It is His faithfulness which undergirds our hope and assurance that there is cleansing for us in the blood of Christ. However, His faithfulness is effective for us individually only if we have faith in Him.

5. The Results of Holiness

    a. Christian perfection

        1) Of peace. He is the very God of peace. II Thes. 3:16 adds the thought that from Him there is perfect peace in every circumstance.

        2) Of faith, 3:10. It is perfect in seeing cleansing from all sin in the blood of Christ. That is, it is fixed on a perfect Object and Person. Further, it is perfect in being free from doubt.

        3) Of love, 3:12. It is not only free from impurity and carnal self-love, but it is abundant and overflowing in quantity.

    b. Establishment in grace, 3:13. It does not guarantee infallibility, but it produces freedom from inward sinfulness that inclines to weakness before temptation. There are still many exhortations to observe, but the heart is fully yielded and ready to obey them. It is faith versus doubt, and strength versus temptation.

    c. Preservation in blamelessness, 5:23. A character has been cleansed, and it can be kept clean. We live in a sinful world; there are suggestions of sin on every side. Like a pair of glasses in the dust, our minds may have deposits on them from the suggestions of sin, but there is constant cleansing through the blood of Christ so that sin does not take root and grow. See I John 1:7.

      d. Holy conduct, Chapters 4 and 5. We are to "quench not the Spirit." He is given to guide and keep us. If we will faithfully observe His promptings, we will be kept holy in action. We are not to despise prophesying. God has given us the resources; we must faithfully use them.

      e. Boldness at His coming, 3:13. See also I John 4:17. If we are like Him, and if we love His appearing, and if His Spirit dwells within us, there will be joy when He appears and not shame. A bride is surely joyous when the bridegroom appears, and she can be united with him.

B. The Second Coming of Christ.

  1. Each chapter ends with a reference to His coming.

  2. The motivations of His coming.

      a. To service, 2:19. If we have won souls to Jesus, it will be a crown of rejoicing at His coming. Let us give our best to witnessing of His salvation, and give our best to winning souls for Him! It is God's approval and His reward at the coming of Christ that will be the greatest possible return for all our service here on earth. A workman here is glad for payday; he works with that in view. The follower of the Lord works with that day of reward in view, also.

      b. To holiness, 3:13. This is not to say that those who have not yet received a second benefit will not be able to enter heaven; if they are walking in the light, they will be permitted entrance there. However, holiness is the preparation for admission, and if we refuse it, we are not ready for His coming.

      c. To comfort in sorrow, 4:18; 5:11. Before this message of the resurrection of the body, men despaired in death; now there is wondrous hope. The Thessalonian Christians were bothered by the thought that their friends and loved ones who had already died before the second coming might be left behind when He appeared. Paul writes to give assurance that the "dead in Christ" shall rise first, and we that live unto the coming of the Lord will be united with them in the air to meet the Lord and be with Him forever. What a bright hope this is! What light we have beyond the grave, whereas the sinner has only darkness and terror beyond.

d. To watchfulness, 5:1-11

   1) Significance of the day of the Lord. In the Old Testament as well as the New, the term is used to signify the end of the present age and the ushering in of a new age of peace and victory. It is to bring punishment upon the wicked and blessing to the righteous. In the Old Testament it was conceived as primarily an external display of power which should give the Jews an uncontested place of authority among the nations. In the New Testament it is shown to be primarily a spiritual victory and not a political one first of all. While it is truly objective, it is not just for the Jews but for all who shall live in the will of God.

   In the New Testament it is also shown to be divided into two appearances of Christ: the rapture and the revelation. I Thes. 4:13-18 clearly shows a rapture or the taking of Christ's own people out from among the people of the world. I Thes. 5:3 and II Thes. 1:7-10 speaks of a revelation to bring judgment on the ungodly. These are two aspects of the day of the Lord, and between them is apparently the work of the antichrist and the time of tribulation upon the earth.

   2) The deception of the world. They shall be saying "peace and safety," emphasizing security here on earth. (The word for safety really means security here.) Sudden destruction or anguish shall come on the world that has gone on in its own false security. The Bible shows elsewhere that God shall bring such shaking phenomena upon the earth—earthquakes, signs in the sun, etc.—that men shall have their security totally disturbed. They shall not escape. There will be no place for the world to hide from God and His Christ, Who has been rejected (Rev. 6:12-17).

   3) The figure of watchfulness. Sinners are like men in darkness who are asleep when a thief comes and takes what he wants. First they have become drunk at night, which makes them sleep the more deeply and so be less likely to be awakened by the thief. Men of this world are so drunken on pleasures, possessions, and carnal attachments that they are totally unaware of the significance of these times for the soon appearing of

Christ. Saints of God are not in the dark; they have the light of God upon this age, and they have responded to the light. Their characters are open before God. The Christian is like a soldier who is on night watch. He must have faith, hope and love. Paul emphasizes these three graces often, especially in this epistle (see I Thes. 1:3.) His intense desire is that these elements may be increased in the life of the Thessalonian Christians.

Soberness and watchfulness are enjoined, 5:6, 8. Watching involves alertness and attention. It is commonly coupled with prayer. We must not let that day find us careless and sleeping, spiritually. Watching is primarily a mental attitude, while sobriety is a moral attitude of allowing nothing to defile our "spiritual garments."

e. To mutual encouragement and hope, vv. 9-11. The day of the Lord is not designed to bring wrath on people but to bring salvation to people. "He willeth not the death of any (see Ezek. 33:11). God has planned salvation for all men (I Tim. 2:4). He prepared hell for the devil and his angels, not for men. Heaven was prepared for all men; they miss it by refusing Mercy.

Christ died and rose again to provide a way for us to escape wrath and enter into eternal salvation. For the reason of this hope, we should do our utmost to encourage all men to seek salvation from wrath.

There was danger that the Thessalonians might be moved from their stedfastness in Christ by the afflictions they were enduring (3:3). Paul recognized that if this were so, his labor would be in vain. That is, he recognized that these Christians who had so definitely been converted could backslide and his labor for them would be lost (3:5). The grace of holiness and spiritual establishment he holds forth as the antidote to such liability to backsliding.

3. Waiting for His coming, 1:10; 4:11, 12. As a result of Paul's teaching about the second coming of Christ, the Thessalonians were inclined to feel His coming was so close that they should just cease the normal activities of life and simply wait for Jesus to come. This meant that some were just becoming indigent spongers on the charity of others, so Paul wrote to set them straight on this matter. It is true we are to be waiting for His coming with hope and anticipation, but we are not to cease

from industry and honest labor, for we know not the exact time of His coming. Christians should be an example of industry and charity to the world, and in no case should their beliefs make them drones or spongers on the mercy of those who are unbelievers. This would be a great reproach to our testimony.

IV. Practical Christian Duties

Paul almost always closes his letters with exhortations and commandments for practical Christian living. This is appropriate, for Christianity has no value whatsoever if it does not change our lives. Theory that does not bring moral alteration is vain and to be rejected, but the religion of Christ does change the lives of its adherents, who by faith in Christ experience regeneration and entire sanctification.

A. Progress in the Christian Life, 4:1, 9, 10

There is no place to settle down and just maintain a status quo in our Christian experience. We are to be advancing. The purification of our hearts prepares us for maximum growth.

1. Progress in our walk—action, 4:1. The duty is to please God, but we are to increase more and more. It is to be the constant inquiry of our lives how to please God more. Jesus had this goal, and He succeeded always to please His Father. We are not to stop at just what He will allow but to please Him—to make Him happy with our lives. It is not a matter of choosing between the good and bad. We must select between the better and the best. Our goal is not just to be just obedient but pleasing.

    In Col. 1:10-12 we are told some of the things that please God: being fruitful in every good work; increasing in the knowledge of God; having patience and longsuffering with joyfulness; giving thanks unto the Father.

    In Heb. 13:15, 16 we are shown some other things that please God: giving the sacrifice of praise with our lips continually; doing good and communicating to others (helping them in any trouble). People who do these things are the people who are constantly looking for ways to be helpful and to bring honor and praise to God. Such is a truly mature Christian life.

2. Progress in our attitudes, 4:10. Love may be made perfect, as it will be if we are filled with the Spirit, but there is still room for enlargement continually. It is the deliberate exercise of love which enlarges it. To love those who love us and do good to us does not necessarily enlarge love, but to love those who do evil

to us will enlarge it. This is the work of the Spirit in us which causes love to grow. If, on the other hand, we respond in narrowness or selfishness, love will diminish.

B. Proper Conduct and Relationship Within the Church, 5:12-22

1. Respect for the ministry, vv. 12, 13, 20. The command to know them which labor among you means to become acquainted with those who have been appointed supervisors. They have needs which must be met and they have responsibilities which must be recognized and respected. It would never be appropriate for the laity to stand aloof from the ministry. There must be respect and fellowship as in a family.

It may be that in Thessalonica the people had been reproved for their idleness and had failed to respond. Evidently the "prophesy" or messages of the leaders was being slighted in some cases, so the exhortation not to ignore prophesying was timely. It is just as true today. The word which a minister receives from God should be received as from God and not just from the man. Paul emphasizes a similar point in 4:8. The minister should be very sure that he gets his messages from God so he may rightfully receive the kind of respect Paul requires.

The minister is to be respected not only for the sake of the sacred office which he fills but also for the work which he performs. It is an extremely important work, one which requires the blessing of God; therefore, it should receive the respect and gratitude of men.

2. Respect to one another, vv. 14, 15

a. Unruly ones (or lazy ones) are those who literally fall out of ranks, like soldiers in an army. When this happens, the strength and efficiency of the army is greatly reduced. It is the duty of the members to watch and warn their fellow members. Too often this is neglected and considered to be the duty of the minister only, but again and again in the New Testament we are told to exhort one another and to watch for the good of one another. We should have enough love and humility to aid those who are seen to be drifting or dropping by the way. See Gal. 6:1.

b. The "feebleminded" are those who are discouraged and downcast. There are almost always some like this in the churches. They have fought against temptations or loneliness or subtle insinuations of the enemy, and it seems they cannot go on any further. We should be watching for such as this, and rather than criticizing, we should be quick to encourage and comfort them as we would lift up a child who had fallen.

    c. The weak spiritually are those who are unstable and specially liable to yield before temptation. They need strength. While they are growing in faith we need to support them, pray for them, counsel them, and show them loving concern in hopes they will one day come to stand alone.

    d. We are to be patient or longsuffering toward all, even the disagreeable sinners about us. In no case should we show the same kind of ill temper or ugly conduct as may be shown to us; we should rather show love and kindness in the name of Christ and for His honor. It is a good chance to show the true nature of Christianity and transformed character.

3. Personal traits manifested by the Spirit, v. 16-22. This is a brief list of vital traits of the sanctified life. We should often measure ourselves by them.

    a. "Rejoice evermore." In persecutions, such as the Thessalonians were facing, to rejoice would be a sure evidence of a supernatural life. This, however, is what the Spirit helps us to do. Paul and Silas rejoiced in prison, and God brought them forth. Jesus, faced with His own death and departure from His disciples, commanded them to be of good cheer, for He had overcome the world (John 16:33). Such joy comes not from circumstances but from the inward reality of Christ. As we cultivate the spirit of rejoicing, it will grow, enabling us to praise God in every circumstance.

    b. "Pray without ceasing." The term "without ceasing" is used outside the New Testament with reference to a person with a hacking cough—he has an impulse to cough continually. While he may not be actually coughing at every moment, the tendency is there, and he soon gives way to it. Likewise, the Christian may not be praying audibly or even consciously at all times, yet the tendency is there, and at odd moments or when awakening in the night, the mind naturally turns to God. This will cause the person to maintain personal prayer, family prayer, church prayer meeting attendance, etc. The life of the Spirit is a life of prayer. Without prayer, we can not maintain His fulness.

c. "In everything give thanks." This is particularly important as is shown by the fact that it is given as the will of God. A thankful spirit enables God to work for us; a complaining spirit cuts the nerve of faith. A man with a carnal heart will be inclined to complain at circumstances; one who is filled with the Spirit will rather incline toward praise rather than complaint. Remember how God was grieved with those in the wilderness who constantly complained rather than praise God for His help, past and future. There are some today in the churches who have a similar spirit. They are given to criticism, and this spirit is infectious, bringing a cloud into the lives of many. Remember that this is the sanctified life that is being described. The Spirit will enable us to praise God in every trial if we cultivate His presence and operation in our lives.

d. "Quench not the Spirit." The word refers to the putting out of a fire. We are not to let this fire go out, but it will, however, if we do not keep supplying fuel and allowing the atmosphere of heaven to flow freely into our lives. We quench the Spirit by refusing any of His unique operations in our lives, the maintenance of unity, the work of intercession, or the manifestation of His liberty to glorify God in all things. Barnes says aptly, "Anything that will tend to damp the ardour of piety in the soul; to chill our feelings; to render us cold and lifeless in the service of God, may be regarded as 'quenching the Spirit.' Neglect of cultivating the Christian graces, or of prayer, of the Bible, of the sanctuary, of a careful watchfulness over the heart, will do it. Worldliness, vanity, levity, ambition, pride, the love of dress, or indulgence in an improper train of thought, will do it . . . . Anyone, if he will, may make elevated attainments in the divine life; or he may make his religion merely a religion of form, and know little of its power and its consolations." (*Barnes Notes on the New Testament*, Grand Rapids: Kregel Publications, p. 1104)

e. "Despise not prophesyings." We have already mentioned this, but we should add that prophesy is the bubbling forth of the message of God through the Spirit. If it comes from the Spirit it has something for us, and we should be eager to receive it, not ignore it.

f. "Prove all things." The foregoing counsel not to despise prophesyings must practically be balanced by this exhortation. There are false prophets, and no Christian should take it as his standard to believe everything that is taught to him. There must be testing of those things given us to believe, just as in a laboratory metals are tested by fire to determine their merits. John makes a similar exhortation in I John 4:1. We should test by the Word of God, by the character produced, by the inward approval of the Spirit (discernment) by the general teaching of those who are spiritual, and by the general doctrines of the Word.

The Second Epistle to the
THESSALONIANS

Introduction

I. Author
Paul is the author of this epistle.

II. Date
II Thessalonians was written shortly after I Thessalonians, probably during 51 or 52 A.D.

III. The Occasion for the Letter
Paul seeks to solve some problems which were prevalent at Thessalonica, part of which arose because of misunderstanding of his first letter.

IV. Outline of the Book (Themed "The Problems of a Young Church")

A. The Problem of Suffering (Chapter 1)

B. The Problem of the Coming of Christ (Chapter 2)

C. The Problem of Waiting (Chapter 3)

The Study of the Second Epistle to the Thessalonians

I. Paul's Introduction, 1:1,2

The introduction is almost identical with that of I Thessalonians. Silas and Timothy were with him, so he includes them in the greeting.

Grace and peace are common words of greeting with Paul. Grace refers to the spiritual blessing which comes from God; peace, in the largest sense, embraces the wholeness or health which is ours as a result of grace.

II. The Problem of Suffering

This is one of the most common questions which thinking people ask about God and His dealings: why does He allow men to suffer? Why is it that sometimes the righteous suffer more than the wicked appear to suffer? Why does God allow the wicked to persecute the righteous?

A. The Suffering of the Righteous, v. 4 ff.

Apparently some of the Thessalonians were asking such questions, and Paul feared lest they should become discouraged with their lot.

1. The fact of their righteousness. Paul begins in a gracious, proper way, by praising them for the good things manifest in them. He was joyous because of their rapidly growing faith. This was one of the characteristics of this church from the beginning, and now it seems even more manifest, for the word "groweth exceedingly" is a very strong word indicating good health and rapid enlargement.

   Together with their faith is love, which also abounded. He had pleaded for this in the first letter, and now it is apparently manifest.

   They were showing patience in their persecutions. While evidently some were questioning their situation and the reasons God allowed it, the church was not turning back but was going on in spite of the difficulties.

2. The fact of their suffering. From Acts 17:5-13 and from I Thes. 2:14 we learn that the Thessalonians had suffered much from their own countrymen and from the Jews of the synagogue.

Persecutions are strictly religious sufferings, whereas *tribulations* may be from any source.

3. The reasons for their suffering

   a. Faith and patience grow under pressure. Doubtless one of the reasons why their faith grew so exceedingly was that they began their Christian life under the stress of persecution. God is more interested in our spiritual enlargement than in our comfort.

   b. Suffering for Christ will enlarge our glory in the world to come.

   This fact is often pointed out by St. Paul. See, for example, II Tim. 2:12, "If we suffer, we shall also reign with Him."

   Our endurance of suffering demonstrates how much the kingdom of God is worth to us in such a way that the world can see it. We always show our evaluation of things by how much we are willing to give or suffer to attain them. The most eloquent testimony of Christian reality ever given to the world has been in suffering for the sake of Christ and His kingdom. Not only do we show how much the kingdom of God is worth to us, however; we also show that we are worthy of the kingdom (v. 5). The quality of a person's faith is shown by his willingness to suffer for his Lord.

   Because of this fact, Paul prays (vv. 11, 12) that they might always live that kind of life that is worthy of the glory to which we are called. To be worthy we must fulfill "all the good pleasure of goodness, and the work of faith with power." This could better be translated, "the good resolve of goodness." The Thessalonians were to resolve to fulfill all goodness in spite of persecutions. Their faith must be shown by works. As it was, God would provide the power for such a life. Here is a fine summary of the Christian life: *proper resolve, good works showing our faith, and power from God to make it all possible.*

       c. It proves the coming judgment. As the Thessalonians felt, it is not right that the righteous should suffer at the hands of the wicked. Therefore, our sense of justice requires that there be a judgment at which God gives the wicked proper punishment for persecuting the righteous, and God gives the righteous appropriate reward for enduring suffering for Christ's sake. This is evidently the sense of Paul where he says their suffering is a manifest token of the righteous judgment of God. Since it is right that there should be such a judgment, and since God is righteous, then there must be such a judgment. The suffering of the righteous here and now proves that there must be a coming judgment at which the situation shall be reversed: the wicked shall suffer and the righteous be rewarded. The righteous God will surely bring this about.

B. The Suffering of the Wicked, vv. 6-9

    1. The fact of their wickedness. Three things are said about them: first, they troubled the saints, v. 6. They were responsible for bringing on the Christians sore suffering. In this they were essentially persecuting Christ himself (see Acts 9:4). Second, they knew not God (v. 8). They could have known Him, for the Gospel was preached there and others came to know God through that Gospel. Paul analyzes this situation in Rom. 1:18-21. They could have known God, but they did not want to because of the obligations that would have followed. Third, they obeyed not the Gospel. Note, the Gospel requires obedience. When a man hears the Gospel, it is more than an intellectual stimulus; it is a moral revelation of his own sinfulness and the grace of God which alone brings deliverance from the wrath to come. When a man obeys not the gospel, it exposes him without excuse to that wrath to come—the Gospel is the only escape.

    2. The fact of their suffering

       a. It is righteous of God to let the wicked suffer, v. 6. A law in the moral realm is that what a man sows, he also shall reap. These wicked people had brought suffering on others; they had also refused salvation from future judgment upon all sin. It is entirely proper that they should suffer for so doing. Moral beings are responsible for their actions, and it is to God that all are so responsible.

b. It is separation from God and the glory of His power, v. 9. This is entirely proper. God has made man a being of choice. When he chooses to go apart from God and refuses God's way, part of his punishment is to be allowed to go that way forever. Note the truth of Prov. 1:30, 31. The wicked shall be filled with the fruit of their own way. If they choose to go away from God, that shall be their way forever. A time is coming when God shall seal this judgment. The wicked shall be separated from God and from the righteous in whom the glory of His power has been displayed.

The revelation of Christ, accompanied by His mighty angels, will be a time of separation. He shall reveal His judgments on those who bring suffering to the righteous. (See 2:8.)

The Bible teaches plainly that angels will have an important part in cleansing the earth of its sinfulness. (See Matt 13:41, 42, 49, 50; 16:7.)

c. It is fiery punishment. Added to the logical consequences of sinfulness is the divine punishment of those who continue in their sins. It is important to recognize that God is just in meting out severe punishment upon unrepentant sinners. First, it is just because all sin is sin against God. It is His law that is broken by those who sin, and it is He who will punish for the breaking of His law. Added to all the other sins is the worst sin—refusing the Gospel. The Gospel is provided in love for the sinner; it is God's desire to save the sinner from the sure punishment that must come. When God's love is refused, His wrath is the rightful consequence. If men do not want to face God's righteous vengeance, they should respond to His love and hear the Gospel.

The fact that punishment is everlasting is clearly taught here. Destruction is not an end of being; it is a breaking down and separation from all that is good.

The flaming fire is the cloak or garment of Christ as He is seen in the judgment. The darkness shall be penetrated by His brightness. Nothing shall remain hidden before Him.

This is a truth so majestic and awesome that it should fill us with reverence for God and impel us to proclaim the Gospel which saves men from the wrath to come. As Paul said, "Knowing the terror of God, we persuade men."

C. As a conclusion of this presentation, Paul exhorts the Thessalonians to rest from their fears, even in the midst of persecution, v. 7, knowing that a judgment day of the Lord is coming when all wrongs shall be corrected.

He further exhorts the believers, in the light of that judgment, to continue fulfilling the goodness of the Lord. He prays for them (vv. 11, 12) that the name (nature) of Christ may be seen in them. The fact that grace is sufficient to enable us to mirror the very brightness of God's glory is a wonderful claim. We can be glorified in Him, and He in us.

To glorify the Lord is to show what the nature of the Lord is like. At His coming He will be magnified by what we are, and we shall be made to wonder and marvel at Him.

III. The Problem of Christ's Suffering

It is rather amazing that such a young church knew so much about the coming of the Lord. It is evident that Paul considered it an important doctrine to give so much time to it when he was at Thessalonica such a short period of time. This should be a lesson to us who live so much closer to the coming of the Lord: our people need to be aware of this momentous event and live in complete readiness for it.

A. The Problem of Deception

1. In his first epistle Paul endeavored to correct the error that Christ would so soon be here that the Thessalonians decided just to wait passively until His coming. It is likely that even after his letter that the error was not thoroughly corrected.

2. There was a further error: some believed that the day of the Lord had already come. Some were crediting Paul with a special revelation (by spirit), a special message to some of them (by word), or a special letter which was evidently forged (see 3:17) to the effect that the day of the Lord had already come. The Thessalonians were undergoing trib-ulations, and it was easy for some of them to feel that this suffering was the great tribulation already begun.

3. Deception has always been common concerning the second coming of Christ and the end of the age. Jesus warned about deceivers (Matt. 24:4, 5, 11, 24). Peter said there would be scoffers who would deny Christ's coming (see II Pet. 3:3, 4). Paul also warned against them in II Tim. 3:13. Approximately one-third of the entire Bible is given to discussion of the day of the Lord, however, so we should understand the main events thereof, even if we do not reach perfect agreement about all the details.

B. The Prophesied Events

It is well at this point to endeavor to give a broad outline of the events associated with the coming of the Lord. Paul mentions several of them in these two epistles.

1. The rapture of the Church, v. 1. The word "coming" is "parousia" in Greek and signifies the presence of Christ. The "gathering together" of the saints unto Him obviously refers to the same event as Paul describes in I Thes. 4:16, 17. Luke 21:36 also speaks of this event. At the rapture the church is caught up into the air to meet the Lord and to return with Him to the marriage supper of the Lamb (Rev. 19:7-9).

2. The falling away, or apostasy. It is probable that this comes even before the rapture; at least, it begins before the rapture. Paul refers to this time in II Tim. 3:1-5 as a time when men not only become unbelieving but also are in revolt against the truth. In II Tim. 4:3, 4, Paul says they will not endure sound doctrine but will insist on teachers who teach what they want to hear, turning to fables. Evil men and deceivers shall wax worse and worse. It is doubtless true that we are in the beginnings of this time now. There is an increasing revolt against conservative views of the Word of God.

3. The revelation of the man of sin. The word "reveal" here comes from Greek words meaning to take off the cover. It means to be manifested openly, whereas before he has been secret. The same word also refers to the revelation of Christ.

   a. His character. He is called the "man of sin," which depicts his character as in direct opposition to the holiness of God and inspired by Satan himself. This thought is strengthened in v. 4. He will be a religious man with great appeal (see Rev. 13:13-15). He will even sit as God in the temple. This is connected with the abomination of desolation (see Dan. 9:27 and Matt. 24:15).

He is also called the "Son of perdition" as Judas was (John 17:12). This signifies the certainty of his final doom. (Compare with Judas in Acts 1:25.)

  b. The development. The mystery of iniquity was working at the time of Paul. Through the ages there has been a behind-the-scenes operation, promoted by Satan himself, to defeat Christ and bring in Satan's own kingdom on earth. The antichrist is Satan's false messiah, who is to take the place of Christ in the earth according to His plan. The spirit of antichrist was already evident in Bible days, as John says in I John 4:1-3. There are a number of developments going on now which are surely a part of Satan's scheme to bring antichrist to a place of universal authority. There is the doctrine of evolution, which belittles God and magnifies man as the highest being. There is the ecumenical movement, which is promoting a union of apostates. There is the United Nations, which is bringing the world toward political union under antichrist powers. There is the growth of a controlled economy, which is preparing the way for the mark of the beast (Rev. 13:16, 17). All of these and others will continue until all is ready for the antichrist to assume his position of power—militarily, economically, politically, and religiously.

  c. The hindrance. Paul says there is a force in the world which is preventing the antichrist from taking power yet. There have been differing ideas of what this force is, but the best interpretation is that the restrainer is the Holy Spirit (or perhaps God in three Persons) working in the church, opposing the working of Satan. Thus, when the church is taken away in the rapture, the great hindrance to Satan's working will be removed, and he will be free to come to his revelation.

  d. His activity

    1) How he gains control of men. Verses 9 and 10 are a most awesome portrayal of his working. He will come with mighty power, duplicating the miracles of God to prove his religious authority. Remember, he is a false

messiah. (See Rev. 13:13-15) where he is shown to have power to call down fire from heaven and give speech and life to an image. Note that he has the gift of miracles, of prophecy, and of tongues—all from Satan.) There is also healing (v. 3) and resurrection (Rev. 17:8). All whose names are not written in the Lamb's book of life shall worship him (Rev. 13:8). Deception will come to a universal climax in him.

2) God will allow this deception to affect all those who did not receive the truth when it came to them, because they loved unrighteousness. These verses indicate all will be damned then who do not receive the truth now. It is true that many will be saved during that time by laying down their lives in resistance to the antichrist's plan (see Rev. 7:13, 14), but it is doubtful that careless rejecters of the truth today will be in that number. Men are not saved by fear but by faith in Christ. Those who are confirmed in unbelief now will be given to deception then, and God Himself will do nothing to remove that deception from them.

e. His destruction. Verse 8 gives the glorious assurance of God's sovereignty and victory over the antichrist. The "breath of His mouth" is a figure like a sweeping hurricane. Antichrist cannot stand against the Word of Christ which will take him away. The brightness of His coming will completely arrest and paralyze him—Satan and his hosts work in the dark. Then antichrist shall be banished to the lake of fire (see Rev. 19:20 and 20:10). Destruction does not mean annihilation but inoperability. We can rejoice in the knowledge of that great day of victory.

4. The revelation of Christ, v. 2 and Chapter 1:7. After the revelation of the man of sin and the period of tribulation, which shall prevail under his persecution of the Jews who turn to Christ (as well as others), Jesus shall be revealed and will dispose of the antichrist. This is the time when Christ comes with His saints to set up His millennial kingdom of earth. This is referred to in 1:10 as well as in I Thess. 3:12, 13; 5:23; Jude 14; and Rev. 19:11-15. Enoch was a type of those who go in the rapture, and by his translation he missed the tribulation of the deluge. He prophesied of the revelation of Christ with His saints.

C. The Security of the Believer, vv. 13-17

1. God's choice. The thought here is not that God has chosen some and rejected others on an arbitrary basis; rather, it is that He has chosen to save men rather than to forsake them. See I Thes. 5:9 for a clear statement of this choice of God. Note what has followed that choice.

2. God's calling. This is effected through the Gospel; this is God's appeal. In Mark 16:15, 16 it is stated that the Gospel is for all creatures. The believers shall be saved and the unbelievers damned. In Acts 2:39 we are informed that God's call is for "all them that are afar off." The command of the Gospel is for all men to repent (see Acts 17:30).

3. Belief of the truth, v. 13. As we have seen in Mark 16:15, 16, not all who are called by the Gospel will believe. Some will rejected the message, as Paul shows in v. 12.

4. Sanctification of the Spirit. This work of separation and cleansing begins in regeneration and is completed in the second crisis when the Spirit comes in His holy fulness.

5. Establishment. This is partly God's work (v. 17), and He accomplishes it through the grace of holiness (see I Thes. 3:13) as well as through the Word and other ministries of His grace. It is also partly our responsibility (v. 15). God gives us solid ground to stand on and gives us strength, but we must exercise our will to appropriate all of the grace available for standing firm. We are to hold the traditions. This does not mean the notions of men but the truth that had been given to them. (In those days the common people did not have the Scriptures, so they had to depend on what they heard—the traditions.)

6. Final salvation and glory, v. 13. This is the good hope (v. 16). The term "salvation" often refers to this final glory with Christ, as it does here.

IV. The Problem of Waiting

There is evidently a continuation of the problem treated in the first epistle (4:11-12; 5:14), so Paul deals firmly with that: the fact that some of the members were settling down in laziness, refusing to work, under the pretext that Jesus was soon to come. The Church was saddled with the responsibility of caring for such lazy ones.

A. The Disorderly Ones

1. Their practices, v. 11. "Disorderly" means "falling out of ranks." They were not serving the church or helping themselves. The term "busybody" is a play on the word "busy." These people were busy, but not for good purpose. Perhaps they were busy going about justifying their own position instead of listening to Paul's teaching and doing the proper thing.

2. Their discipline, vv. 14, 15; also v. 6. Here is a case of Paul exercising apostolic authority to bring about correction of a bad situation. He instructs the members to cease having familiar fellowship with that person, not to cause him to lose heart, but to cause him to feel his error with the hope that he might be saved from it. They were first to "mark" him. This literally meant to brand, and certainly meant that there was to be some recognition given to his error so nobody could mistake it. It is an example of New Testament discipline which was for the purpose of saving the one involved. They were to still love the person as a brother.

3. The command to the person, v. 12. The rule for such persons was that they should eat their own bread, and in order to do so, they should work quietly—that is, without the agitation concerning Christ's immediate coming.

    Paul gives his own example, vv. 7, 8. If he, the apostle of the Lord, worked so diligently to bring them the gospel, they should be willing to work diligently, also. He recognized it would be acceptable for him, God's minister, to receive material support while he preached the Gospel, but in order to be a good example of working, he did not exercise this privilege (see his explanation in I Cor. 9:7-18).

B. The Occupation

There is much for the Christian to do while he waits for the Lord to come. The waiting is not to be an inactive one but one of active watchfulness while working.

1. Prayer, vv. 1, 2. In many of Paul's epistles, Paul asked for prayer for himself and his ministry. His was not a professional ministry which he learned and then could carry on habitually. He knew the going forth of the Word must be with the power of God, or it would not accomplish its ordained purpose.

   "Have free course" literally meant to "run." It refers to rapid progress with impediments out of the way. He knew the time was short and there was so much to be accomplished that there must be supernatural strength in his ministry. The Word must be used, but without prayer it would plod heavily rather than run swiftly. This is an important concept: *a professional knowledge of the Word and how to declare it is not enough.* If there is spiritual victory, there must be prayer that is effective. He wanted the Word to go swiftly and be victorious in its going.

   Further, he wanted deliverance from wicked men. There were evidently those who were opposing his ministry—this was usually the case, and he knew there must be prayer in order for victory to come. He always recognized that this was a spiritual warfare and not one fought with flesh and blood. Prayer was the only thing that would bring victory over human opposition.

2. Progress, v. 5. They were to advance in love. This love may refer to God's love for us or our love for Him. The two are inseparable in true growth. This request is a form of prayer by Paul. As they prayed for him he was praying for them, that they might increase in love. The whole of religion is involved in the true love of God in the heart and life.

3. Well doing, v. 13. They were not to grow faint, no matter how severe their persecution was. On the contrary, they were to "do the noble thing," as is the true meaning. Often there is the temptation to settle down in discouragement and relax our efforts for Christ. This exhortation is a prohibition of such a mood.

C. The Preservation

It is never casually taken for granted that believers are assured of Heaven. There is a necessary persistence, patience, and endurance.

1. God's faithfulness assures us of sufficient strength, v. 3. In 35 references to God's faithfulness in the Bible, there is always a background of human peril or need. Here are a few of such cases.

    a) When a storm of poverty, distress, grief, or loss sweeps over us, God is a strength and a refuge, giving comfort and healing. See Is. 25:1-5.

    b) When people make great, hopeful promises to us and then fail, betraying our confidence, God is faithful. See Jer. 42:5.

    c) When severe temptations assail us God is faithful. See I Cor. 10:13.

    d) When others fall and forsake the way of the Lord and the load falls more heavily on us, "Let us hold fast the profession of our faith, for he is faithful that promised" (Heb. 10:23).

2. We should note that there is establishment accompanied by preservation from evil. There is no such thing as establishment for the believer while he continues in evil doing. We can thank God that the life of holiness—preservation from evil—is a stable life. It is not a life of doing a handstand on a flagpole in a high wind; it is a life of solidly resting in the faithfulness of God and living victoriously by His strength.

    Verse 5 literally means the steadfastness of Christ. Christ's own steadfastness under trial and opposition becomes ours as we trust and grow in conformity to Him.

3. There is peace in every circumstance. Verse 16 literally means peace in all circumstances. How wonderful this is! We may come to places and times when the body is endangered, but the soul may still be kept in peace by the God of peace Himself. The mind may be perplexed by deep problems, assailments, and uncertainties, but beneath it all is this deep soul peace.

    This is not peace apart from God's presence. The Lord Himself is always with us. Our faith is secured, our hope restored, our courage increased by the awareness of this fact. Our physical eyes do not observe, but the spiritual eye of faith rests on Him, and in that contemplation we have peace and stability. "The Lord is with you." This was always the source of strength for that early church, whether in jail, the fires of martyrdom, or the duty of each day. "The Lord is at hand," Phil. 4:5.

V. Conclusion

In conclusion Paul certifies that his own hand has signed the letter. Inasmuch that there had evidently been a false letter circulated, he gives assurance that this one is genuine. His usual gracious benediction and "Amen" close the letter.

Review Questions
I and II Thessalonians

1. What were the circumstances surrounding the establishment of the church at Thessalonica?
2. What kind of city was Thessalonica?
3. What were the reasons for writing each of these epistles?
4. Give the general subject of each chapter in II Thessalonians as well as the general theme of each epistle.
5. What were some of the charges that were evidently made against Paul by some opposers in Thessalonica?
6. State some of the characteristics of Paul which appear in I Thessalonians.
7. Describe both the "human entrance" and the "divine entrance" when the Gospel went to Thessalonica.
8. What does Paul mean by "election?"
9. Give the characteristics of the church at Thessalonica as Paul describes it.
10. What two great doctrines does Paul treat substantially in the letters?
11. In Paul's treatment of the doctrine of holiness, what reasons does he give for the necessity of holiness?
12. What evidence is there in I Thessalonians that holiness comes by an instantaneous work of grace?
13. What are the results of the experience of holiness in a believer's life?
14. What motivations arise from the fact of Christ's soon coming back to earth?
15. What is meant by the expression, "The day of the Lord"?
16. The Thessalonian believers had evidently been mistaken in their thinking about Christ's second coming. What error had they believed?
17. The believers wondered what would become of those who had already died as Christians before Christ's second coming. What was Paul's answer?
18. Paul gave many practical Christian exhortations. What did he mean by those who are unruly (I Thes. 5:14)?
19. In the expression "quench not the Spirit," what figure of the Spirit is suggested?
20. What three special problems are considered in II Thessalonians?
21. For what reasons did God allow the righteous to suffer such persecutions?

22. Show from II Thessalonians, Chapter 1, that God's punishment of sinners is righteous and everlasting.
23. What errors about the coming of Christ appear from our study of II Thessalonians?
24. There are four great events concerning the end time which are prophesied in II Thessalonians. What are they?
25. Explain the terms, "The mystery of iniquity," "The man of sin," "The falling away," "The son of perdition," and "He who now letteth."
26. Why will God allow the antichrist to deceive men?
27. What is the relation between the rapture and the revelation?
28. Explain the security of the believer as Paul presents it.
29. What discipline was to be given to those who were disorderly?
30. What assurance did the believers at Thessalonica have that the letter of II Thessalonians really came from Paul?

The First Epistle to
TIMOTHY

Introduction

I. Author

It is generally agreed among conservatives that Paul was the author. However, there are some problems related to his authorship. The event referred to in the opening verses—Paul's having left Timothy at Ephesus while he himself went on to Macedonia—does not fit into any of his missionary journeys as recorded in the book of Acts. So if Paul were the author, he wrote it after he was released from his first imprisonment at Rome. Also, there are marked differences in vocabulary from Paul's earlier epistles, which have caused some to believe that various personal letters of Paul were combined by the hand of another into this epistle under his name. Many personal references in the epistle convince us that the writing is that of Paul.

II. The Time of Writing

If, as indicated above, it was written after Paul's first release from prison, then it must be as late as 63 A.D. The problems and errors referred to are so much the same as in II Timothy that it appears they were both written near the same time. Thus, it was perhaps near the year 64 A.D.

III. The Recipient of the Letter

The letter is plainly addressed to Timothy, and he was probably between 30 and 35 years of age when the letter was written. His home was in Lystra, where Paul may have made contact with Timothy's family on Paul's first missionary journey. No mention is made of Timothy until the second journey. Their friendship was very close and beneficial to the Apostle. It is apparent that Timothy was converted under Paul's ministry and that after the second missionary journey

Timothy was with Paul or on errands for him during most of the rest of Paul's ministry.

IV. The Reason for Writing

A. The Purpose Stated in the Letter, 3:14, 15
Here Paul says he writes so Timothy may know how to behave himself in the church of God.

B. The Combatting of Heresy
In both epistles to Timothy and the epistle to Titus there are repeated references to dangerous error. Timothy was left at Ephesus to counteract the error, and this epistle strengthens Timothy's offensive against the false teachers. It appears that the errors are linked with Gnosticism, which was at this time increasing in its influence. Although it is not named as such, it seems possible to relate most of Paul's descriptions to that error.

V. Outline

There are a number of key words in the epistle: faith, salvation, conscience, doctrine and holiness. The one which occurs most frequently is "Godliness" and related terms. We have chosen to outline the book about this significant word, entitling it "The Minister and Godliness."

A. Paul's Introduction

B. Law, Gospel and Godliness

C. The Warfare for Godliness

D. Church Order and the Promotion of Godliness

E. Godliness and the Business of the Church

F. Gain and Godliness

G. Paul's Conclusion

The Study of the First Epistle to Timothy

I. Introduction to the Epistle, 1:1, 2

A. The Writer

It was customary in letter writing for the writer to begin by stating his own name, whereas now we customarily put the writer's name at the close.

1. The official nature of the letter. If this had been a purely private letter, the reference to his apostolic office would perhaps not have been included. Since Paul is authorizing Timothy to deal with heretics and false teachers, the authoritative note is important. Timothy may use the letter as a type of credential in dealing with the error.

2. The authority of his apostleship

   a. God our Savior. This concept is common in the Old Testament, but it is no less true, although not so common, in the New Testament. Though Jesus purchased our salvation and is known as the Savior, the Father planned our salvation, and it is His love that motivated it. So Paul refers often in the pastorals to God as Savior. (See 2:3; 4:10; Titus 1:3; 2:10, 3:4.)

   b. Christ our Hope. Paul had an exceedingly exalted view of Jesus. For Him, Jesus was the basis of all things good. He that had Jesus had all he needed. In Ephesians 2:14 he called Jesus our peace. In I Corinthians 1:30 he said that Christ is made unto us wisdom and righteousness, sanctification and redemption. All our hopes are centered in Him, and in every difficulty, He is our hope of victory.

B. The Recipient

Timothy is called a true child. It accents the genuineness of the young man, as well as Paul's claim to have been his spiritual father.

C. The Benediction

Grace is the attribute whereby God gives us so much of good which we do not deserve. Mercy is the attribute whereby He withholds the penalties which we have deserved and showered love on us instead. Peace is a term for comprehensive well-being;

everything for man's highest good is included. It is tranquility and harmony within the love of God.

II. The Law, the Gospel, and Godliness, 1:3-17

  A. The Law and Godliness, vv. 3-10

  1. Its perversion, vv. 3, 4, 6, 7

   a. The situation at Ephesus. Before Paul left Ephesus on his third missionary journey, he warned that false teachers would arise. Now it is evident that the prophecy has come true. He does not identify the error by name, but it appears that the descriptions fit the error of gnosticism which was gaining prestige and influence at this time. We may note some of the characteristics of the error here, as it features prominently in the background of a number of New Testament writings.

   b. The errors of Gnosticism

   1) Gnostics believed that matter was essentially evil. This was their way of accounting for the fact of evil in the world. Matter was also eternal, so that God was not the creator of it.

   2) Since God is essentially holy, He could not have handled matter, so He did not directly create the world.

   3) Gnostics believed that there were a series of emanations from God reaching progressively downward and each one becoming farther removed from the character of God. These emanations, or aeons, were personalities, each having his own genealogy and his own name. At the bottom of the list was an emanation far enough removed from God that he was able to handle evil matter and make a world out of it.

   4) In order for man to get to God, he had to ascend the scale of emanations. To do so, he must have knowledge of a special kind (Gnosis), including the essential passwords to move from one emanation to the next higher. Only a person of the highest intellectual ability could expect to have this knowledge and thus get to God.

5) Gnosticism was thus marked by intellectual snobbery or pride. Endless speculations and questions about the emanations and their genealogies was considered a sign of the kind of wisdom that was important.

6) Since matter was altogether evil, the body was considered to be evil, also. Two different conclusions were drawn from this. One was that the body should be subjected to a severe asceticism. The desires and instincts, particularly sexual ones, were to be extinguished as far as possible. On the other hand, some felt that since the body was essentially evil and could never be otherwise, it did not matter what the body was involved in; the spirit was good, independent of any conduct of the body. On the basis of such thinking, it was concluded that all kinds of gratifications were not relevant to true morality.

7) Since the body was considered evil, there was believed to be no resurrection of the body possible, only that of the spirit.

b. The combination of Judaism and Gnosticism. It is evident that some of the Jews were involved in the Gnostic heresy. There were reasons why the error would appeal to them. Many of the Jews believed it was knowledge of the law and Jewish food regulations which comprised the necessary knowledge and asceticism to find favor with God. In Jewish writings they had built a great store of silly fables which were supposed to be spiritualized applications of the Old Testament teachings. They also worked at length on their genealogies, since their ancestry was so important to them. Many of the Jews felt that their sins could be easily overlooked if they could prove their descent from Abraham. People believed that their salvation depended on their being able to trace their descent from Abraham, so they were involved in "endless genealogies." Also, one of the favorite occupations of Jewish scholars was to construct an imaginary biography for every name in his genealogy. It is obvious how wasteful and useless this was, yet it was considered of great value to them.

Paul could rightly say that those who desired to be teachers did not really know what they were saying.

2. Its true purpose, vv. 5, 8-10
   a. Positively, the purpose of the law is to bring about love out of a pure heart and of a good conscience and of faith unfeigned. It seems likely that the term "commandment" here refers to Timothy's command to the people, but it also applies to the larger command, the Law of God.
      1) *A pure heart* is one whose motives are absolutely pure and unmixed. There is nothing of sin left in it to pollute the motives or actions.
      2) *Love* flowing out of a pure heart is the essence of holiness. Love, we are told, is the fulfilling of the law. This is the grace which is poured into our hearts by the Holy Ghost which enables us to fulfill the law and to show forth the spirit of Christ.
      3) *Conscience* basically means a knowing of oneself. A good conscience is one which can know the inward moral nature and be unashamed of what it knows. This can only be true of those people who have been cleansed by the blood of Jesus Christ.
      4) *Unfeigned faith* is that which has no element of hypocrisy about it. The Christian is sincere in his desire to find the true, to obey it, and to communicate it. Faith with disobedience is not pure. Taken together, these words give a wonderful summary of the life of holiness.
         It is when people swerve from such a high purpose of the dispensation of God (Godly edifying) that they are turned to vanity and jangling. A moral breakdown frequently inspires the turning aside to error as an effort to compensate for the pain of an injured conscience.
   b. Negatively, the law is to expose, condemn and check lawlessness and ungodliness. The "Thou shalt not" commands of the law were meant to be a barrier against evil, of which some examples are given here. The first three pairs of evils are against God and righteousness; they are evils of attitude. The remaining ones are evils of conduct, evils in society.

       1) The *lawless* is one of those who know the law but deliberately breaks it.

       2) The *disobedient* refuse authority.

       3) The *ungodly* is one who deifies God and withholds respect from Him.

       4) *Sinners* are those who have character without moral standards. It shows the results in one's own character of misconduct.

       5) The *unholy* is worse than the lawless in that he violates sanctity and decency. He is in contempt of the basic principles of right and wrong.

       6) The *profane* is one who corrupts things by trampling them underfoot. He does this to God's day, God's name, and the life which God has given him to live.

           The remaining list of sins shows the kind of world the Christians of that day lived in. The same sins are prevalent in our society, but it is as possible to live holy and free from sin now as it was then if we take of the offered grace of God and victory in Christ.

B. The Gospel and Godliness, 1:11-17

    1. The relation of law and Gospel. The law is opposed to all that is contrary to sound doctrine, and this sound doctrine is according to the gospel. That is, the law and gospel are in agreement in standing opposed to sin. The false teachers raised no effective barrier against sin, but both law and gospel do. Whereas the law had no power to make men righteous, the gospel does. In this fact the Apostle never ceased to exult. There seemed to be a spirit of praise which erupted within the heart of Paul whenever he thought of the Gospel's power, and here he shows how much it has done for him.

    2. The characteristics of this gospel, vv. 10, 11

       a. It is a gospel of sound teaching. The word "sound" means health-giving. It produces moral cleanness and health. Other religions were associated with the worst kinds of immoralities, but the Gospel of Jesus Christ makes men clean. Any religion today which does not lift men above the level of sin and make them clean is not being true to the Gospel.

  b. It is a glorious gospel because it gives forgiveness for past sins and victory over sin in the future with a prospect of eternal blessedness with our Savior.

  c. It is from God. The Almighty is the prime Mover in this glorious plan.

  d. It is committed to men. What a responsibility pertains to the minister of the Gospel!

3. The example of Paul, vv. 11-16

  a. His call to the ministry

   1) He was chosen of God ("Committed to my trust"). This choice was made before Paul was ever converted, and it never ceased to amaze him that it should be so. We can all praise God that we have been chosen also. Not all have been chosen to be an apostle or an evangelist or missionary, but all have been chosen to eternal life.

   2) He was trusted of God ("counted as faithful"). This is especially amazing when we learn how great a sinner Paul had been. If God could use him, He can use anybody who will come to Him.

   3) He was appointed of God ("putting me into the ministry"). It was for service, not honor, that he was chosen, so the praise should go to God and not to the servant. Paul is faithful to give all praise to God; we should do likewise.

   4) He was enabled by God ("who hath enabled me"). Never did the Apostle feel that his achievements were to his own credit but to the credit of Him Who enabled Paul with His own power. We should feel likewise. The reason some men do not have any more power is that they would take to themselves too much of the honor that comes from the exercise of power.

  b) The call to the ministry of the gospel is all the more wondrous in the light of Paul's past life. There is here a list of three sins which in the original were given in ascending scale. A blasphemer is one who, literally, speaks injuriously. Paul had spoken so against Christ and His Church, and worse still, he had forced others to do so (Act 26:11). As a persecutor his sin passed from speech to action.

He could not touch Jesus himself, so he expressed his hatred in pursuing Christians as one chases animals. In Acts 22:4 Paul stated, "And I persecuted this way unto the death, binding and delivering into prisons both men and women." "Injurious" is an extreme word, indicating a sadistic satisfaction in hurting others, not for any gain it brings the injurer but just for the gratification of lust for violence. His passion against the Christians was thus quite unbounded, a violent, irrational, insatiable desire to see them die in anguish or languish in prison. To satisfy this passion he pursued them to strange cities and determined to see them exterminated from the earth.

c. The salvation of a sinner. Paul's effort here is to put the power of the Gospel over against the futility and emptiness of the false teaching that was being propagated at Ephesus. His stress is that in his own salvation God had shown what could be done through the Gospel.

God's *mercy* was displayed. Paul gives two reasons why he received mercy. One was that he sinned in ignorance of Who Jesus really was. The second was that he was in unbelief. The Jewish idea was that willful, presumptuous sin could not be forgiven, and that no sin at all could be forgiven until there was contrition and confession. From this viewpoint, Paul says he received mercy. He was ignorant, and when he saw Who Jesus was he was broken in contrition (cf. Heb. 10:26-29).

The reason for this display of mercy was so God could make an example of its greatness in saving an extreme sinner. Paul stated that his sin was the greatest. Doubtless this was true: Paul was the greatest sinner there was in those days, perhaps in any time. God wished to make him a "first" example of His longsuffering in saving a sinner. The word "first" is the same translated "chief" in v. 15. The chief sinner became the chief example of God's saving grace. Paul does not say he is the most outstanding saint, but we could safely add this comment. NOTE: It does not fit into the true meaning of this passage to insist that Paul still was at the time of writing the chief of all sinners. He is the chief example of a saved sinner.

God's *grace* was displayed. It abounded in overflowing measure, he says. To save such a sinner, God showed a super abundance of grace. This grace brought faith where there had been unbelief, and love where there had been hate. It was such a transformation that could not come from education or moral resolution but only by revelation and transformation.

The *longsuffering* of Christ was displayed. Christ on His throne might properly have destroyed this persecutor of His Church, but He wanted to show His longsuffering—His delay of punishment while He patiently waits for the possible repentance of the sinner. If sinners today could get a view of these wondrous attributes of God in Christ, surely they also would repent.

The *pattern* displayed to men. It may be summed up in this saying which was apparently somewhat of a proverb at that time: "Christ Jesus came into the world to save sinners." Perhaps it was becoming a part of an embryonic creed in that early church. This saying is absolutely trustworthy, universally, without doubt and necessity of delay. What a wonderful declaration! This Paul held in contrast to the false teachers as a way of true salvation.

Life everlasting may come to all who believe in Christ. If Paul could be saved, then anybody anywhere may be saved who will believe in Christ.

4. A tribute to the King, v. 17. The mention of life everlasting seems to catch Paul away from earthly things into the realm of the spirit and eternity and the reality that will be paramount there. The great and glorious God, in all His glorious attributes, and Christ, in Whom all the fulness of the Godhead dwelleth, receive the outpouring of praise here, and shall forever more.

We may comment here how much higher the true message of salvation from sin is than any of the false messages that men proclaim today in order to get a following. There is still no higher message than holiness. This is the message which Paul was proclaiming as announced in v. 4 and demonstrated in his own example—a man brought from the chiefest of sinners to the level of the Christ-life where he could say, "Be ye followers of men, even as I also am of Christ" (II Cor. 11:10).

III. The Warfare for Godliness, 1:18-2:15

A. The Charge of Paul, 1:18-20

1. Its nature. It is from a father to a dear son, Timothy. The name Timothy means "honor to God." It may be that Paul's use of the

name is accompanied with emphasis on its meaning. Timothy is charged to live up to his name in the present place of labor.

It is according to prophecy. This apparently means that as some of the prophets of God were in meeting about the problems of Ephesus, Timothy was considered to be the proper person to go and attend to matters there. Thus he had an appointment similar to that related in Acts 13:1, 2 concerning Barnabas and Paul.

2. Its object. Timothy was appointed to a warfare for the faith. It includes the problem of the false teachers, but since the term "warfare" is used there is more than just one battle involved. It apparently includes the entire conflict of truth against error, of Godliness against ungodliness.

In this warfare which goes on continually, the soldier must have faith and a good conscience. These are the elements mentioned in v. 5 which mark the purpose of the command. It means that in order to be a good soldier of the cause of holiness the soldier must have the graces of holiness in his own heart. If the minister's own conscience condemns him, he loses the power of his message. As Paul says in II Tim. 2:6, "The husbandman that laboreth must be first partaker of the fruits."

Two examples are given of men who, having failed in faith and a good conscience, made shipwreck of the faith. They may well be the same as are mentioned in II Tim. 2:17 and 4:14. If so, they not only opposed Paul but led others astray into error. It is typical for men who fall short of true holiness and whose consciences are therefore not clear to begin propagating error vigorously, for in this way they seek to justify their actions and to alleviate the pain of an injured conscience. The extreme seriousness of such action is shown by Paul's decision about them. The meaning of "delivering them to Satan" is not clear. It may mean excommunication from the church and therefore putting them into the world under the god of this world, or it may mean that he pronounces some affliction on their bodies which hopefully will bring an awakening in their consciences. (See a comparable case cited in I Cor. 5:5.) It would appear that the first meaning is preferable, for these two men were not involved in such physical immorality as the other case and might not thus contract bodily disease as a result of their error. If Paul, by apostolic authority, pronounced affliction on these men, it would not be an affliction from Satan.

B. The Campaign of Prayer, 2:1-8. The word "therefore" links this chapter to the charge which has gone before. It is in keeping with Paul's thinking that prayer is a major part of the warfare of faith. In fact, in Eph. 6:18, after he has given elaborate description of the armor of the Christian soldier, the only reference he makes to the actual warfare is that of prayer, and he lists there two of the kinds of prayer which he uses here. The term "first" refers to importance and not to time. Prayer is the most important element in victory in our warfare. We can do nothing well unless we pray well! There is always a danger of putting too much emphasis on human ability and energy, giving them more and more time, while prayer is neglected. Let us not be taken in this danger! It must be prayer "first of all."

1. The kinds of prayer, v. 1

    a. *Supplications* are prayers made from a sense of personal need. Prayers are made toward God specifically, with reverence for Who He is. Thus in the first two terms we have emphasis first on the personal need which prompts prayer and then the approach to God in prayer.

    b. The term *intercessions* refers to a special quality of prayer whereby we have boldness and confidence to enter the presence of a king and submit a petition. The basic idea is not of requesting something for another but of intervening in the presence of the king to gain what we desire from him. The audience is confidently sought and received. The words of v. 2 make it clear, however, that this as well as the other kinds of prayer are not just for ourselves. All prayer that is in faith should be marked by *thanksgiving*, not only for what has been received but also for what has been expected by faith.

2. The objects of prayer

    a. Kings and rulers. This was a prominent part of prayer in New Testament days when the king was conceived as the minister of God. It is important today as well. When kings and rulers rule in the fear of God, it is a great factor in bringing quiet and peaceable living.

    b. The purpose of seeking a life of quietness and peace is so that Godliness and honesty can continue and be manifested. *Godliness* is a very important term and denotes the proper respect toward God, our fellowmen, and ourselves. It has been defined as "reverence towards the one and only God, and the kind of life He would wish us to lead" (Eusebius). William Barclay says "it describes the character of the man who never fails God, man or himself." (*Letters to Timothy, Titus, and Philemon,* Edinburgh: The Saint Andrew Press, p. 70.)

Honesty means more than truthfulness. It refers to grace and dignity that come not from this earth but from a relation to God. For such a man, life is lived always in the sight of God. his attitude toward God and man is always right. There is due seriousness about life and its obligations, though it is not a gloomy life. Such a man inspires respect, though he is not consciously seeking it.

These two terms taken together picture the ideal man in his relation to God and to men. It is such a man that Paul holds up as the ideal through this epistle.

c. All men

1) The universality of salvation, vv. 3-6. Such praying accords with the plan of God that all men should be saved. Here is a strong contradiction to the false doctrine of a limited election and unconditional predestination to salvation. God wants all men to be saved and has devised means so that it may be so. It does not state that God will save all men, as the universalists believe, but that His plan provides for all. They may either accept or reject the plan.

Beyond merely being saved from sin, God's design is that men should come to a knowledge of truth. It is never God's plan merely to give men an escape from hell. He wants to make something of them, and an increase of knowledge accompanies maturity. See II Pet. 3:18.

a) The unity of God. Here is a brief doctrinal statement that must have been something like a creed of the early church. Because there is only one God Who provided the plan of salvation, there is only one plan of salvation. This is hard for many to receive. I once had a Hindu student say that there are many true religions, and Hinduism is one of them. But Paul insists that the Gospel of Christ is God's only plan of salvation.

There is one mediator. The Gnostics taught the existence of numerous emanations between God and man. Even the Jews taught that there are numerous mediators, including angels. Today the Catholics teach the mediation of priests and of Mary. But this is false, as Paul says. Only one Mediator exists. Unless we come through Christ, we can not come to God!

    b) The presentation of the Gospel. The ransom price of Christ was for all. Note the repetition of the word *all*—six times in vv. 1-6.) There is no other way of salvation. So this plan must be testified, and the due time to tell it is now, since Christ has come and wants men to be saved. Our labors in prayer and proclamation are a mandate from God in this day of salvation.

2) The appointment to the Gentiles, v. 7. This exclusiveness of the Gospel is not the idea of Paul or of any other preacher. It is not bigotry to declare it so, for this is God's plan and His declaration. Paul did not design the Gospel. He was appointed to his office, and he *received* his message.

He was a *preacher*. The word means a herald, one who speaks on behalf of another. He was an *apostle*, speaking with authority from another. He is a *teacher* of the Gentiles to bring to them the truth, backed by his faith in God and total commitment to the message. This man Paul was unreservedly committed to bearing the truth, even at the cost of his life. There was no time serving or self sparing in him. He was "all out for Christ." May it be so with us as well!

3. Qualifications in prayer, v. 8. It is specifically referring to men versus women. It would seem to refer then to public prayer in this place, for surely women are as fully entitled to access to God in prayer as are men. (See I Cor. 11:5; I Tim. 5:5).

One posture of prayer is suggested: standing with open hands upraised, showing sincerity and dependence upon God. Three qualifications of effective prayer are given.

    a. Holy hands. We are dealing in a warfare for Godliness. One who is effective in warfare must himself be on the side of

Godliness and therefore must have holy hands. This refers to those whose conduct is free from sin. A sinner may come to God, but first on behalf of his own sins before he will be heard in prayer for others. "If I regard iniquity in my heart, the Lord will not hear me" (Ps. 66:18). Sin in one's life cuts the nerve of faith, obscures the face of God, and makes prayer ineffective.

    b. Without wrath. There can be no anger toward our fellowmen. We must be right with men before we can be right with God. Prayer is hindered if there is a broken relation with other men (see Matt. 18:19, 20, 35; 5:23, 24). Possibly the wrath could be directed toward God as well, for one who would labor in intercession will be tempted at times to accuse God of being tardy in His workings. We must have an unshakeable faith in His dealings.

    c. Without doubtings. This probably refers to uncertainties as to the truthfulness of God's promises or of the grounds of our praying. We must pray in faith to be effective. Prayer in faith is an effective means of fighting the warfare for Godliness.

C. The Campaign of Modesty and Good Works, vv. 9-15

The writer is still involved in a discussion of the warfare for Godliness. "In like manner" links what he is saying to what has gone before and back to the charge of 1:18. It is possible that there may be some reference to public worship here, but the principles apply more broadly than just in the public worship.

Women have a most important place in the warfare for Godliness. See the connection of v. 10. We can thank God that the Gospel has brought an equal right of access to God for women as for men, though their respective positions differ. So important are women in the warfare that historically they have often been the avenue through which men have been led into spiritual defeat and loss. Verse 14 is an example, in which Eve was deceived and led the man into sin and death. We could give many examples: Num. 25:1-3, in which Israel was defeated because of the enticements of the women of Moab (see Num. 31:`5, 16; Rev. 2:14); Is. 3:16-26, in which God tells of the fall of Israel before her enemies and the part of the women in being immodest (see Is. 4:3, 4, in which the holiness of the city includes the cleansing of the filth of the daughters of Zion); and Rev. 17:3-6, in which the source of all apostasy is summed up as a harlot woman arrayed in gorgeous apparel and jewels.

In the days of John Wesley, after nearly fifty years in the ministry, he saw the Methodists begin to yield to the tendency to dress like the world and even the formal church people around them. He entreated them passionately not to do so, saying, "And is there no harm in all of this? Oh God, arise, and maintain thy own cause! Let not men or devils any longer put out our eyes, and lead us blindfold into the pit of destruction" (source unknown).

Yet those who observed the increasing apostasy of the Methodist Church declare that it began in such matters as dress, whereby the Word of God was carelessly set aside. And when it was set aside in such matters it was soon set aside in weightier matters, even the most fundamental doctrines.

Wesley gave the following reasons for refraining from the wearing of jewelry and costly apparel: 1) It engenders pride, and where it is already, it increases it; 2) It increases vanity—the love and desire to be admired and praised; 3) It tends to beget anger and uneasy passion. Only when you have cast off your fondness for dress will the peace of God reign in your hearts; 4) It tends to create and inflame lust; 5) It is directly the opposite of being adorned with good works. The more you lay out on your own apparel, the less you have left to clothe the naked, etc; 6) It is directly the opposite to the "hidden man of the heart," to "the mind which was in Christ Jesus," and the whole nature of inner holiness. Instead of growing more and more heavenly minded, you are more and more earthly minded. Insensibly you sink deeper and deeper into the spirit of the world. (J. Wesley Bready, *This Freedom—Whence?*, New York: American Tract Society, pp. 178, 179.)

Adam Clarke said, "Christians must not imitate the extravagance of those who, through impurity or littleness of mind, deck themselves merely to attract the eye of admiration, or set in lying action the tongue of flattery." (*Clarke's Commentary*, Vol. VI, p. 592.)

Cyprian of Carthage (A.D. 248) said, "Conquer dress since you are engaged in conquering the flesh and the world."

Charles Finney said, "The fashions of the world are directly at war with the spirit of the gospel, are contrary to a profession of salvation, are a manifestation of a broad and complete approval of the spirit of the world, and show that you differ not at all from ungodly sinners."

George D. Watson said, "Ear-rings, finger-rings, bracelets, gold chains, charms, trinkets, etc., are not articles of clothing. They add nothing to brains or beauty; they add nothing to comfort or convenience; they neither give protection, nor health, nor beauty to the human body; they are all absolutely without rational use, and conducive to nothing in the universe but vanity."

Wesley acknowledged that the world and perhaps close family members would mock and laugh at the simplicity of the Christian, but he warned that they who would rather have the applause of friends than of God were not worthy of being called followers of God.

We are saying here that women have a large part to play in the defense of Godliness, and their modesty is strategic. John Adams, second president of the United States, said that the position of woman "is the most infallible barometer to ascertan the degree of morality in a nation." H.C. Morrison, founder of Asbury Seminary, said, "The last step in the degradation of a nation before appalling calamity and catastrophe, is immodesty and indiscretion in women. Suggestive dress means, in the end, the ruin of a people." This truth is not just a pet hobby of a foolish preacher; it is the sober reflection of many and honored leaders, especially in the holiness movement from its beginning. Holiness ought to be separate from the world in such matters!

1. The responsibility of women, vv. 9, 10

   a. To adorn themselves in modest apparel. *Adornment* means ordering and arranging, preparing of things. With respect to women it refers to the preparation of their appearance. *Apparel* refers to external deportment in appearance, manner and dress. *Modest* refers to that which is proper in dress and behavior, not calling undue attention to one's own person or making an offensive display of the flesh or person.

   b. To have shamefacedness and sobriety. This qualifies the term *modesty* and refers to the inward attitudes of modesty and seriousness, keeping all things proper with self-restraint.

   These terms do not rule out attractiveness. The word *adorn* indicates attention and preparation. The Bible makes much of the beauty of good women. Salvation is even said to increase beauty. There is nothing wrong with beauty which is God-given. The emphasis here is on what is proper and what is improper in adornment.

   c. The exclusion of fancy and expensive adornment. These terms in v. 9 are specific, but they indicate a pattern which extends to other types of apparel as given in Isaiah 3. The broided hair was hair into which strands of colorful cloth or threads of gold were woven to make a fancy appearance. It would exclude the jewelry which is so common today.

    d. The adornment of good works. Good works are truly becoming to the profession of holiness. Good works will appeal to mankind and to God! How much more there would be to put into good works if the adornment of jewelry were left off! And how much more pleasing to God it would be!

2. The restrictions on women, vv. 11-15

    a. Their place in relation to men. The tense of the verb "to teach" shows that a continuing place of authority is meant. In other passages it is shown that women have a proper sphere of teaching (Titus 2:3, 4; Acts 18:26), but they are not to assume authority over the men of the church. There are two reasons for the place of women in relation to the men:

        1) The man was first formed, then the woman. She was made as a helpmeet for him. This means she should assist but not rule over him.

        2) The woman was deceived and led the man into sin. He was not deceived but went into sin for her sake and at her invitation. The woman has great power to assist or to beguile and lead into sin. She must never assume an authoritative role over man in the church.

    b. Their salvation

        1) In child bearing. It does not mean that childbearing in itself is the means of salvation but that the proper sphere of womanhood is in bearing children and making a Christian home. How great is the influence of a Godly mother! Her influence can be of untold value if she takes this sphere as a calling from God.

        2) In personal holiness that is maintained. Salvation is as much for women as for men. The Gospel has emphasized this fact. But the life of holiness must be accompanied by the proper modesty if the woman really prizes salvation.

I Timothy 149

IV. Church Order and the Promotion of Godliness, 3:1-16

A. The Office of the Bishop, vv. 1-7

1. The responsibility, vv. 1, 5

    a. The term *bishop* means overseer. It refers to one who has the supervisory care of the church (see I Pet. 5:2; Acts 20:28). A similar term is *elder*, which refers to the same office but indicates rather the personal dignity and maturity of the person who holds the office. Originally only older men were placed in such offices among the Jews, but in the New Testament sense other qualifications were considered more important than mere age. The man had to have some maturity "not a novice," but he could be young, as Timothy himself was (see 4:12).

    b. The "care of the church of God, " v. 5, makes plain what his duty is. The passage in I Peter shows that it is not a position of "lordship," not a place to display autocratic authority but rather a place to serve. It is in this sense that one who seeks the office seeks a good thing. It is a responsible place of service where much good can be done if the person is truly qualified. The qualifications are such as to prohibit one's seeking the office for personal pride or gratification.

2. The qualifications, vv. 2-7

    a. *Blameless* means to be one "not to be laid hold of," one who is not justly open to censure or criticism. If the enemy can take hold of the man with blame, his ministry will suffer. He must be exemplary. This will not prevent one's being slandered, but it is important that the report be false.

    b. *Husband of one wife* is generally taken to mean not married to more than one wife at a time. Other meanings are possible.

    c. *Vigilant* literally means "unmixed with wine." The man must be fully rational, watchful and in command of his faculties. It literally means "wineless," but the application is broader than that.

    d. *Sober* means discreet and prudent, well-balanced and regulated. It refers to one who does not quickly jump to conclusions that are indefensible or false but one who is thoughtful, serious and deliberate.

e. *Of good behavior* means that he orders well his outer life. It describes the man whose character is blended and integrated into something orderly and beautiful. The former term, sober, refers to inner control, and this one refers to outer attractiveness. As Barclay says, "The leader must be a man in whose heart the power of Christ reigns, and on whose life the beauty of Christ shines."

f. *Given to hospitality* means a willingness to receive and care for strangers. In those days, hotels were dirty and disagreeable and costly. When Christians traveled, it was important that they find some Christian friend who was hospitable. It is easily seen that the bishop has important services to render outside the sanctuary.

g. *Apt to teach* shows a necessary ability and a duty as well. He is to preach to get men saved and teach to help them grow. This requires study as long as a man is in the ministry. Without it, he is not worthy.

h. *Not given to wine* can be interpreted literally and can also mean "not quarrelsome or violent." The elder must not do anything that would make him less vigilant or that would spoil his conduct and influence.

i. *No striker* means that he is not to be domineering or quick-tempered; he is certainly not to strike with his fists.

j. *Not greedy of filthy lucre* means that he is not motivated by love of money. He is not a minister because it is a paying position but because it is a service to Christ and to others. (This seems not to be in the original texts.)

k. *Patient* means gentle, mild and considerate of the feelings of others. It has been called "sweet reasonableness." It denotes a spirit that is willing to act in love rather than to act rigidly and legalistically in applying the law. It seeks to look to a man's motive before punishing a deviation from law.

l. *Not a brawler* means peaceable, not looking for a fight. Not contentious over personal matters, he still does "contend for the faith" but in a spirit of love.

m. *Not covetous* means not money-loving. This phrase appears in the original and means essentially the same as *not greedy of filthy lucre*.

n. *One that ruleth well his own house.* Qualities of leadership, discipline, and teaching should be first evident in a man's home before he is qualified to exercise the same in the church. Reasoning from the lesser to the greater, Paul shows that if the man can not exercise proper leadership and control in the home, he surely cannot do it in the church. It is often true that poorly disciplined children in the home of a pastor greatly hinders his ministry.

o. *Not a novice* means that he must not be one newly come to the faith. He must have some spiritual maturity so that the office will not sway him or influence him toward pride of position. The "condemnation of the devil" seems to mean the same kind of snare the devil fell into when he sought to lift himself up and disqualified himself forever for the favor of God.

p. *A good report of those that are without* means that he must by his honest and disciplined life give the impression to the outside world that his is a good character. If men of the world have just cause to criticize the carefulness or honesty of the minister, then the church is reproached, and the minister himself may become discouraged and fall away.

B. The Office of Deacon, vv. 8-13

1. The qualifications, vv. 8-12

a. *Grave* means to have a dignified character.

b. *Not double-tongued* is a new characteristic, one not found in the list for elders. It means not speaking with two voices, saying one thing on one occasion and something contradictory on another.

c. It will be noticed that the qualification "apt to teach" for the elders is not mentioned here. Otherwise the lists are similar. It would seem that a deacon may properly be promoted to the position of elder if he should meet the added qualification of aptness to teach.

d. *Women who are grave* may refer either to the wives of deacons or to deaconesses. The latter seems more probable.

Women who instructed female converts, attended women at baptism, and visited other women were put in the office of deaconess in the early church. They were not to be inclined toward gossip and slander but be careful and serious about their work.

- e. *Let them first be proved* means essentially the same as "no novice" in the case of elders. It does not indicate a formal test but rather the test of a faithful life.

- f. *Faith in a pure conscience* speaks of a divine revelation (mystery) to his own soul. The condition for this revelation is a pure heart. Truth is weakened if a man has an unholy heart, and revelation can not be clear and effective unless the heart is pure. It may be seen again how strongly Paul emphasized the life of holiness.

2. The reward, v. 13. Those who serve well in this office (and the same doubtless refers to other offices as well) earn a good standing among men. That is, they will be looked upon with respect and gain honor rightfully. They will be a credit to the church and to Christ. They have boldness in the faith. They will have confidence in coming before God or in standing before men.

C. The Majesty of the Task, vv. 15-16

1. The purpose of the letter, v. 15. The whole purpose of this letter and of all pastoral epistles is given here: that the man of God may know how to conduct himself in the church. The word "behave himself" refers to the entire conduct, especially before men. One who qualifies for an office in the church must have good conduct both before God and man. Fellowship must be maintained in both directions, but fellowship is based on character; hence the man of God must have good character.

2. The nature of the church, v. 15

- a. *The household of God.* In Old Testament times God dwelt in a material tabernacle or temple. Now he dwells in the Church! Some translations have "household of God." This would be true also. The members of the Church are all in one family of God. The love of God will be manifested in love for the brethren.

- b. *The church of the living god.* The "ecclesia" means the "called out" ones. All who are in the church have been called out of the dead world; they are saved from the world; they are separated from the world by nature and citizenship.

    c. *The pillar of the truth.* In Ephesus, where Timothy was, was the temple of Diana, one of the seven wonders of the world. It had 127 pillars, each the gift of a king. All were made of marble, and some were studded with jewels and even overlaid with gold. These pillars were for more than support (a thought which follows) but for display as well. Many times statues of famous men were placed high on the pillars to be seen. The church is to adorn and display the truth for all to see.

    d. *The ground of the truth.* Here the idea is that of a support and establishment, which keeps a building from being moved by any contrary element. The church is to hold and keep the truth inviolate against all opposition, not allowing it to be compromised or diluted by its enemies.

3. The mystery of Godliness, v. 16. This appears to be one of the hymns sung in the early church. The church at Ephesus was old enough to have the beginning of a creed and a hymnology. In this letter we have evidences of both.

    The words "without controversy" mean that the truth expressed here is certain beyond debate and now is a matter for the boldest declaration.

    A mystery is something which is now revealed that was not before clearly known. It obviously refers to Jesus Christ himself. He is the revealed essence of Godliness, the power by which it is to be lived.

    a. *Manifest in the flesh* refers to the incarnation. God's nature was brought down where men could see it in the Person of Christ Jesus. Jesus was true man.

    b. *Justified in the Spirit.* The meaning is not clear. It possibly means two things: 1) The life of righteousness which Jesus lived was by the power of the Spirit. His life was a sinless life, not by His inherent deity but by the aid of the Spirit. Likewise we may have the Spirit's help in living the Christ-like life. Jesus was a real man, yet a holy man. 2) It may mean that Christ's claims for Himself were vindicated by His resurrection, which was by the power of the Spirit.

    c. *Seen of angels.* Those who worshiped Him while He was in the Heavens watched with eagerness as He came to earth.

They shouted aloud at His birth, strengthened Him in His temptation and again in Gethsemane, and doubtless waited eagerly His return to glory.

    d. *Preached among the nations.* The message of Christ must go to all nations; He does not belong exclusively to Jews, Asians, bond or free. He is the Savior of all men who will believe.

    e. *Believed on in the world.* All over the world men have believed on Him. This is a testimony to the effective evangelization wrought in that first century church.

    f. *Taken up into glory.* This refers to the ascension. We have in this song of faith the story of Jesus from His coming to His going again into Heaven. It is impossible for us to conceive the glory which is Christ's in Heaven because of His having come into the world to suffer and die for a lost race. It is far greater than if He had never come. And the Church is to behold that glory and share it with Him as His chosen bride!

V. Godliness and Doctrine, 4:1-16

  A. False Doctrine in the Last Days, vv. 1-7

Consistently, the Bible speaks of the closing of this age and the opening of the age to come. *This* age and *this* world, in contrast to the age and the world to come, were common themes with Paul as well as with other writers. Here and elsewhere, Paul sets forth some of the perils of the last days which evidently were beginning in those days. It is made clear that such conditions would get worse and worse (II Tim. 3:13).

    1. Its nature, vv. 1-3. This is an awesome passage indeed It shows that men who turn away from the faith of God may be so overcome of demon spirits that they have their minds subject to the errors conceived by those demons. It is not doctrines about demons but doctrines introduced by demon spirits into the minds of men. Demons are the source and hypocritical men are the channels (II Tim. 4:4).

Note that these men would *depart from* the faith. They were once followers of the faith, but they turned from the faith and were taken over by demon spirits! How serious a thing it is to back up from the truth!

Their consciences were seared with a hot iron. They had a mark on their conscience that could not be removed, and they had no more feeling of danger. The brand produced a callous that reduced sensitivity. There are men like this today who once preached holiness but pulled back from truth!

Their specific teaching came apparently from the Gnostic emphasis on asceticism or the inherent evil of the body. They taught the imposition of unreasonable abstinence as a means of righteousness. It should be noted that Roman Catholics teach something of the same today.

2. Its rebuttal, vv. 3-5. Paul points out that marriage and meats are from God and are good, as was the whole of God's creation. To avoid the possibility of misuse of these blessings, though, Paul shows that they are to be used prayerfully and thankfully as gifts from God. They may be sanctified or made sacred as a means for the promotion of godliness if they are properly received. *All of life becomes sacred by such an approach to the gifts of God.*

3. The minister's responsibility, vv. 6, 7. He has a great responsibility for the flock when such error appears. Positively, he is to "put the brethren in remembrance of the truth." This indicates a method of teaching by counseling, advising, and persuading rather than dictating. Before he can faithfully and effectively teach others, he must himself be nourished in the truth and doctrine. This is a general rule.

Negatively, he is to avoid "old wives' fables," such as are indicated in 1:4. They do not produce Godliness, and the minister cannot grace them by giving time to them.

B. The Teaching of Godliness, vv. 7-11

1. Its profit, vv. 7-9. There may be some profit in discipline and denial of the body for a short time. Paul himself observed fastings often, and he "kept the body under." This has Christian value, but it is never in itself a means of salvation or of giving the spiritual life priority. The way to victory is to receive the Holy Spirit to animate and control us, body and spirit, not just to punish the physical body.

Godliness profits us here and hereafter. Bodily exercise at best has some value in this life, but Godliness profits eternally. How infinitely better spiritual victory is than just bodily asceticism. In those days there were gymnasia where men exercised the body to gain athletic prowess. Paul is here exhorting such an ardent exercise of the spiritual life unto Godliness. Here let it be said that Paul had no place for a tepid, half-hearted Christianity. He called for all-out exercise unto Godliness. Jesus did the same (see Luke 13:24). When we consider what exercise men will endure to win athletic laurels, it is a challenge to do more for Jesus and the life to come.

"This is a faithful saying . . . ." Here is Paul's way of saying, "This is extremely important. Let us observe it carefully." Are we pursuing holiness in such fashion today, or are we just casually considering this life for God and holiness?

2. Its reproach, v. 10. Paul includes himself along with Timothy and gave the reason for the intense labor and suffering which accompanied it. It was all because of the trust which they had in God and the reward they foresaw for the faithful.

God is the Savior potentially of all men but actually only of those who believe. Hence Paul determined to believe and keep on believing with all that it involved.

C. The Minister's Duty, vv. 12-16

1. To others, vv. 12, 13. Timothy was young in comparison with Paul, but he was probably mature by the necessary standards as laid down in Chapter 3. He was probably between 30 and 35 years of age, and a person could be considered young until he was 40 years of age. Paul's advice is that Timothy must silence criticism by irreproachable conduct. His conduct is to be so exemplary that he causes men to see their own faults instead of his.

The first two items of example refer to the outer life, the speech and conduct or word and deed.

The last three (spirit should not be included) refer to the inner life. *Love* is unconquerable benevolence: the will to do good and show concern for others, no matter what they do to you. *Faith* or loyalty is unconquerable fidelity to Christ, no matter what it costs to be true. He keeps on serving with all his heart no matter how the battle seems to be going. He never leaves his post until victory comes in the name of Christ. *Purity* means faithfulness to the standards of Christ, coming from within the heart. It includes chastity but involves more: purity of motive and sincerity of purpose. This is holiness upon which Paul is insisting, and the same is applicable to every one who would be a minister of the Gospel today.

Now Paul stresses some of the elements which Timothy must attend to in the public services of the Church. We see here something of what those early services must have been like. There was to be *reading* of the Scriptures. The false teachers would endeavor to bring in their endless genealogies, but Paul stresses the Word of god. *Exhortation* applies to the type of public address which followed the reading of the Word. It was designed to move people to action, not merely to entertain or even just to inform. *Doctrine* refers to faithful teaching of fundamental truth. it would appeal to the mind and heart primarily, while exhortation would move the will.

2. To himself, vv. 14-16. It is a likely possibility that the gift here referred to was something special from God as a result of the laying on hands of the presbytery or body of elders. And it may have been the elders at Ephesus along with Paul who did this at the time he was sent there as Paul's representative (1:30).

   a. The danger: neglect. It is so easy to rest on past victories and gifts. We must always be watchful lest having received blessings we become presumptuous as if the source of blessing were in ourselves. It is in Christ.

   b. The remedy

      1) Meditation. The minister must engage his mind and heart in searching out truth. It is alive and must never be allowed to become dull and dead.

      2) Concentration. There are many duties which the minister can get involved in that are somewhat beneficial, but they must never draw him away from the duties set forth in vv. 12-14. Be holy in your life; be holy in your ministry. Be a champion of holiness! Give everything to it!

         If a person does these things there will be progress in his own life which people will observe. The man of God must grow in grace himself. Woe unto him if he stagnates and makes the Word of God appear dull and unchallenging! Woe to him if he does not lead people forward!

      3) Take heed to thyself. This refers back to v. 12. He must be sure he is a good example. His life preaches more loudly than his lips, and more will see than will hear him.

4) Take heed to the doctrine. He is to *continue* in these things, seeing that his people never stop feeding and growing. We are saved, in the fullest sense of the word, not just by a crisis but by persevering to the end. The minister must first of all save himself and keep saved, lest he become a castaway (I Cor. 9:27).

VI. Godliness in the Business of the Church, 5:1-25; 6:1, 2

A. Courtesy in Human Relations, vv. 1, 2

1. The necessity of reprimand. Although reprimand is a difficult thing, it is at times most necessary. One of the duties of the bishop is to oversee and to correct error (see v. 17). The rule here is not that of an overlord but of a shepherd who wishes to save from error.

   There is a strong tendency for people to reprimand in a sharp and painful way, with harshness prevailing over love. When we feel the wrong keenly, the indignation may flame into hurtful words and acts. It is most vital that at such times this exhortation of Paul be taken seriously.

2. The family relations in the church. The terms Paul uses to refer to the various groups are family terms and show how strong are to be the bonds of fellowship and loyalty in the Church.

   a. The elders. Here the term refers truly to older men and not necessarily to office holders in the Church. Young Timothy would be called upon to correct older men, and there would naturally be resentment from the older ones for this. Consequently, older men and women must be entreated kindly and in love as one's own parents. Correction should show a loving desire to help rather than to hurt.

   b. To contemporaries—younger men. There should be the attitude of brothers. Display of lordly superiority is not appropriate; rather, they should manifest a loving, sharing helpfulness by the grace of God.

   c. To the opposite sex there must be manifested purity at all times. So many men of God have been drawn into sin because of indiscreet relationships with those of the opposite sex. The minister must deal with the errors of women, but he must have regard for the highest of purity in such cases. The Arabs speak of a chivalrous man as one who is a "brother to girls." William Barclay says, "It is a fearful thing when physical things dominate the relationship between the sexes, and when a man cannot see a woman without thinking in terms of the body." (*Letters To Timothy, Titus and Philemon*, p. 121.) Today when women dress so immodestly it is almost impossible for a man to meet such a woman without being affronted by the display of the body! Temptations for young men are great, and the man of God must be all the more discreet and watchful.

The word "purity" here refers to chastity but to more as well: it includes the whole concept of a pure heart and conscience.

B. Treatment of Widows, vv. 3-16

1. *Widows indeed.* The term indicates a person who was not only widowed but who was also given a place of official service in the church. She was something like a Bible woman in our present churches, having the duty of watching over younger women in the church, giving time to prayer, and helping others in trouble.

   Before a widow was placed on this roll of service and total support, she had to meet certain qualifications.

   a. Age of 60 or over. She should be able to concentrate on spiritual life and service and yet have strength for that service.

   b. Having been the wife of one man. This probably means she was never an adulteress, though some think she could not have been married more than once, for by doing so she would have forfeited some of her dignity in that age.

   c. She must have been a woman of good works and hospitality and a good mother when she was independent of church office in order to qualify to fill such an office. The office does not bestow any special qualifications; they must have been manifested beforehand.

2. Widows with children, v. 4. Such were not to be placed on the roll for support by the church. The children and grandchildren ("nephews" meant descendants such as grandchildren) were to show their piety by supporting their parents and grandparents. This did not prohibit the widows from serving the Church, as is mentioned in v. 10, but they were not put on support for so doing.

Those who do not manifest proper care for their own families, whether it be children providing for parents or vice versa, have given a practical denial of the faith. The word "infidel" here does not mean a denial of the existence of God but rather an unbeliever. The unbelievers care for their own families, and Christians surely should do no less. There can be no separation between personal conduct and Christian faith. Those who do not maintain the most obvious charities in their homes are not showing a proper life consistent with Godliness.

3. The widow living in pleasure, v. 6. This is not a description of immoral living, in the sense of grosser sins. It describes one who lives daintily, with undue emphasis on eating and drinking expensively. One who pampers the appetites is not to be placed on relief from the Church. Such a person, Paul says, is dead. She is not a true Christian and should not be treated as such. To spend God's money to pamper human appetites is out of place. Sacrifice is the rule in the kingdom of God.

4. The younger widows, vv. 11-15. These were under the age specified for full-time support. The reasons are given. A younger widow, having pledged to give full-time to the work of the Church, is likely to be overcome with a desire for social activities and marriage and thus to violate the pledge of faithful service in the Church. Rather than to trust in God and continue in prayers day and night, she might tend to wander about in gossip and meddling rather than to be faithful to the work of God.

Paul does not by this forbid marriage, for he rather recommends that the young widows do remarry. But he wants to avoid the condemnation that will come to the one who proves unfaithful, and he wants to avoid the reproach on the church that would come by the failure. When a servant of the Church "turns aside to Satan," it is always a tragedy for the individual and for the Church, also.

So it is recommended that younger widows marry again. In those days a widow without adult dependents was in a very difficult position. It was not easy for them to gain employment, unless they went into prostitution. The two best courses were to serve the church or to marry again. Paul recommends the latter as an honorable estate and most likely to prevent scandal.

In v. 16 he takes up the rare case where ancestors had widows as their descendants. The reverse of v. 4 is thus considered, and again there is to be support from within the family and not from the church.

C. Respect Toward Elders, vv. 17-25

1. Proper support, vv. 17, 18. The double honor includes that of the position itself and that from faithful service therein. The one who does well in preaching and teaching is worthy of full support. He quotes from Deut. 25:4 and from the words of Jesus in Luke 10:7.

2. Necessary discipline, vv. 19-21, 24, 25. To protect elders from retaliation, it was necessary that witnesses not be recognized singly. There must be two or three witnesses to the same error.

   It was also necessary, if the sin were proven, to deal with it. The tenses of "them that sin" is progressive, indicating continuous and obvious sin. These it is necessary to rebuke openly so the correction is as obvious as the sin. The church must never give the impression of condoning sin in any measure in any of its people! Paul does not say in what way the correction is to be made; it will vary with the sin—its nature and degree. But there must be proper discipline.

   The importance is shown in v. 21. This work is done not only before the individuals concerned and before the world but before God and the (unfallen) angels. There can be no partiality because of high office or prestige. It is better to admit a grievous error and correct it than to keep it protected and incur the disfavor of God. At the same time there should be no lust for exposure and damage to the person involved. There should certainly be a desire to save the one concerned (see Gal. 6:1, 2).

   In vv. 24, 25 it is shown how important full investigation is. Some sins are very obvious, while others are not easily detected. It is important that the character of the man be known. This is emphasized elsewhere as well as here (see I Thes. 5:12). It is also true that the good deeds of some are more easily seen than those of others. Whether or not they are all known here, they will be surely seen at the judgment of God, even if not at the examination of men.

3. Precaution in ordination, v. 22. It is so important for elders to be godly men that proper investigation must be made before any is ordained to the office. If they should have concealed sin in their lives and they are ordained, the ordaining officer is in a sense a partaker of therein. The exhortation of vv. 24 and 25 is appropriate here, also.

The exhortation "keep thyself pure" applies to the abstinence from involvement in "other men's sins," but it has a wider application in purity of motive and singleness of life for Godliness.

Here Paul inserts a purely personal note which seems to have occurred to him, perhaps in contemplation of the heavy responsibility which lay on young Timothy. It relates to the use of wine for his stomach and frequent infirmities. It by no means encourages uninhibited use of wine, but neither does it support a total abstinence, even from medicinal wine. As Barclay puts it, "Paul is saying that there is no virtue in asceticism which does the body more harm than good." (*Letters to Timothy, Titus and Philemon*, p. 139.)

D. Instructions to Servants, 6:1,2

In that day there were many slaves who were Christians. It was important that they understand the proper display of Godliness in their situation. In this short instruction we have some principles which are very important now.

1. Slaves with unbelieving masters. Theirs was a hard lot many times. They worked hard, had nothing hopeful to look forward to, gained no significant possessions. They were oppressed and could be killed without fair trial if suspected of unfaithfulness or insurrection.

   Christianity brought the freedom of slaves in various parts of the world, including the British Commonwealth and America. However, the instruction for these slaves was to put Christianity ahead of personal interest. The Christian was to come to feel the gross wrong of slavery, but if Christianity at this time had inspired the slaves to rebel, it would have brought great discredit to the cause of Christ and perhaps have brought civil war. It was more important for the slaves to show a Christian spirit under hard and unfair conditions than to become warriors in their own personal interests. In due time the leaven of Christianity permeated the country and the evil of slavery was overcome.

   In like manner, Christians today should first of all show a true Christian spirit in the face of injustice. Their first concern should not be to fight for personal rights but to exalt and demonstrate the Spirit of Christ in their place. The influence of Christianity should then penetrate to expose the evils and remove them, not as a matter of personal vengeance but as the spreading of the truth, supported by Christian example.

2. Slaves with believing masters. It might be easy in such cases for the slaves to impose on the goodness of the master and count themselves as equals, demanding considerations for themselves out of self-interest. It was all the more important that they serve their masters faithfully, since both were Christians.

VII. Gain and Godliness, 6:3-19

A. The Idea that Gain is Godliness, vv. 3-5

In this section Paul refers again to the false teachers at Ephesus. Having set forth the requirements of true Godliness, he insists that they who teach otherwise are to be rejected, for they are evil men.

1. They reject the doctrines of Godliness. This is not done on intellectual grounds but rather on moral grounds. The description of the man follows. It is because of his character that he rejects the right doctrine. His heart is out of tune with it. How often this is the case: a man, because of his own character defect turns from the truth and begins to justify error, providing an excuse for his false character and conduct.

2. They have degenerate characters. Here is an awesome contemplation: the character of men who reject the truth rapidly degenerates until they no longer have the capacity for discerning the truth. Look at the characters of these false men.

    a. They were proud. Their chief concern was to have a personal following, and they were willing to distort the truth in order to do so. Truth was no longer the anchor of their lives or their pursuit. Selfish advancement was more desirable for them than the truth. They were willing to put Christ down if they could be lifted up. Such is still the character of pride. Wherever men seek to lift themselves to high office or places of prominence, they do so at the expense of the honor of Christ. How terrible is pride in the Church!

    b. They knew nothing. Divorced from the truth, they were making a great show of declaring error. They became unaware of how great was their error, pursuing selfish advantage by use of words empty of helpful moral content. They could go on endlessly talking about doctrine and never help a soul get nearer to God. Unless we are helping men toward God, our labors are vain also.

        c. They produced discord. Their main concern was to get a personal following, not to display saving truth. If they could not win an argument by logic, they attacked the character of their opponents and thus generated strife and railings.

        d. They supposed gain was Godliness. Their highest standard of evaluation was money. If they made money from their following, they considered themselves successful. In that day in the Greek world, there were many orators who traveled about making high speeches for money. There were men in the church who carried over the same activity and sought to profit from people by their clever speeches. To them, gain was the highest goal. There are men today who do the same thing. They use the church as a base for making money, capitalizing on some real or feigned gift from God. There are commercial "healers" of this type who get a huge following from eager people and play upon their gullibility in a search for gain.

B. The Fact That Godliness With Contentment is Gain, vv. 6-10

    There are considerations which make Godliness profitable even in this life.

    1. The reason, vv. 7, 8. Life in its beginning and in its ending is independent of material gain. Hence there is nothing in material gain which is essential to life itself. Life's goal and its true purpose is far above material things.

        If we have the basic essentials for the ongoing of life, the true Christian will have contentment. The meaning here is a statement of fact and not an exhortation. Having Jesus Christ, the Christian is filled with joy. His life consisteth not of the abundance of things which he possesses.

    2. The exception, vv. 9, 10. There are those who have as their highest goal the accumulation of earthly gain. While the gain of wealth seems very attractive to them, it is in reality a snare which pulls them toward a precipice of drowning. The love of money is recognized in many cultures as a root from which every form of evil may arise. (This is the true meaning.) Love of riches can easily pull men away from God and bring them many disappointments. Here are some:

       a. The thirst for wealth is never satisfied. A Roman proverb said that getting wealth was like drinking sea water. The more a man drinks, the greater becomes his thirst.

       b. The idea that wealth brings security is false. It may bring fear of loss and thus be a source of insecurity.

       c. The drive to gain produces selfishness in many cases, and this in turn alienates a man from his friends and leaves him lonely.

       d. The man may be led to dishonesty and thus to a guilty conscience. At the end of life there is departure and loss of all he has lived for.

C. The Charge to Seek True Riches, vv. 11-19

   1. The man of God, vv. 11-16. Timothy is here given this appellation: the man of God. It is essentially an Old Testament term but here applied to this fine man of New Testament times.

       a. He is to flee the snare of riches. Seeing the point of danger, he is not to stay even close to it. This should be a rule for the man of God. If he knows a place of temptation or danger, he is not to see how close to it he can stay but is to hurry away.

       b. He is to follow positive virtues. Righteousness and godliness relate to attitude toward God. The first is *character* conformed to the will of God. Godliness is devotion to God in worship and *conduct*. Faith and love are the great graces that spring from the heart where God is enthroned. Patience and meekness are shown outwardly toward men, especially men who oppose the way of Godliness. *Patience* here means victorious endurance and constancy under trials of all kinds. *Meekness* or gentleness is that spirit which does not fight back for its own sake but strongly defends the cause of God and others. It knows how to forgive and how to fight for righteousness.

       c. He is to fight the fight of faith. The figure here is taken from the arena where athletes contest for victory. The verb *fight* is in present tense and indicates a continuing contest. "Lay hold" is aorist and shows that the prize at the end is eternal life. This is the true value to be sought at all costs. Note how energetically Paul puts the matter. With him

Christianity is never a matter of mild interest or superficial concern. It is intense, continuing, and all-important. May we give all to win the prize!

d. He is to keep the charge faithfully. He made a good confession, probably at the time of his baptism, before many men. Now Paul charges him before God and before Christ to keep the charge given unto him until Jesus comes. As Jesus made His good confession before Pilate, Timothy may be brought before judges and tribunals for his life, and he is to be true. Probably the whole content of the Gospel is contained in "this commandment."

The incentive which moves us to this faithfulness is the coming of Jesus Christ. Repeatedly Paul uses this grand event as the incentive to watchfulness and faithfulness. Almost never is readiness for death used in the New Testament; it is always readiness for Christ's coming. How much more should we consider that event today. That appearing of Christ is in God's hands; we know not the time, but we must always be ready.

Something of the challenge of reward is given in this high tribute to the person of God. His glorious attributes are given, not so much in an analytic way as in a song of overflowing praise. Potentate refers to His unique and underived authority. He alone is supreme as Lord and King. He alone has deathless life. He can not be reached through human senses. Men will never discover Him in a scientific pursuit but by the pursuit of faith through Jesus Christ. He shall have honor forever among His redeemed saints! What joy it will be to come into His presence to receive the crown of life!

e. He is to keep his trust, vv. 20, 21. The term refers to a deposit which is to be kept for another, inviolate and complete. Timothy is not on his own business; He is doing work for the great God Who has just been described. *Science* here means "knowledge," and probably again refers to the gnosis of the Gnostics who loved to argue and contend. Winning an argument, along with gaining riches, were their goals. Paul would emphasize that our purpose is not to win arguments but to win men for Christ. Some have erred and gone back from God, but Timothy can win if he is true.

2. The Christians of wealth, vv. 17-19. There were some of these even at that time in the Church. There is no evil inherent in having wealth, but there are necessary admonitions for those who have wealth. It can be a snare, but if the admonitions are followed, it may be of great service to God and His cause. Here are some rules:

   a. Men must not be proud of their wealth. They must not be lifted up in vanity, using their wealth to make a vain show of who they are. It was common then, as it is now, for such people to want to dress and act in such a way as to show off their wealth and impress others with their finery (see James 2:2, 3).

   b. They must not depend on their wealth for security or happiness. The riches of God are the true source of joy and satisfaction. Christians should surely know this and constantly apply the truth.

   c. They must use their wealth for good. It is to be handled as a stewardship. God gives the power to get wealth, and it is to be used to do good for eternity. Jesus stressed this fact in Luke 16:1-12, the parable of the unjust steward. There is power in the use of money to "lay up for ourselves a good foundation against the time to come." We can make deposits in Heaven to be enjoyed eternally by our benevolent use of money down here. But those who spend it on themselves in vain show or lavish living are unfaithful as stewards and have lost the true concept of lasting treasure. Some person has said, "What I kept I lost; what I gave I have."

   Again, it is seen that the true goal to seek and the prize to be gained is eternal life. With that, everything else shrivels in comparison.

   May we at all costs fight this good fight and enter into eternal life with treasures stored there awaiting our arrival!

Review Questions
I TIMOTHY

1. Does God have special mercy on those who are ignorant of the law?
2. Are the ignorant entirely exempted from penalty?
3. In 1:3, Paul says they should teach no other doctrine? What particular doctrine does he mean they should teach?
4. What idea is contained in the term "commit" in 1:11 and II Tim. 2:2?
5. Does 2:4 mean that all men will be saved, as the universalists teach? What Bible verses help you answer this? (See Mk. 16:16, John 3:36.)
6. What is the meaning of "ransom" in 2:6?
7. Did Paul ever permit women to speak or serve in the church? Give scripture references. (See I Cor. 11:5, Titus 2:3, 4; Acts 18:26.)
8. Would it be possible for a deacon later to become a bishop? If so, what extra qualifications would he have to meet? If not, why?
9. For what proper reason might a man desire to become a bishop? What would be some improper reasons?
10. What does Paul mean by "latter times" in chapter 4?
11. What group of people today follow the errors shown in 4:3?
12. In what sense is God the Savior of all men?
13. In what two different ways is the word "elder" used in chapter 5?
14. What important qualification of an elder is not required of a deacon?
15. What is "the condemnation of the devil"?
16. Two kinds of exercise are mentioned in chapter 5. What is the advantage of each?
17. In what way might a slave cause the name of God to be blasphemed?
18. In what two ways is the word "gain" used in 6:5, 6?
19. What is the meaning of the statement, "The love of money is the root of all evil"?
20. When is the man of God to "lay hold on eternal life"?

The Second Epistle to
TIMOTHY

Introduction

I. Author

It is generally agreed among conservative scholars that Paul was the author, although some believe that II Timothy is a collection of some of his letters by a later person. The reason for this position is the uncertainty about his having been released from the imprisonment recorded in Acts. This letter does not fit into that imprisonment at all. However, there is sufficient reason to believe that Paul was released from that imprisonment and that he later was taken back to prison under more severe conditions, where he finally died. We believe fully in the Pauline authorship.

II. Time of Writing

II Timothy was written not long after I Timothy, as indicated by Paul still being in prison, by the similar errors which Timothy is facing, and by similarities in expressions. However, this epistle includes reference to some incidents related to the imprisonment, such as his first appearance before trial and his impending death, so there must have been some lapse of time. It is commonly thought that it was written about 66 A.D.

III. Purpose of Writing

There is something of the official note in this letter: the identification of himself as the apostle and the charge to Timothy to be faithful and fulfill his ministry. However, this letter is much more personal than the first one, filled with notes about Timothy's family, Paul's tears, and Paul's situation in prison. He wants Timothy to come to him and bring his cloak, books, and parchments. Paul is lonely and desires companions in his dark hours, yet he wants to leave a letter of great confidence and encouragement with Timothy, who will have to continue his work without the presence or help of the Apostle.

IV. Outline: The Workman of God

A. Introduction

B. The Preparation of the Workman

C. The Conduct of the Workman

D. The Perils Facing the Workman

E. The Resources of the Workman

F. Conclusion

The Study of the Second Epistle to Timothy

I. Paul's Introduction

A. The Writer

1. The Apostle of Jesus Christ. Although this letter is largely personal, there is this official note about it, perhaps because Timothy needs the encouragement of the great leader and apostle to continue in the hard task that is his, especially when the Apostle is gone.

2. According to the promise of life. This is a unique element in Paul's introductions. It is noteworthy that Paul is not primarily preaching the threat of hell but the promise of life. He believed in the former, but his great passion was to present the grace of God which was revealed in Jesus Christ.

B. The Recipient
Timothy is again addressed as Paul's son, and a dearly beloved one. What a credit to Timothy that the last letter of Paul's of which we have any record was addressed to him.

C. The Benediction
This is essentially the same as in the first epistle, and customary for Paul.

II. The Preparation of the Workman, 1:3-18

A. Parental Background, vv. 3-5

1. Paul's parentage, v. 3. Paul was grateful for his parental heritage in the truth of God. He was a devout Jew, and apparently his parents were, also. Although now he is in prison, having been charged for heresy by his own people, the Jews, he insists that his conscience is clear. He believed that Christianity was the proper outgrowth of Judaism, and he was being true to his ancestors as well as to God by proclaiming the Christian faith.

2. Timothy's Parentage, v. 5. Evidently while Paul was on his first missionary journey, Timothy's grandmother was the first to believe on Christ Jesus, and the mother and son followed. They

were devout Jews who placed their faith in Christ. What a wonderful heritage it is to have true Christian parents! Many of us would not be where we are today if we had not received good Christian training from our parents. It is possible for people with godless parents to find God and be true Christians, but it is a great advantage if the parents are exemplary Christians.

B. The Confidence of a Great Leader, v. 3-5

It must have been a mighty challenge to Timothy to have Paul express so warmly his confidence in Timothy's faith. That confidence is the inspiration of Paul's prayers, which continue night and day. Doubtless much of the strength of this young man in the face of hard circumstances came to him from God because of Paul's prayers. It is a challenge and source of strength to any Christian to have another express confidence in him and pray for him.

C. The Gift of God, vv. 6-7

1. Its reception, v. 6. The gift here mentioned is probably the same as mentioned in I Tim. 4:14, and is thought to refer to the ministerial gift, with the abilities and enablements to be a good minister. The laying on of Paul's hands may refer to the ordination of Timothy at Lystra, or the appointment to special service in Ephesus. At any rate it was a special commissioning to special work for God and the ministry.

2. Its content, v. 7. The gift was by the Holy Ghost and produced in the soul of Timothy certain essential qualities. It did not produce fear, and so Timothy should not be marked with fear and cowardice in this hour of sore persecution against the church, and of loneliness when Paul shall leave him behind.

It is a gift of power. There will be strong energy to go forward in the face of difficulty. This is not necessarily ability to work supernatural wonders, but power to go forward and endure in spite of all difficulties. There is ability and energy to stand firm against strong pressures, and to persist in loneliness and the departure of others from the field. Barclay says, "The Christian is characteristically the man who can pass the breaking-point and not break." Application of power is shown in v. 8.

It is a gift of love. The power must operate in keeping with love. I Cor. 13 is a vivid description of love. It takes power to live that life, and the Spirit's gift of power is to be directed

II Timothy 173

along that line. The man of God who has problems to face and constant burdens to bear, must have a heart of love for God and His people, or his labor will be largely in vain. There are some laborers whose service is marked more by sheer toil than of love. The Spirit of God puts love into our hearts.

It is a gift of a sound mind, or of self-discipline. No man is fit to rule others unless he has learned to rule himself. Paul had learned this well, and he encourages Timothy in the same. God's Spirit requires this of us if we are to be successful, and He energizes us for it. The power of God is to be directed by love and governed by self discipline. Then it will be effective.

3. Its rekindling, v.6. The figure is that of a fire which needs to be stirred up lest it go out. The workman of God needs to keep himself and his gifts stirred up in zealous purpose and application, if he is to remain effective.

D. The Call of God, vv. 8-18

1. Its basis: the purpose of God, v. 9. We were not called, any of us, because we were worthy of it. Surely St. Paul was not more worthy of place as a messenger of Christ than others of his day in the Church, for he had been most severe in his persecution of the church and of Christ. It was by God's purpose, to get glory to His name. This purpose was eternal, before the founding the world, that Christ Jesus should be the Redeemer, and that we should be His ransomed children, giving praise for His wondrous salvation.

This purpose was not revealed until Christ was manifest in His appearing. The Greek word, epiphaneia, was used to express the manifestation of an emperor on the day of his accession to the throne. The appearance of Christ in the flesh did not have that royal setting, but Paul saw that the outcome of that appearing was greater than the appearance of any emperor. For Jesus came to abolish death and establish life eternal, through the Gospel.

2. Its nature: a holy calling, v. 9. The meaning is a call to holiness. The words "saved" and "called" are both in the aorist tense, denoting instantaneous and effective actions. It is plain that when God saves men from sin, His purpose and choice is that they should live a holy life. He calls then to holiness. Here as in the first epistle Paul soon comes to the theme of holiness. It is momentous with him, for it springs from the eternal purpose of God. This call is not because we were holy, but because God

has purpose and grace to make all kinds of men holy! The unending marvel of the power of Christ is that it takes men like Paul and makes holy men out of them. We should always be praising Him for it.

3. Its expression: the Gospel, vv. 8, 10. St. Paul loved the Gospel, and wanted always to be identified with it. (See 2:8)

   a. It is a gospel of power. In the days of Paul there were many suicides. Even the philosophers recommended the right of suicide when the conditions of life became unbearable. The Gospel introduced a power that could and did take men through the most intolerable conditions, and kept them singing while they passed through them. Men can be Christians under any kind of circumstances brought against them, even unto death.

   b. It is a Gospel of salvation from sin, and the call to holiness. It has power to make men whole and clean.

   c. It is a Gospel of grace. We are not saved because we deserve it, or because we are natively good, but because of God's goodness and love toward us. It is all of grace. None need therefore despair of salvation if they desire it.

   d. It is a Gospel of life and immortality, v. 10. The Gospel changed the world's view of death. Without the Gospel, death is an intolerable enemy of mankind, with nothing hopeful beyond. Now we can see light and life beyond, and death is the gate to eternal life and joy in the presence of God.

   e. It is a Gospel of service, v. 11. Paul uses three terms to denote his activity and service through the Gospel. A preacher: the term means a herald who brings announcements from a king; a messenger who goes between opposing armies to present conditions of peace; and an advertiser of wares that are to be sold. So the preacher speaks on behalf of God, presents to men the terms of reconciliation, and advertises the good things of God's grace. An apostle: a special messenger. He spoke on behalf of another. A teacher: this function pertains to that period of growth after being saved. The man of God must teach as well as evangelize, or the converts will be lost. "Feed my sheep," Jesus said.

4. Its cost: suffering, v. 12

   a. Paul's condition in prison. He had been called for trial once and had been spared death by being thrown to lions. This was evidently because of his own defense, because the ones who he had hoped would come to help defend him did not come. Now he is evidently faced with another trial, and the outcome is a foregone conclusion: he is to die. He was apparently in a dungeon prison where he was hard to find.

   b. His courage. He was not ashamed to be in such a case. It is based on his knowledge of Christ. He had believed in Him, and he knows Him personally. Such knowledge is a sustaining power in suffering and sorrow.

   Paul had made a deposit or commitment of his life and results of his ministry to God. In those days the most sacred of duties was to keep the trust which another had committed to him, and to be prepared to return it safely. Paul has made a commitment of his all to Christ. While others are now ready to take his physical life, he knows they cannot take his soul, or the results of his labor away. These are with God. It is wondrously encouraging in such an hour to know that God understands the life and has the outcomes in His hands!

5. Its responsibility, vv. 13-18. Here St. Paul uses again the word "committed" but this time it is God's commitment to man which is meant. The trust is two-way. We give something to God and He gives something to us. We trust Him and He trusts us. How blessed is such a partnership! Timothy has been entrusted with the doctrines of the Gospel. He is to hold securely and never lose the form of sound words. The exact words in which the Gospel is expressed may and should vary, but the pattern must not be changed. He must be constant in faith and love which are in Christ. These must show forth as they would from Jesus if He were here, for we are in His place, representing these graces!

   By the help of the Holy Ghost Timothy is to keep this charge inviolate. Today when so many men are changing the expression of the Gospel, to make it suit this modern age, they should be reminded that this is not ours to change. It is committed to us to keep changeless, and the Holy Spirit will give us grace to fulfill this task and keep the charge.

a. Some who failed this responsibility. Paul had evidently called some men from Asia to come to Rome to testify in his behalf, to show that he was not a political troublemaker, or a heretic who was dangerous. But these men were fearful and refused to stand up for the work of Paul. All we know of the men are the names of two of them. Their names are preserved for all time in connection with their weakness and cowardice. If our lives were to be summed up in one sentence, what would that sentence be?

b. One who stood firm and faithful. Onesiphorous was a man whose name meant "help-bringer," and he was just that. It was dangerous at that time for a person to seek out Paul in prison and to be found with him, but this man hunted until he found Paul, then often came and refreshed the spirit of this prisoner. He was a man whose habit was to help others. In this dangerous situation he put personal safety in the background and kept up his habit of helpfulness. How good are men like that in the church! Not all can be eloquent preachers, but all can be helpful if they have the spirit of Onesiphorous.

Some have suggested that Onesiphorous died in connection with this dangerous journey and that Paul prays for his departed spirit. This does not follow from what is said. Paul's prayer is that Onesiphorous may find his reward when he stands before God, for surely he did risk his life, and the family risked the loss of a husband and father when he took this dangerous journey to Rome.

III. The Conduct of a Workman, 2:1-26

Here as in other places Paul places responsibility on the young workman and challenges him to be faithful. Paul sets forth some of the labors that are before him and urges him to be strong in these various capacities. The strength comes from Christ, but Timothy is to appropriate and exercise it. We all have this responsibility in our places.

A. His Employment, vv. 1-7

1. As a teacher, v.2. In those days there were no printing presses and books such as we have in abundance today. The truth of God's Word was not in the hands of the multitude. If the truth was to be perpetuated, those who had been taught it must teach it in the same form to others. Thus the emphasis again and

again here to be true to the form of sound words and to pass it on to others. It is a figure somewhat like the passing of the Olympic torch from Greece to whatever place the Olympic games are to be held. Although we have books and teaching aids today, the responsibility still rests on parents and workmen to teach faithfully the truth. Books do not replace teachers.

2. As a soldier, vv. 3, 4. Paul had been chained to a Roman soldier in prison, and he saw here a figure of some vital Christian characteristics.

   a. The soldier concentrated on soldiering. He was that and nothing else—not a farmer or trader on the side. The Christian should concentrate on being a Christian, and a man of the ministry should concentrate on that. As we have seen, Paul did make tents on the side since he had no regular support as a minister, but it did not detract from his concentration on the ministry.

   b. The soldier was obedient to his superiors. This is an essential condition for soldiers, and it is for the workman of God, also. He must be *absolutely* obedient to his Master, seeking always to please God.

   c. The soldier was given to sacrifice. Family and friends, business and ambitions, are expendable for him, because his life is expendable. So it is with the Christian workman; he is "all on the altar" for God. Paul "counted not his life dear unto himself." When the Roman soldier joined the army, he took the oath of loyalty to the emperor. So does does the workman.

3. As an athlete, v.5. The term used indicates a professional, not an amateur athlete. The professional gave his entire life to the work. He was totally disciplined to the cause of winning. No athlete would aspire to be a mediocre one; his entire purpose was to be the best. No workman should allow himself to settle for a second-rate ministry, merely going through the motions in a half-hearted way. He must strive, which means the utmost intensity. Men train for years, hours per day, for one victory. The minister must put his all into the work.

   The athlete must abide by the rules, also. He cannot expect to win by injecting his own ideas and variations into the game. The minister is not called to produce innovations and changes in the rules, as so many seem to feel today. He is given the truth and must abide by it. He must go on even when he is weary until the finish is reached. The winner must have this spirit and the endurance to match it. The man of God has this extra strength from the Spirit.

4. As a husbandman, v. 6. The original will allow either of two constructions. The laborer must first labor and then partake of the fruits; or, the laborer must be the first to partake of the fruits of his labor. The first meaning accords best with the context. If a man expects fruits, he must labor diligently unto weariness. (This is the meaning of the term.) There are natural enemies to face; weeds grow of themselves, but the harvest of the husbandman will not come unless there is labor. So it is in the ministry; there are foes to face and labor to be expended. Evil seems to flourish of itself, but righteousness does not. Labor is required.

Having given these four figures, Paul stresses the necessity of understanding and applying the truth. In all of them there is the hope of victory, but there are requirements to meet first. We are not to take these figures as merely mental curiosities; there are spiritual lessons from God for us in them, and we need spiritual understanding to see and appropriate them. If we do apply the lessons, we can have victory in our ministry as Paul did and as he expected Timothy should, also.

B. His Endurance, vv. 8-26

1. Of suffering, vv. 8-13. When Paul wrote this last epistle he was a criminal in the eyes of the Roman law. It seems evident that when Nero burned Rome on July 19, 64, the blame for it was placed upon the Christians, and they were severely persecuted as a result. As a leader of the group, Paul was arrested, perhaps while he was at Troas. (See 4:13). It appeared that there was no way of gaining release, when the charges were so false and backed up by such high authority. It is for being a Christian that he was bound and condemned. So he could truly say it was for the Gospel's sake.

   a. The cause of suffering, vv. 8, 9. The suffering is for the sake of the Gospel. Here is a magnificent presentation of "my gospel." He says to remember Jesus Christ. We have seen that this letter is a kind of "memory book." There has been memory of Timothy, of his mother and grandmother, of the gift of God, and now of Jesus Christ Himself. Falconer calls these words "the heart of the Pauline gospel." Timothy is to remember Christ risen. This does not refer to a past event in history, but to a present reality: the presence of the risen Christ. What a valuable asset in trouble! He is to remember Christ's humanity, of the seed of David. It is this which links Him vitally to us in our humanity, makes Him to feel our infirmities, and makes Him a faithful and merciful High Priest in things pertaining to God. It is these facts which make the Gospel "good news," even if the preacher is in prison and sentenced to death for it. It is always good news--to be proclaimed with joy and boldness! Paul had a personal attachment to this Gospel, and was glad to suffer for the sake of presenting it. He is to remember the victory of the Word. The minister could be bound, but not the Word. It is not the body of the workman that is of greatest moment, but the Word he bears. The workman may be killed, but the Word cannot. The man can be closed in behind walls, but the living Word cannot, and the written Word cannot either. Luther said, "The body they may kill; God's truth abideth still; His kingdom is forever." So the workman need not lament even imprisonment as if the end to all had come. God's truth cannot die; and since His Church is founded on truth, the Church cannot die either.

b. The effects of suffering, vv. 10-13. Salvation is brought to the elect, that they may share the eternal glory of Heaven. The elect here seem to be those who are truly saved. Jesus said, "Many are called, but few are chosen," (Matt. 20:16). John, in his vision of things to come, says, "They that are with him are called, and chosen and faithful," (Rev. 17:14). The thought concerns endurance. Paul is enduring suffering for others, that they also may be encouraged to suffer and endure unto the end. He recognized the danger that some might depart from Christ in the midst of such sufferings, but his hope is that his own sufferings with joy may encourage others to endure to the reception of the glory to come. In other words, he wants the elected to be faithful unto death, that they might receive the crown of life. Those who are called have the Gospel invitation; those who are elected, answer the call; those who are faithful endure to the end and receive the crown.

There follows what seems to be part of an early Christian hymn. If in our sufferings we are true, even unto death, we will share His glory. If we turn away in suffering, we will lose our reward. He will be true and a perfectly safe anchor, no matter how severe the persecution we may be called to endure. But if we lose faith and deny Him, He cannot then receive us, for He is unchanging in His principles. He must reject the man that rejects Him, for God does not change; it is the man that changes.

2. Of false doctrine, vv. 14-26. In this section again there is a clear and strong reference to the Gnostics and the kind of error they proclaimed. There is a continuing contrast between the proponents of error and the true workman of God. We will show the contrast in four different ways.

   a. The use of the Word, vv. 14, 15. The false teachers "strove about words to no profit." There are those who are ever occupied with much talk, delighting in argumentation, logical discussion and analysis, but who never apply the truth effectively in their lives. There is ever a danger that we will be satisfied to behold the sparkle of rhetoric and the novelty of new ideas and new expressions, but that we will not be changed in character for the better thereby. Such were the Gnostics: their discussions not only were unprofitable; they actually subverted faith. They caused faith to become weak or even lost. The error was thus a damning and extremely serious error. Paul took a strong stand against it, because it threatened the faith of the believers.

   The true workman, in contrast, is one who labors intensely to show himself to God as one who has been tested, purified, and fit for service. This is by "rightly dividing the word of truth." The words have a variety of meaning, referring to a straight road, or a properly squared stone. Taken with what is said about error, it refers to the fact that the true workman uses the Word in such a way as not to distort it, but to build a building, or structure or truth which is solidly founded and truly built. He is true to the Word.

   b. The characters produced, vv. 16-19. The false teachers use the Word in such a way that their message produces deadly effects. These people "progress" or chop their way forward with great zeal, but the results are like a cancer—they increase in deadliness. The combination of zeal by the errorists and the gullibility of the credulous causes increase of the false teaching, which would increase, according to the apostle.

Hymenaeus and Philetus were two of the false teachers, who are unknown otherwise. They taught that resurrection had already occurred, possibly at the time of baptism. Since matter was believed to be evil, they could allow for no resurrection of the body. (If this Hymenaeus is the same as in I Tim. 1:20, it seems that the excommunication did not accomplish a remedy.)

In contrast Paul refers to the building which God had directed, which he calls the "foundation of God." There are different interpretations of what it means, but it appears probably to mean the Religion of Jesus Christ, built on the foundation of the Gospel. In spite of error and false doctrines, the religion of Christ will always endure. False teachers may assail it, but it will endure. There are two seals, or marks of the architect on it. First, there is the seal, "The Lord knoweth then that are His." This seal shows divine ownership and genuineness of character. Those who belong to God are safe, for He knows them, and they are secure in Him. This is a fact to be believed. Second, "Let every one that nameth the name of Christ depart from iniquity." This means clearly that God's people are not to continue in sin. There is to be an end to sin for them. Taken with the first seal, it shows that security and purity go together. There is no security for those who go on in sin. This seal is a command to be obeyed.

c. Fitness for service, vv. 20-22. The great house refers again to the religion of Jesus Christ. Associated with this religion are not only the ones known of God to be His, but there are also some who are not His, though they have associated themselves with the congregation of the righteous. Such were the false teachers like Hymenaeus and Philetus. Jesus taught the same truth in the parable of the wheat and the tares, in Matt. 13:24-30, 36-43. The vessels of gold and silver stand for the true servants of God; those of wood and earth are representative of false teachers and other persons who are not God's and whose destiny is to be condemned.

The true servant of God must purge himself of these false people. He is able to discern them, though they are associated with the true Church. He must purge himself from them; that is, he must be totally free from their error. He must not enter into fellowship with them as if they were true. By this purging and separation he will be worthy of God's using as His servant.

The vessels unto honor are characterized by sanctification (being set apart for God's holy use, and cleansing from all sin), and by fitness for divine service. They are prepared for whatever service God may need them for.

Not only must the true servant separate himself from external error; he must also flee away from internal lusts. This refers not just to sexual desires, but from all lusts peculiarly strong in youth, which would draw them away from truth and holiness. Examples are: impatience, self-assertion, love of argument, love of novelty, love of fine clothes and other possessions, ambition for material success, and others. Instead of giving himself to these, the servant of God must pursue, as a hunter pursues his game, the positive graces here mentioned. None of these are permanently and rigidly fixed even in the life of the fully sanctified. We must follow them and see that they grow and enlarge. The fellowship of such people will be with the holy who are given to prayer. Note the emphasis on holiness which is repeatedly stressed. Prayer and holiness are here vitally related.

d. Aim of service, vv. 23-26. The aim of the false teachers is to generate controversy with the hope of securing a following. To do this they pursue questions in their ignorance of the truth of God's Word. Tragically there has been much of this in the church down through the years, and it still exists today. So much of controversy is about minor matters that are magnified all out of proportion to their importance. The matter of speaking in unknown tongues today is one such issue. It draws the attention of people away from the true fulness of the Spirit and what it will accomplish, and places greater emphasis on that which is of very limited value at best, and which causes much division and loss in the churches. The error is gaining a greater and greater following, and that in itself is what causes it to be so highly recommended today. But popularity is never the test of truth. It wasn't in Paul's day, and it isn't now.

The aim of the true servant of God in dealing with error must be:

1. To be gentle. He must not yield to the temptation to become quarrelsome, as the errorists are. By so doing he would come down to their level, and reproach his position in the truth.

2. Apt to teach. He must be able to present the truth that will expose the error.

3. Patient and meek. The errorists may slander him, but he is to take it graciously, not answering back in equally slanderous terms.

4. To recover the errorists from their captivity in error. The devil has taken them captive at his will, in effort to oppose God's work. The true servant is not in a human battle against personalities; he is in a battle to recover men from Satan's captivity. May we today see our true purpose in this light. Those who are in error are in reality working against themselves, and unless they see it and repent, they will be eternally lost. The servant of God will work with the hope that mercy may be extended to them and that they will repent and be recovered.

IV. Perils Facing the Workman, 3:1-17

Having dealt with the errors immediately confronting Timothy, Paul turns to a consideration of dangers farther ahead, even to the end of the age. No specific time is given, but the term "last days" would include the days in which we now live, leading up to the coming of the Lord.

A. Empty Formality, vv. 1-9

In Romans 2 Paul sets forth a list of the horrible sins of the heathen. The list in II Timothy is quite similar, but it applies to those who have a form of religion. It is amazing that the predictions are so true at this present time. All of these sins which Paul mentions are evidenced among professedly Christian people. We have neither time nor space to give detailed attention to all eighteen conditions; however, we may note some facts about them and make some observations.

1. The entire description begins and ends with the love of the individuals concerned. They love themselves; they love pleasure more than God. The word translated "covetous" really

means "lovers of money." What people love determines their character. A false love can lead to the grossest of degeneracy, as is pictured here. The true religion of Christ makes men holy because their hearts are perfect in love; they love God supremely and their neighbors as themselves.

2. The described condition gets worse and worse, in keeping with what Paul says in v. 13.

3. When love is directed to a wrong end, such as to self and money and pleasure, the proper loves disappear. Natural affection, such as that between parent and children, disappears. It is so today; the family as a stable institution is disappearing in many countries.

4. Self-centered people become blasphemers (lovers of insult to men and God), trucebreakers (implacable in hatred), false accusers (reveling in slander), proud, heady, and highminded (going beyond all restraint in word and action).

5. It should be noted how the beginning items of the list are now gaining prevalence even in conservative circles. Self-love and materialism are eating away at the strength of the church. They can cause the effective loss of the power of the Spirit. When this happens, the others of the series can follow. The only real cure is perfect love!

6. The man of God is to turn away from such dead formality. This is in marked contrast with the instructions of 2:25 where Paul advised gently dealing with the teachers of error. In this latter case, men have gone too far into apostasy to be helped. They are unapproachable and antagonistic to the truth to the point where the workman must save himself from them. When people recognize such irremediable apostasy, they should by all means depart from it. Their case is clearly shown in v. 8.

7. They prey on women who are poorly informed and ready to follow lustful men. It is amazing how much of false religion of this kind there is today. Many false teachers, by radio and magazine, appeal to the support of those who are emotional and ignorant.

Such women ever learn from the teachers, but they will never come to the truth, for the false teachers do not proclaim the truth They have selfish interests which conflict with the truth, so they oppose it.

8. There is one encouragement about such error: it can not always endure. Truth *must* finally prevail! Jannes and Jambres (magicians who opposed Moses when he appeared before Pharaoh) were eventually exposed for their failure, and so shall these false teachers be. In the last days, truth is soon to appear, even if error is gaining. We can be encouraged by this fact.

B. Active Persecution, vv. 10-12

1. The cause, vv. 10, 12. Paul was persecuted because of his holy life and doctrine. Here he refers to Timothy as a disciple of his own teaching and training. Paul had not only given him the truth academically, but he had also trained Timothy in it, showing him how to live. Paul had clear purpose in his life which was never altered even in the midst of severe persecutions. How wonderful it is to have life with high purpose. It is worth suffering. The most miserable people today are those who are wealthy but who have no real purpose. Paul had such, and so did Timothy; so will we if we follow Jesus.

All who will live Godly will suffer persecutions. This is quite a startling generalization, and one that needs clear understanding. Paul has just been describing a time in the last days when men will love pleasure, comfort, ease, and self. They will not want hardship and will consider hardship as unnecessary even in the name of religion. Instead of tolerating persecution, they will do whatever is necessary to remove it. We are in such a day now when people do not want to endure the reproach and scorn of the world. They adopt the styles, customs, manners, and pleasures of the world, still calling themselves Christian. They do not want to bear the scorn of being modest and of living by principles that are contrary to the ways of the world. Let a person disown the immodest styles, the immoral activities, the Christ-dishonoring conversation and amusements of the world, and let him give his reasons for so doing, and he will be branded by the world as a fanatic and a fool. He will feel the hatred of the world. Remember the words: *"all* that will live godly in Christ Jesus shall suffer persecution." Jesus said similar things: "Because ye are not of the world, but I have chosen you out of the world, therefore the world hateth you" (John 15:19).

2. Paul's case, v. 11. He gives three illustrations which occurred near Timothy's home. He had to flee from Antioch and Iconium to avoid lynching, and he was stoned at Lystra.

3. The defense, v. 11. God will rescue the man who trusts Him. He may suffer, but his glory will be enhanced thereby. God knows His workman, and He watches to deliver Him at just the right time and in the right way. See 4:18.

C. Seducers, vv. 13-17

1. Their character, v. 13. The seducers are illustrated by the two mentioned in v. 8, Jannes and Jambres. These were men who used their magical arts to imitate the gifts of God. One commentator (Harvey) says, "They directly opposed the true gospel by setting up their magical arts in rivalry with the gifts of the Spirit, as the old Egyptian sorcerers had done in the contest with Moses." Adam Clarke says these seducers are "pretenders to magical arts; probably persons dealing in false miracles, with whom the Church in all ages has been not a little disgraced."

They are deceivers, spreading their error among those who are undiscerning and unspiritual. Their use of pretended gifts and miracles prevails over the minds of those who are not spiritually discerning. So the error increases greatly. Then its very magnitude prevails over those who want to be with something big and popular. Such men are deceived themselves.

Such conditions will grow worse and worse in the last days, Paul says. It is clear today that there is a great increase in such false workers. There are those today who pretend to do the miracles and gifts of the Spirit, whose lives are not pure and holy. They are not seeking the supreme glory of God. One of the greatly advertised radio preachers in America, who was declared to have the gifts of healing and tongues, was found in adultery, and died in deep sin. This movement is placing increasing emphasis on the false gifts and less and less on holy living, until there is a great increase of sinfulness among its adherents. The movement is having an increasing influence over those who are not themselves deeply spiritual, and who are thus easily deceived.

2. The defense against them, vv. 14-17

   a. Paul's teachings and example, v. 14 . It would appear that St. Paul is included among those from whom Timothy had learned the truth. Perhaps the mother and grandmother are also included. The truth of God is not some novel thing that just lately appeared to capture the attention of men. It has been taught across the centuries. Truth began in the heart of God and it will not die as long as He lives!

b. The Holy Scriptures, vv. 15-17

   1) They were learned in childhood. This was customary with the Jews, and is extremely vital in indoctrination.

   2) They can make wise unto salvation. This is the greatest characteristic of the Word: not its account of creation, or its history, or prophecy of the future, but the fact that it is able to bring men to salvation.

   The word "reproof" in v. 16 is related to salvation; it means conviction for sin. A man was once caught at night in a forest in Sicily by thieves and ordered at the point of a gun to light a fire and burn his copies of the Bible. He lit the fire, then asked if he might read some from each copy before he dropped it into the fire. He read Psa. 23, the good Samaritan story, the Sermon on the Mount, and the story of the Prodigal son. At the end of each reading a thief would ask for that copy to keep, saying, "That's a good book; give it to me." Not one book was burned; the thieves went away with all of them. Years later those same men turned up again, and the leader of them was a gospel preacher; the reading from the Word had been his turning point.

   3) They are "God-breathed." This means that the presence and operation of God's own Spirit is inseparably connected with the Scriptures. Such a condition applies to all of the Scriptures, not just certain portions. God used the writers, holy men who were moved by His Spirit, but the Scriptures themselves are here said to be inspired. That is, the men did not detract from the inspired quality of what was written.

   4) They are profitable in developing workmen. Correction here refers to the removal of doctrine. The Bible must remain the final test of every theory and statement.

IV. Resources of the Workman (Chapter 4)

We have already discussed some of the perils of the last days. In this final chapter we have a further discussion of perilous conditions, plus the resources which are available to the workman in facing them.

A. In Apostasy, vv. 1-5

1. Characteristics of the apostates, vv. 3, 4. In Paul's day there were traveling teachers, called Sophists, whose purpose was to seek students who would pay them for teaching. Then the teachers labored to build arguments and teaching which would support what the student wanted to do. In our day again there are such teachers who labor to support the people in what they want to hear. We are living in a time of vaunted Progressivism, when religion to be popular must be ever coming up with new and "enlightened" views, but must never condemn the personal moral sins of the individuals. It is the sins of society which are in vogue now, not personal sins.

   These are religious people, nominally Christian, who will not hear the Word when its rugged truth applies to their personal lives. They deny its authority, and turn away to whatever they want to hear, because they are motivated by lusts.

2. The charge to Timothy, vv. 1, 2, 5

   a. Preach the Word, v. 2. This charge is made before God and Christ.

   Timothy is reminded of 3 things about Christ. First, He is to be the judge of living and dead. Our ministry is to be judged by Him. It does not matter whether or not we please ourselves or others, if we do not please Him. This is of supreme moment. Second, He will soon appear. The word refers to the coming of a king into His realm as conqueror. Cities through which he would pass would make elaborate preparations for his coming. Likewise we should be ready in all things when Jesus appears. Third, Jesus is coming to a kingdom. If we are to have a part in it, we must be faithful here. Our place there is determined by our work here.

   b. Watch in all things, v. 5. It means to be steadfast, sober, and alert. While others are changing and always looking for the novel and sensational, God's man must be unmoved and unruffled by the cry over novelty and the emphasis on progressivism. Much of what is called "progress" is in reality a move toward apostasy.

    c. Do the work of an evangelist, v. 5. This means to bear good news to men in sin. The workman must never become so preoccupied with problems and dangers that he loses the note of joy and hope in the good news for sinners. He is to oppose error, but always he is to love the lost and seek them for Christ.

    d. Make full proof of thy ministry. This means to be faithful in attendance upon every aspect of the ministry. The workman must never become lopsided, so that he leaves off some important emphasis of the Gospel. Some are in danger of spending so much time opposing certain errors that they do not present the whole Gospel. Paul said that he declared the "whole counsel of God," (Acts 20:27).

3. The resource: the Word of God, v. 2. At a time when people in general are turning away from the Word, the man of God is not to seek something novel to substitute, but is to specialize on the Word. He must never depart form it. Preaching the word is adapted to accomplishing certain important things:

    a. Reprove. This means to make the sinner aware of his sin. While the false teachers encourage and cover sin, the workman of God must expose it. There is a dangerous tendency today for preachers to avoid the popular sins, so as not to make sinners uncomfortable. Barclay says, "Somehow or other the sinner must be made to feel disgusted with himself and sin." Charles Finney said, "The deceitfulness of sin renders the inquiring soul exceedingly exposed to delusion...Do not fear to be thorough. Do not through false pity put a plaster where the probe is needed...If the Holy Ghost is dealing with him, the more you search and probe, the more impossible it is for the soul to turn back or rest in sin." Walter Bagehot once said, "The road to perfection is through a series of disgusts."

    b. Rebuke. This is an even stronger term, showing reprimand. The preacher must thrust the sword of the Spirit, exposing the full measure of sin. The ministry of the Spirit is to reprove the world of sin, but the preacher of the Word is

His means of doing so! If we fail here, we have quenched the Spirit in His operation.

    c. Exhort. This is the positive side. After exposing sin, the sinner must be encouraged, not in himself but in the hope of salvation. He must be shown what to do. Jesus used this method with the woman of Samaria, Nicodemus, and others. Peter did also after Pentecost.

    d. Longsuffering. The preacher must keep at it, being true to the truth and being compassionate on the needy at the same time. The Scriptures, he must remember, can make sinners wise unto salvation, so he must keep presenting the Word.

B. In Facing Death, vv. 6-8

1. The circumstances, v. 6. Paul uses a sacrificial term here. It meant to pour out as a drink offering. Paul was now ready to pour out his life as a final offering to Christ. He had given everything else to Jesus; now he will give his very life. It is clear that Paul did not think of the Romans as taking his life away from him. Like Jesus, he could say, "No man taketh my life from me; I lay it down of myself."

When he said, "The time of my departure is at hand," he was using a word with several meanings and uses.

    a. It meant unyoking oxen at the close of the day. Likewise, there would be release from wearying labor so that rest could be enjoyed.

    b. It meant loosing fetters so as to allow freedom. Paul looked forward to the end of all bondage. He had spent about five years in prison, plus other painful opposition, and it was now at an end.

    c. It meant loosing the ropes of a tent so camp could be moved. Paul had been moved often with no certain abiding place. Now he was ready for his last move! That would be joy for this tentmaker preacher!

    d. It meant pulling up anchor and loosing the mooring ropes of a ship in harbor and launching out on the deep. Paul was leaving the port of earth and moving toward heaven!

2. Resources, vv. 6-8

    a. Consideration of the past. He now uses the figure of the Greek games. He has fought a good fight. He has put everything into the effort, sparing nothing to win. He is not ashamed of the performance.

    He has finished the course. There are many who begin; there are many less who continue to the end. It takes far more discipline and effort to finish than to begin, but here was a man who finished. This was his goal from the beginning, see Acts 20:24.

    Paul had kept the faith. This too probably refers to the games. It would then mean that Paul had kept the rules. He had not violated the principles of right and holiness. Paul had said to Agrippa, "I was not disobedient to the heavenly vision." He had done his duty correctly.

    What a consolation at the point of departure. Jesus had the same satisfaction as He faced death (see John 17:4). It does not matter so much how long we live but whether or not we have finished our work.

    b. Consideration of the future. There is reference to the laurels given in the Greek games. Paul expects not a perishable crown but an imperishable one. It is the reward of righteousness which he expects. It is the Lord Himself Who will present the crown. Paul labors above everything else to receive the final approval of his Lord Whom he loved so much. So should we.

    All may receive the same crown if they meet the conditions. One of the marks of such readiness is eagerness for His appearing. Those who are so engrossed in earthly things as to have no lively interest in the return of the Lord do not give sound evidence of being prepared. There must be not just a casual curiosity but a genuine love of His coming.

C. In Loneliness, vv. 9-13

  1. The circumstances. There was not only loneliness but also heaviness because of the record of some who had failed not only Paul but the Lord as well.

    a. The failure of Demas, v. 10. We read also of him in Philemon 24 and Col. 4:14. In the former passage he is mentioned as a fellow-laborer, but now he has forsaken

Paul and gone away, having loved this present world. The original means that he let Paul down in a time of great need and in a crisis. It was a crisis event in the lives of both men. It seems his love of the world is in contrast to those who love Christ's appearing. Men cannot love both. Those who love the world do not have the love of Christ. This man was a backslider. We can only hope he returned to the Lord, if not to Paul.

  b. Only Luke is with me. This is a glowing statement about a man who was much with Paul. We do not know much about him except that he wrote Luke and Acts, that he was a physician and a fellow-laborer. He stayed when others failed. May God give us more such men who do not fail in the test!

    The way this is said it is apparent that Paul was lonely for other friends. His solitude and condition are weighing on him. Though a rugged and faithful apostle, he still was human, and physical circumstances had their effect on him.

  c. The need for Mark. This is the man who failed once but who has evidently recovered from the early failure. It is good to know that while some fall not to rise again, others rise from early failure. God is able to turn human failures into successes by His grace! No man need stay the way he is!

2. The resources, vv. 9, 13

  a. The coming of friends. How precious is the visit of a friend in time of loneliness! In one of my early pastorates there lived a couple much too old to get to church. I endeavored to visit them regularly. They often mentioned how glad they were to see me, saying, "Most people have forgotten us since we are so old and can no get about much." To be forgotten is a deep hurt. Paul wants and needs company. He was human and needed comfort; He was a Christian and needed fellowship.

  b. The reading of books. The books he wants may have been the early forms of the Gospels, and the parchments were probably copies of the Old Testament Scriptures. He wanted His loved Scriptures even in old age. What a lesson this is to keep our mind filled with the Word even down to old age!

Note the very personal incident here: the call for a cloak. Winter was coming, and he needed warmth in the dungeon.

D. In Injustice, vv. 14-18

1. From Alexander the coppersmith. We do not know what this man did exactly, but it appears that he must have been an informer against Paul. (The word *did* in "did me much evil" often had that meaning.) He also came and testified against Paul in the trial, opposing what Paul said. Paul leaves his case with God and predicts that God will give him what he deserves. It is not in the form of an imprecation in the original, apparently.

2. From faithless friends, who forsook him. When Paul first appeared before the judge he needed some friends to witness for him; perhaps he even sent for them. But they failed (see 1:15).

   In this case, like Stephen, Paul prays for God not to requite them for their neglect and unfaithfulness.

3. The resources, vv. 17, 18

   a. The presence of the Lord. When nobody else would stand with him, Paul was conscious of the presence of God. Such was the strength: that Paul could use that trial as an occasion to preach the message of God's salvation "that the Gentiles might hear."

      He was delivered out of the mouth of the lion. It is not sure what this meant; it may mean the lions of the amphitheater which devoured many Christians at that time. It may mean Nero or the devil, or just any great danger. There is some support for each one of them. In fact, he was delivered from each of them at this first appearance.

   b. The Holy Scriptures. It is noticeable that Paul uses here several portions of Psalm 22. Note the comparisons:

Paul's Words	**Psalm 22**
All men forsook me, v. 16	Why hast thou forsaken me?, v. 1
No man stood with me, v. 16	There is none to help, v. 11
I was delivered out of the mouth of the lion, v. 17	Save me from the lion's mouth, v. 21
The Lord shall deliver me from every evil work, v. 18	He trusted on the Lord that He would deliver him, v. 8
That all the Gentiles might hear, v. 17	All the ends of the earth shall turn unto the Lord, v. 27
He will preserve me unto His heavenly kingdom, v. 18	The kingdom is the Lord's, v. 28

It may be recalled that Jesus referred to this same Psalm in His passion on the cross. So Paul even in looking to death drew comfort from the Scriptures and was identified with His Master and Lord.

c. The assurance of future deliverance. In v. 18 he declares his unshaken confidence in God's faithfulness. He does not intimate deliverance *from* death here, but *through* death. God is going to remove him from the presence of all evil forever! In that kingdom there will be glory forever, and Christ will be the center of it. But Paul anticipated His share; for having been identified with Christ here, he could share the glory there. This was his desire, and it was Christ's, also. See John 17:24.

Barclay well says, "It is always better to be in danger for a moment and safe for eternity, than to be in safety for a moment and to jeopardize eternity."

VI. Final Greetings

There must come the final goodbyes. Paul gives his personal love to his dearest friends who had meant so very much to him in days past. Aquila and Priscilla were co-laborers who had risked their lives for him (Rom. 16: 3, 4). Onesiphorous had sought him out in prison at great risk. Erastus had once been his messenger to Macedonia (Acts 19:22). There is some strong evidence that Pudens and Claudia were a royal couple; Pudens a highborn Roman notable and Claudia a princess from Britain. If it is true, it indicates how much Christianity was penetrating the high circles of government. How great the price, but how wonderful the results!

Paul again asks Timothy to come before sailing on the sea was stopped for the winter. He closes with the word "grace" which he loved so much.

Review Questions
II TIMOTHY

1. How does the tone of II Timothy differ from that of I Timothy?
2. Was Paul's great passion to preach the threat of hell or the promise of life?
3. How could Paul be grateful for his parentage?
4. How does Paul encourage Timothy in 1:3-5?
5. What two things might the "laying on of hands" refer in 1:6, 7?
6. What characterizes the gift of God to Timothy?
7. For what cause was Paul suffering?
8. What one thing do we know about Onesiphorous? About Demas?
9. What examples does Paul use when speaking of the conduct of a workman?
10. Who was most likely the Roman emperor at the time this epistle was written?
11. To whom does Paul refer when he says he suffers for the "elect's sake"?
12. What are the effects of suffering?
13. Contrast the proponent of error with the true workman of God.
14. What are some dangers characterizing the "last days"?
15. What characterizes the seducers who wax worse and worse?
16. What is the greatest characteristic of the Word?
17. What characterizes apostates?
18. What was Paul's charge to Timothy in chapter 4?
19. What does the preaching of the word accomplish?
20. Paul mentions several resources available to him in prison. Name three of these.

The Epistle to
TITUS

Introduction

I. Author

There are two opinions about the authorship of this epistle, as there are about those to Timothy. Many believe that Paul was released from his first imprisonment at Rome and that thereafter he wrote these epistles. Others do not see sufficient reason for believing that Paul did gain release from prison. Also, they see differences in language between these epistles and the others of Paul. They are inclined to believe that a later person, a personal friend of Paul, took parts of personal letters from him, added to them, and issued letters in Paul's name. This kind of action was not uncommon in those days and was not considered dishonest. We are inclined to favor the first opinion, although there is no final proof. In either case, the letter deserves a place in the sacred canon, for the material is of great value.

II. Time of Writing

Assuming that Paul did write it after release from his first imprisonment and before his second imprisonment, it must have been written about 64 or 65 A.D. We have said that I Timothy was written about 64 A.D., and the great similarities between that and this indicate that they probably were written about the same time, with Titus being written perhaps a bit later.

III. The Recipient of the Letter

Titus is so designated, and we have no reason for doubting it. We do not know much about him, but the following facts are known.

  A. He was a partner and a fellow laborer of Paul, traveling with him in the way Timothy did. See II Cor. 8:23.

- B. Paul chose Titus to organize the collection for the poor saints in Jerusalem. This means he was a trusted and able man. See II Cor. 8:6, 16, 17.
- C. From Gal. 2:3 where we are told he was not compelled to be circumcised, we learn he was a Greek and converted from heathenism. This means he was neither Jew nor proselyte before his conversion.

IV. The Occasion for the Letter

In 1:5 we are given the reason why Paul left Titus at Crete: to set in order the things that were lacking. This epistle evidently serves to instruct Titus particularly how to do this. Further, there is instruction for combatting error, as there was in the epistles to Timothy. Evidently the same errors are in view: Gnosticism and the Jewish variation thereof.

V. Outline

From the purpose which Paul stated, we take the following topic as the organizational theme for this study: Order in the Church

- A. Paul's Introduction
- B. Order in the Preaching Ministry
- C. Order in the Laity
- D. Order of the Church Before the World
- E. Paul's Conclusion

The Study of the Epistle to Titus

I. **Introduction, 1:1-4**

A. The Writer

Paul typically refers to his official position and to his personal relationship to Christ.

B. His Epitome of the Gospel Plan

1. Election. Paul uses this word frequently, and it is important that we understand it. There are three kinds of election.

    a. Individual election to an office, as seen in Jeremiah and John the Baptist. It is not involved here. See Ps. 89:19, 20.

    b. National election to a place of responsibility and privilege. In this sense the people of Israel were the elect of God. See Is. 45:4; Romans 9:11; 11:26, 28.

    c. Individual election to salvation through grace. See Rom. 11:5-7. The nation of Israel rejected the Messiah, the Way to personal salvation, so the nation was set aside. However, some individuals of Israel, as well as some Gentiles, received Christ as personal Savior.

    This election is of grace and depends on faith and obedience of the individual. It is this form of election with which we have to do in our text. The personal responsibility involved is clearly shown in II Pet. 1:10. (Compare v. 9.)

    Before God ever made the world, He had already perfected His plan for the saving of the lost through Christ.

2. The subjective content of salvation

    a. Faith of the elect. That is, the faith by which they choose to be saved. Election is not only God's choice but ours as well.

    b. Knowledge of the truth. This is a New Testament word for knowledge which indicates strong, clear, and experimental knowledge. Such knowledge of salvation comes through the operation of the Holy Spirit.

- c. Such knowledge is accompanied by a transformation of character so that Godliness follows. It is not merely theoretical knowledge but experimental knowledge which has godly character with it.
- d. Hope of eternal life. This again is not theoretical but spiritual. It is a lively hope, as Peter says in I Pet. 1:3.

3. The timing of salvation

- a. It was planned before the world began.
- b. It was manifest in due time. This same truth is set forth in Eph. 1:10. There are some significant facts about the time when Christ came and the Gospel plan was declared.
    1) Most of the world spoke Greek, so the spread of the Gospel was facilitated. Then the Greek language became a dead language, so that the New Testament books have been preserved in an unchanging language.
    2) The Roman Empire was so extensive that people could freely travel from country to country without difficulty. There were virtually no uncrossable boundaries. The spread of the Gospel was thus aided.
    3) Travel was easier than before because the Romans had built many roads and discouraged robbery so that travelers could travel without fear.
    4) The world was largely at peace, which meant that men were quite free to travel without fear from place to place.
    5) The world was tired of its old religions and philosophies. These had proven inadequate to change men's basic characters. There never was a time when men were more open to the message of salvation. God moved at the right time.

C. The Recipient, v. 4

Titus is called "mine own son after the common faith." This apparently means that Titus was converted under Paul's ministry. It is not known where this happened, but some think at Iconium. The word "common" here means "general," and indicates that the faith of the Gospel is for Gentiles as well as Jews. This is appropriate, since Titus was evidently a Gentile.

D. The Greeting, v. 4. This is typical of Paul. It is worthy of note that grace speaks of gifts from God which are not deserved, and mercy speaks of the withholding of judgments that are deserved. Together, they provide total peace for the believer. In all of them, grace, mercy and peace come from the Father through the Son.

II. Order of the Preaching Ministry, 1:5-16

A. Qualifications of Bishops, 1:5-9

1. It will be noted here that an elder is the same as a bishop. The term "elder" refers to personal spiritual maturity, and the term "bishop" (overseer) refers to the official responsibility. "Elders" were honored in Old Testament times as those who were old men. In the New Testament, while the term is retained, it is only in a relative sense that the men were to be old. They were to be spiritually the most mature men in the company.

2. It was common to have more than one elder in each city to be in charge of the spiritual and moral responsibilities of the flock. At the same time, it was recognized that they did not do all the work of the church. They were overseers and examples (I Pet. 5:2, 3), leading and feeding the flock, not just dictating or doing all the work themselves.

    The qualifications have been dealt with in the study of I Tim. 3:1-7, so they do not need to be dealt with in detail here again. There are a few here which are slightly different from the statements in I Timothy.

    a. *Having faithful children,* v. 6. Ability to supervise the flock must first be manifested in ability to supervise his own little flock at home. If he cannot do the latter, he has not the qualification to do the former.

    b. *Not accused of riot* literally means not accused of profligacy or wastefulness. The family must be thrifty and not wasteful. It must be disciplined and properly controlled.

    c. *The steward of God,* v. 7. Elders are not merely human appointees. In no case are they politicians, seeking to climb an ecclesiastical ladder. They are appointed under the authority of the Holy Ghost (Acts 20:28), and they are answerable to God for their service. They are not human lords but servants, and they must conduct themselves in that way.

d. *Not self-willed*. This is fully in harmony with the preceding qualification. The word means one who is *conceited*, thinking too highly of his opinions; is *contemptuous*, thinking too lowly of the opinions of others, and is *arrogant*, acting out of his wrong estimate of himself and others. Such a person cannot be a good steward and is not worthy for the office.

e. *A lover of good men*, v. 8. The term may include either good things or good people. He has spiritual discernment, seeing the difference between good and evil and always choosing the good. He does not use good or evil as means to other ends but chooses good as an end, knowing that it please God. Some men will choose evil means to ends which they consider good, but we must remember there is no need of employing *wrong means* of doing a *good thing*. In Rom. 3:8, Paul denies that we should do evil so that good may come.

f. *Just and holy*. The first refers to conduct, and the second refers to the heart. Inwardly and fundamentally he is allied with truth and holiness.

g. *Holding forth the faithful Word*. This indicates that the Word itself is adequate for all of its intended uses, as Paul says in II Tim. 3:16. Here two special uses are given.

   1) To exhort or encourage believers. This is very important. The minister of the Word should so preach as to encourage, not to discourage. It is possible to be so negative in pointing out errors and deficiencies as to produce defeat and discouragement. On the other hand, it is possible to show error in such a way as to produce hope for betterment and thus increase maturity.

   2) To convince the gainsayers. Again, the rebuke is to be done on the basis of the truth and not on the basis of personal opposition. The truth must be so displayed that its conclusions are clearly displayed. The hearers will be convinced of the truth even if they are not willing to follow. For this purpose the elder must be a diligent student, finding the illumination of the Spirit in the use of the Word.

B. Error to Be Corrected, 1:10-16

1. Character of the false teachers. It appears that this is a group similar to those Paul describes in I Timothy: the Jews who had appropriated some of the error of Gnosticism and added some of the Jewish legalism to it. These men as individuals had a sordid character, as Paul shows. He refers to the Greek poet Epimenides, who had been ranked as one of the seven wise men of Greece. He describes the Cretans as pernicious liars. It was widely acknowledge in those days that Cretans were of this sort. In fact, to be a "Cretan" meant to be tricky and deceitful. They were also quarrelsome, greedy and gluttonous. They would do anything for money and then utilize it on their own passions and appetites.

2. Influence of the false teachers. Their talk was vain. They produced no goodness in the lives of the hearers. Knowledge is unprofitable if it does not improve the character; their knowledge did not. Worse still, they deceived men, leading them into error instead of the truth. They upset whole households, turning them away from the faith into error that cannot save.

    Because of this deception, Paul says their mouths must be stopped. This is a strong statement, but when we consider that they were turning whole families away from the truth we can realize how serious was the need to stop their influence. While the man of God does not like to enter contention (II Tim. 2:24), yet there is a time when he must oppose error with the utmost energy and determination. The intent of this exhortation is not physical violence against the deceivers but a strong application of the truth that will silence the error by sound reason. Stephen used this method with his enemies (Acts 6:10).

    A kind of poetic proverb is used in v. 15, possibly taken from the teachings of Christ Himself. These false teachers had long and detailed lists of what was pure and what was impure. They even carried their lists to such extremes as to call marriage and childbearing sins. In Gnosticism, even the body was considered evil, and so nothing related to the body could be pure. Paul states that it is really the heart condition that determine purity. Jesus said essentially the same thing in Mark 7:15. These false teachers made evil to consist primarily in our relation to physical things—abstaining or partaking. Jesus and Paul insisted that evil is first of all in the heart, and so is purity.

If a man is pure in heart, then marriage can be pure, as well as eating meat. If a man is impure in heart, then these things will be impure in their function.

The false teachers themselves were examples of this truth. They were abominable people who turned holy things into cause for unclean jests and suggestions. Cleanliness is beautiful, but they delighted into turning the clean into something unclean, in making the holy appear wrong and the unholy appear right.

They were disobedient men. The mind and conscience were both defiled. They could not think in terms of purity, and their consciences were so depraved that they could not discern the holy. The intellect is the basis for rational decision and evaluation; the conscience is the basis for judging of God's leading. They could not evaluate properly, and they could not hear the voice of God clearly. This was because of disobedience. What a solemn truth this is: when a man will not obey the truth, he soon loses the ability to see and know the truth.

Because of such a condition, these men were reprobate concerning every good work. Nothing they did could be credited as good, because they were evil in every part of their being! It is an awesome condition, similar to the one that Paul describes in Rom. 1:20-32.

3. The means of meeting the error. Paul does not give up hope for such people. He says to rebuke them sharply so that they may be sound in faith. The cutting edge of the truth is to be used to expose the error. Perhaps the false teachers themselves will hear and be converted. However, the meaning seems to be primarily that the believers who were tending to give heed to the false teachers are to be rebuked that they may resist the error and continue in the truth. In any case, it is the truth that is the weapon, and the man of God has great responsibility to resist evil such as they were experiencing.

III. Order in the Laity, Chapter 2

Here is the most practical kind of Christianity, placing duties and responsibilities on every class of person in the Church. The religion of Jesus Christ is not merely an intellectual curiosity but a moral imperative. There is no place whatsoever for antinomianism or the kind of eternal security belief that people are secure without reference to their conduct.

A. Special Duty of Groups, vv. 1-10

1. Aged men, v. 2. They are to be *sober*, meaning literally not given to wine. Beyond this, it means to have a proper sense of values, knowing what is of true merit and what is destructive in the long run though it may yield temporary gratification. They are to be *serious*, meaning that they are to live in the light of God's judgment and of eternity. This does not preclude laughter, but it does include trifling with time and eternal values. They are to be *temperate*, which means self-controlled, having every part of life under the rule of a mind which is sound and wise. The whole of life is to be Christian, always and forever.

   Aged men are to be sound or healthy in faith, love, and patience. While the physical man may wither and age, the spirit of man should gain in strength and dimension. There is no excuse for an old man to become soft and critical or bitter and unbelieving. God will put a person in situations which will strengthen faith, love and patience. If he endures them, he will grow stronger. The Bible says, "Blessed is the man whose strength is in thee. . . . They go from strength to strength . . ." (Ps. 84:5, 7). The years should temper the metal of a man so that he can endure joyfully whatever the Lord permits to come. Paul showed this kind of radiance in his letter to the Philippians. "I can do all things," he said.

2. Aged women, vv. 3, 4. As has been pointed out in the earlier epistles, the Gospel of Christ placed high value upon womanhood. How blessed has been the place of older women in the Church compared with what it has been outside the circle of Christianity! They have several specific duties, which are summed up in the general exhortation to "become holiness." Generally, the men are the teachers and preachers. But nobody has greater responsibility than the women to display holiness in such a way that it is beautiful. Paul emphasized this fact in I Timothy, as did Peter in his first epistle.

   They are not to be false accusers. Women are often in position to spread gossip if they have an appetite for it. Such trait is forbidden to the Christian. This delight to tell something to damage another is a subtle trait that springs from pride and selfishness. There seems to be morbid satisfaction in hurting somebody else. May God deliver our churches from such a poison!

The women are to teach good things to the young. Instead of spreading gossip, they are to spread the grace of goodness through their life and counsel. We should always respect the years of experience which older Christians have and draw upon such wealth. They are naturally equipped with experience to enable them to teach.

3. Young women, vv. 4, 5

   a. The background conditions. In those days there was no place for women in society except within the home or in sinful practices. There was almost no employment for women except in prostitution, so the instruction here is quite circumscribed the conditions of the times.

   b. The permanent injunction. Women have an indispensable role to play, and always will have, as homemakers. Nobody else can properly substitute for mothers in the home where young lives are being molded and characters being shaped for eternity.

   The young women are to show love and obedience toward their husbands. Obedience is the duty and love is the grace that turns the duty into delight. It should be noted here that love should ennoble and strengthen all the relations within the home. Without love there cannot be a true home at all, whatever other bases there may be for the relationships.

   Chaste means pure in heart and action. Goodness is the positive presence of virtue in every area of life. The wife should be self-controlled so that every part of life is exemplary of Christ. If she is not, the Word of God may be blasphemed or spoken against. The home is a place where Christianity must be applied if it is genuine. Many children have been won to Christ because the home has been truly Christian, while many have been embittered because the example was poor.

4. Young men, v. 6. Only one word is said of them, but is is a very important word. To be *temperate* or *sober-minded* means to have all things in life under control. This is especially important in youth when the passions tend to be strong and ambitions excited. Temptations are often directed most strongly at youth, and there is often a recklessness due to lack of experience. Consequently, it is vital to have all things under control of high Christian principle.

5. Titus himself, vv. 7, 8. Titus was a young man, so it was natural to apply the truth to him at this point. He was to be a pattern to others, meaning that there was to be a form of religion in him which others could follow. The power of example is great. Some are inclined to follow the poorest examples, but they should have a good example to follow.

   a. He was to be without corruptness in doctrine. The word means *purity* and is thought by some to pertain to *motive* and by others to pertain to the *content* of his message. Both are surely important. There are unfortunately those who have sound doctrine but impure motives. There are others who have pure motives but whose doctrine is erroneous. God's man must have both. He cannot seek to promote his own personal interests, to make money his goal, or to fight for personal status. He is to be a servant to the truth, to God, and to the people.

   b. *Gravity* refers to the need for commanding respect by his life. He must do nothing to bring reproach on himself, upon his message, or upon the faith of Christ.

   c. A sound message is a healthful message. If the truth is taught with the anointing of God, people will grow to Christlikeness because of it. If, however, the minister is promoting his own selfish interests, fighting some opposition to himself, contending for some minor interpretation, or following religious fads, he will not produce growth or spiritual health. His members will be infected as if he were spreading a disease.

   d. In all these things he is to be such a high example that those who might disagree with him will still see that he is Christlike and genuine. What a noble ideal for a preacher!

   Arminius was a man of this sort. His critics, the Calvinists, imprisoned their opponents because they had gained political power. Arminius had such a grasp of Scripture and such strong character that he could set at nought all his opponents. We need such advocates of the truth today.

6. Servants, vv. 9, 10. They were to be good examples of Christianity if they had unbelieving masters and were not to take advantage of their masters in any way. *Purloining* is taking

things away from their masters. The Christian must set an example of honesty in every detail.

The workman also has the duty of *adorning the doctrine* with his life. This means that practical conduct is essential to make doctrine meaningful. Doctrine that does not produce changed and holy character is vain.

B. The Transformation of Grace, 2:11-14

Duties have been given in considerable detail. Now the power which can bring this kind of change and sustain holy character is vividly set forth. No man can do this in his own power, but there is mighty power in the grace of God to change men and keep them changed. There are two great powers involved here.

1. The teaching of grace, vv. 11, 12. Grace has appeared to all men, or, grace hath appeared that brings salvation to all men. Both are possible interpretations, and both are true. There is no election to damnation. God has intended that all men have the offer of salvation, and it is His desire that all be saved.

    This grace brings truth first. It teaches men. The light of God's revelation shines into the darkness of sin. It shows us duties which have already been set forth but are reviewed here.

    a. Negatively, we are to give up all ungodliness and worldly lusts. All wrong attitudes toward God and wrong conduct before Him must be repudiated. All wrong desires toward the world are also to be given up. Such lusts are reviewed in I John 2:15. They include not only the baser lusts of the flesh but also the desires for wealth, pleasure and honor, such as are not in keeping with a primary interest in spiritual and eternal values.

    b. Positively, we are to live soberly, righteously and godly in this present world. *Soberly* refers to self; *justice* to others; and *godly* to God. It is a summary of our duties in three directions. We are to be true to ourselves, true to the people among whom we live, and true to God Who is supreme over all.

        This is to be done in *this present world*. There is always a tension between this world's standards and God's standards. Most men live by this world's standards, but we can not be conformed to this world if we would be true to ourselves, to others, and to God. Christianity is to be truly lived here and now! The Christian must not let the world pull him down to its level. He is to wield a purifying influence to pull men up to a higher level.

2. The empowering gift of grace, vv. 13, 14. There is not only revelation of truth to show us duty, but there is also the revelation of Christ Who gives power for moral transformation. Look at the powers available in Him.

   a. Redemption from all iniquity. As William Barclay says, "He rescues us from the power which makes us sin." (*Letters to Timothy, Titus and Philemon*, p. 294.) Redemption means the paying of a ransom price to liberate a slave from his bondage. Sin is the bondage in which men are held, and it is the purpose of this wondrous redemption price to liberate men from all iniquity, not just from part or most of it. It is inconceivable that the Great God should make such a wondrous plan and then design to leave men in sin. No, His plan is to free men from sin entirely!

   b. Purifying a special people unto Himself. Freeing from guilt is followed by cleansing from all inward sin so that the redeemed soul is pure in His sight. Such a wonderful transformation is given in a beautiful figure of the captive bride in Deut. 21:10-13. The word *peculiar* here means special or precious. God sees as very special the people who have been redeemed and purified by the blood of Christ.

   c. Zeal for good works. The presence of the Holy Spirit and the constraining power of Christ's love give such zeal, which is the design of God for His people. It is not possible for a person to have the fulness of the Spirit and God's love without their being zealous for good works. If there is no zeal, the fulness of love is surely lacking. We are not saved by good works, but we are saved in order to bring forth good works.

   d. The blessed hope of Christ's coming. In this present world there will be opposition and suffering, but we have a wonderful hope that serves to steady us in the way. Christ is here shown to be the great God, and His appearing will be as glorious as His station deserves. May we truly hope for that day and labor with its glory in view.

C. Speak and Rebuke and Exhort

Timothy was exhorted to teach these things faithfully. To *speak* means to proclaim or declare a message. It is not a matter of debate or speculation, but these things are given truths.

To *exhort* is to encourage men. This message has negatives, but there is also encouragement as Paul has shown immediately before this.

There is to be *rebuke* also, with all authority. Men must see their errors and sin and must feel the horror of it if they are to appreciate the love and forgiveness of God. Titus is so to teach and live the truth that men will respect him for it.

IV. Order of the Church Before the World, 3:1-11, 14

Through this letter runs the thought of our responsibility to live as becometh the doctrine we represent. Every Christian is an advertisement for Christ, and every Christian will be good or bad advertising. Note 1:9 (responsibility of the bishop); 2:5 (responsibility of the wives before their husbands); 2:8 (responsibility of Titus); 2:10 (responsibility of servants); and 2:3 (responsibility of elder women). In 3:2 the responsibility of the entire church is shown to display all meekness to all men.

A. The Duty Specified, 3:1, 2, 8, 14

1. To rulers, v. 1. The Christian is to be a law-abiding person. He must recognize that God has ordained rulers to order social life. If men are to live together in society, there must be laws which limit our individual freedoms in the interest of social harmony. Such law is ordained of God, and the Christian should be a good example in honoring the laws and obeying them. He should respect men in office of authority, knowing that their power is ordained of God. They may be not be Christian, but the office must be respected anyway.

2. To men in general, vv. 1, 2, 8, 14. We are a part of mankind in general, and we thus must show forth our Christian life toward all men with whom we come in contact.

    a. Readiness to every good work. Christianity shows itself in the character of its people, and this in turn is shown by the conduct of its people. The child of God should be always ready to do good works, especially such as show forth the life and love of Christ. In a secular job, the believer will be honest, dependable, faithful and diligent. Aside from regular employment, he will be looking for ways to help others in the name of Christ. This is how the news of salvation spreads. There can never be boredom where people are looking for ways to help others rather than ways to entertain and gratify themselves.

    b. To speak evil of no man. The meaning is not simply that we should not lie or slander a person but that we should not say things about a person, even though he may be guilty, which will injure him. Our motive must always be to help him and not hurt him. Therefore, we can not casually report the faults and misdeeds of a person just to be gossiping about him. Such is a very common error, even among professed Christians, but it is strictly forbidden in the Word. We must be careful to speak of others as faithfully as we would want them to speak of us. John Wesley says that if we relate to another the fault of a third person who is absent, it is evil speaking, and that there is no excuse for such speaking unless it be to protect the second person from some anticipated injury by the third.

    c. To be no brawler. This means that while he will stand up for the truth, he is not aggressive to insist on his own opinions. He is ready to listen to the words of other good man and give them the same right to their opinions as he desires for his. He does not demean or seek to exclude or hurt those who oppose his ideas. There is no resentment or desire to fight back.

    d. To be gentle and meek. He will show kindness to all men: the rich and poor, the neighbor and the foreigner, the educated and uneducated. He does not follow narrow prejudices or bigotry. He represents the grace of Christ to all men.

        He is gentle, having his tempers under complete control. Some men let their prejudices and passions control them, but with the child of God it is otherwise. The inward Spirit of Christ keeps all things regulated for good. How beautiful is such a life!

B. The Reason for the Duty, vv. 3-7

    1. What we once were—a part of this lost world. We have here a most graphic picture of what we once were and what men of the world still are: foolish and disobedient but deceived into

thinking that they are all right and having a good time. They follow the lusts that lead to death as if they were delightful in their fulfillment. There once were hateful and ugly attitudes in us, but we despised others rather than ourselves. How tragic is the estate of such people who are lost but do not know it, who are hateful themselves but hate the light that would show them a better way.

Inasmuch as we have been saved from this world and the death due to us, we are the ones to seek the salvation of those who are still left in the world. This is the consistent message of the New Testament. We are to be witnesses to others in the name of Jesus. "Freely ye have received; freely give," said Jesus. We are saved to tell others of the grace that saved us! Surely this is one of the good works that we owe to others.

2. The nature of salvation, vv. 4-7

    a. From the moving love and kindness of God. Judgment is due us from the holiness of God, but there is also kindness in Him. He delights to withhold justice and give mercy. He wants to show His mercy to sinners of all kinds. This is why He delays His judgments. See II Pet. 3:9. His love here is "philanthropia," a word much used among the Greeks to express the relation of man to man as equals. But God expressed His love from the perfect to the imperfect, from the highest to the lowest, and from the lovely to the unlovely.

    b. A free and bountiful renewing. We were washed with the washing of regeneration. This is the true washing, of which baptism is the outward symbol. The true washing is inward, from guilt and pollution of sins committed.

    There is the renewing of the Spirit. He gives us new life, new desires, new hopes, a new name, and a new character. "All things are become new," says Paul (II Cor. 5:17). This wonderful grace has been given to us in abundance. God loves to be prodigal in His gifts to His creatures who look to Him to receive them! There is no penury or miserliness with Him.

    c. Not by our works. Paul has much to say about good works in this epistle, and especially in this chapter. He makes it plain that we are not saved by our works. If we could be saved by our works, we might then not consider ourselves debtors; we could pride ourselves on our own righteousness. As it is, salvation is all of grace, and we are total debtors for our salvation. How can we meet this debt? God's chosen way is for us to take the same message of salvation to others. We cannot save ourselves by our own works, but we can help save others by such good works, and this is the proper way for us to return our gratitude to God. We can never fully pay our debt, and God does not expect us to, but we owe it to others to work for their good in Jesus' name. Paul said, "I am debtor both to the Greeks, and to the Barbarians; both to the wise and to the unwise" (Rom. 1:14).

    d. There is a wonderful hope before us. We are to receive an inheritance in life eternal. Having come from poverty to such riches, we must have a love that shares with others. Let this be no mere word or formality; let us share it with others truly! So shall we help to pay our debt of love to God Who justified us freely by His grace.

The truth that we are to maintain good works is to be affirmed constantly, Paul says. Let us never forget the duty!

C. The Error That is Unprofitable, vv. 9-11

In verse 8 Paul has spoken of the necessity to "maintain" good works. "Maintain" is an interesting word, referring to the practice of a shopkeeper who stood in front of his shop crying his goods and selling them to passersby. So the Christian is to advertise the way of salvation by his good conduct. He is putting Christ on display.

In contrast, Paul refers to those whose religion is one of talk but which is unprofitable. Good works are profitable, he says, but the talk of the false teachers is unprofitable and vain. There is a kind of speculation about theology that satisfies the mind but does not energize one to good works. Unless our discussion of theology results in better living, it is in vain. There are some who are always fighting theological battles, but they fall short in showing forth the love and goodness of God.

The heretic is to be rejected. The term "heretic" originally meant *one who chooses*. Then it came to mean those who chose the same doctrine and became a sect. Later still it meant those who chose a false doctrine or error. Paul uses it here for those who contend for their own error against the opinions of all others. Those who argue for their own opinions against the truth and against the loving, prayerful counsel of others are truly heretics. Such are to be warned not only once but twice in the sincere hope that they can be saved from error. If they refuse counsel still, they are to be rejected. That is, it is to be made manifest that they are in error and that they have no place as proper Christians, much less leaders. Such people are perverted and condemned. Their own actions and lives condemn them. They do not reproduce the Spirit of Christ but are rather narrow, bigoted, and self-willed. They pursue selfish ambition rather than the honor of Christ and the good of the Church.

V. Conclusion, vv. 12, 13, 15

A. Personal Instructions

Paul was evidently at liberty when he wrote this epistle. Adam Clarke believes he had left Rome and sailed by Crete, where he left Titus. Then he went into Macedonia, where he wrote I Timothy. Journeying westward, he came near Nicopolis on the west coast of Achaia where he intended to spend the winter. From that vicinity he wrote this epistle, which is similar in content to I Timothy. The same errors are much in his mind.

We do not know Artemas or Zenas at all, as they do not appear elsewhere. Artemas and Tychicus were evidently to go to Crete, and probably take the place of Titus when he left to meet Paul.

Zenas and Apollos were to leave Crete and go elsewhere. The Cretans were to supply their needs for travel and food in keeping with new Testament custom. This was part of the good works to which the people were exhorted.

B. The Close

Paul closes as usual with personal greetings and the prayer for God's grace to rest upon those to whom he wrote.

Review Questions
TITUS

1. What facts do we know about the man Titus?
2. Why did Paul leave Titus at Crete?
3. What are the three kinds of election?
4. What qualifications of an elder given in Titus are slightly different than the ones listed in I Timothy?
5. What two special uses of the Word are given?
6. What does Paul mean when he says that the mouths of the false teachers must be stopped?
7. How does Paul advise Titus to meet the error of the false teachers?
8. What are some special duties of "aged men"?
9. How does the general exhortation to "become holiness" sum up the specific duties of "aged women"?
10. How is the instruction to "young women" circumscribed by the times in which Paul was writing?
11. Why is Paul's one exhortation to "young men" so vital?
12. What two great powers bring about the transformation and empowering necessary to live up to these standards?
13. What are the distinctions between *speak* and *rebuke* and *exhort*?
14. Why is the Christian to be a law-abiding person?
15. Our Christian life should be apparent to men in general. In what ways can this be accomplished?

The First Epistle to
PHILEMON

Introduction

I. Author
Paul is the undisputed author. Philemon is a short letter, but one of great charm and value.

II. Time of Writing
This appears to have been written near the same time as the epistle to the Colossians. Greetings are sent from Aristarchus, Demas, Luke, and Epaphras in both epistles. Philemon was evidently written shortly before his release from his first imprisonment, which makes it about 62 A.D.

III. The Reason for the Letter

A. The return of Onesimus, the slave, as the letter clearly shows.

B. It is possible, though not certain, that this is the letter to Laodicea to which reference is made in Col. 4:16. The reasons for this belief are as follows.

1. Archippus is mentioned in both letters, Col. 4:17 and Phile. 2. In the former place it is commonly believed that he was the minister at Laodicea, since the church there is mentioned in the verses immediately preceding. If this is true, it is probable that Archippus lived in Laodicea.

2. In Phile. 1, 2 it appears that Archippus is the son of Philemon. Philemon evidently lived in Laodicea when the letter was written to him. If this is true, the epistle to Philemon was directed to Laodicea.

3. The letter is written to the church in his house as well as to him, so this could well be the epistle to Laodicea.

4. The point is strengthened by a statement in v. 12 which should probably read, "I am referring the case to you." This would mean that Paul wanted the entire church to know of this case in order to assure that a proper Christian disposition was made. Paul would not want the disposition left to one man's decision.

5. We should note that this position is speculative, but it illustrates the kind of interesting research and conclusions which are possible in detailed Bible study.

IV. Justification for Inclusion in the Biblical Canon

From the earliest collection of sacred writings, Philemon has been considered worthy of a place with almost no objection by critics who questioned many other parts of the New Testament. The reason for this is not only that it was written by Paul but also that it is a letter of great beauty, grace, and courtesy in handling a real problem—a display of Christian principles in operation. It is an excellent example of good psychology, sincere affection, effective logic, and human persuasion.

V. The Recipient of the Letter

A. His Home

It is not sure where Philemon lived. As has been said earlier, there is some possibility that he lived in Laodicea. However, it is said in Col. 4:9 that Onesimus was one of them, which would seem to indicate that Philemon also lived in Colosse. However, Laodicea and Colosse were very close together and might well be considered parts of the same community so far as Christian fellowship was concerned. The letter to Colosse indicates that the two groups had much in common.

B. His Position

Philemon had a church in his house. From this and the fact that he had Onesimus as his servant, it has been assumed that he was a man of some means. This is not certain, however. He performed well-known acts of charity, but this may have been possible without any great means (see v. 7). He was evidently converted under the ministry of Paul, although where this occurred is not known (v. 19). It is likely that it occurred at Colosse, although some have thought it was at Ephesus. Paul hopes to be able to come and stay at his house, which may have been rather spacious.

The Study of the Epistle to Philemon

I. Paul's Introduction

A. Paul's Informal Style

Paul calls himself a prisoner of Christ. He almost always introduces himself as an apostle, but in this case he is not appealing to his authority; instead, he is appealing as a humble individual to the sense of fairness and love in his recipient. There is to be no coercion here. While duty is involved on Paul's part, the action on Philemon's part is to be entirely voluntary.

B. The Family of Philemon

1. Philemon is called a fellow-laborer. Some have thought from this that he was a minister or at least an officer in the church. However, the term is also used of any person who works in the cause of the Gospel. See Rom. 16:3 for example.

2. Apphia, a feminine name, is probably Philemon's wife.

3. Archippus is probably the son of Philemon and Apphia. He was a fellow-soldier, doubtless a minister in the church. As has already been stated, Philemon has commonly been connected with the Church at Laodicea, although it may be that he labored at Colosse.

   Philemon is called a fellow-soldier, which figure likens the minister to a soldier in God's army. There are some obvious comparisons: both are engaged in conflict; both require discipline; and both are under the absolute authority of another. Paul may have been reminded of the soldier's duty by the fact that he himself was bound to a soldier by a chain while he was writing.

4. The church in the house may have been composed simply of the household, or it may have been larger by including other residents of the city. The latter was quite common. In this case, the letter must have been meant to include them also.

II. The Story of Onesimus

A. The Runaway Servant, vv. 10-16

Many have thought that Onesimus was a bond slave. This is quite possible but not certain. There were servants who were pledged to work for pay, either of their own choice or at the choice of their parents. Onesimus may have been one of this kind of servants. At any rate, he had left his master under conditions that were not right.

Apparently, Onesimus had wronged his master in his leaving (vv. 11, 18). The name "Onesimus" means "useful" or "profitable." Paul plays on the name and states that Onesimus had been an unprofitable servant. It is also suggested that he had wronged his master. What the conditions were, we do not know. It is possible he may have stolen from his master before he ran away, or he may have been entrusted with funds which he misappropriated.

He had gone to Rome, the big city, where he could easily lose himself amidst the throngs of people.

B. A Convert Returned, vv. 12-21

How Onesimus found Paul in Rome we do not know. It is likely that he knew Paul before from Paul's contacts with that family. It is also likely that he knew of the Roman imprisonment of the apostle. It may be that while in Rome the runaway was disillusioned with his new freedom and needed help. Knowing Paul was there, Onesimus may have looked him up for help. In such case, we know Paul would have endeavored to lead him to Christ and salvation. In this he succeeded; the servant was saved.

Perhaps Onesimus freely confessed all of his misdeeds and obligations. On the other hand, it may be that either Paul or Epaphras recognized Onesimus and therefore the story came out. At any rate, there was a full acknowledgement of the story of the wrong that had been done.

Paul would like to have kept Onesimus as his own servant; he needed messengers and writers. But the sense of obligation to the former master made it imperative that Onesimus be returned to face his past record and make necessary adjustments.

In those days slaves (if he were truly a slave) had no rights of self-defense. A runaway could be put to death without trial. He was considered merely a tool in the hand of his master with no more rights than a donkey or an ox. Thus, there was the possibility that Onesimus would be put to death on the spot when he arrived at his master's house. It was with this thought in mind that Paul wrote the letter with its tender appeal and sent it by Onesimus to Philemon.

C. A Bishop in Ephesus

1. The possibility of Onesimus' return to Paul, vv. 13, 14, 21. It appears that Paul would like to have had Onesimus returned and that he had confidence Onesimus would, in fact, be returned. With the kind of appeal made it seems a definite possibility. If so, Onesimus would have been trained in the gospel and perhaps have taken some place of responsibility in the church in later years.

2. Fifty years later the Christian martyr Ignatius wrote a letter to Ephesus and made reference to the bishop there named Onesimus. He also referred to the meaning of the name—how Onesimus was useful and profitable to the cause of Christ. It is not certain, but possible, that this is the same Onesimus as Paul wrote about If so, it may explain how this little letter got into the Biblical canon. It is quite certain that the early canon was first collected at Ephesus. If Onesimus was there, he may have brought forth the personal letter and had it included in the collection of sacred writings.

Much of this is speculation and should be taken for just that. It is interesting, though, to endeavor to fill in the blanks of the Bible story.

III. The Study of the Letter

There are some valuable lessons to be learned from this letter that are very applicable today.

A. Communication and Increase, vv. 4-7

1. The two-directional expression of spiritual life, v. 5. Paul had heard of Philemon's faith and love. It is love toward the saints and faith toward God. (The arrangement of the words is known as "chiasmus" or cross-reference.) In v. 6 it is shown that his faith toward God found expression in his love toward the saints.

Christianity always has this two-directional application. The Bible often insists that neither one is real or effective without the other. For example, see John 21:15-17 ("Feed my sheep"); James 2:15-20 ("Faith without works is dead"); I John 3:16-18.

2. Communication brings knowledge, v. 6. There are several possible meanings to the word "communication." It may mean receiving a share, giving a share, or just fellowship. The word "knowledge" can also mean recognition by others or increase in knowledge ourselves. Several commentators believe the meaning to be that as we share with others of our love and faith, our knowledge increases and others will be able to recognize the increase. Whether or not this is the intention of Paul, it is a profound truth. If we want love to increase in us, we must express our love to others. If faith is to increase, it must be expressed. It is seen, therefore, that love and faith do not increase as academic products but as moral products. Knowledge increases by expression. People who have little chance for schooling may nevertheless develop large knowledge of God and His grace because they are effective channels. May this process work in every one of us!

   Philemon had found this joy, and Paul prays for it to continue.

   Two words in the text are worthy of special note. The word "effectual" (energetic, powerful in exercise) refers in the New Testament to superhuman power, either good or evil. In Philemon's case it was a divine power working in him and through him for good. He was a channel of God's power.

   The second word is "epignosis," an intensive word meaning "full" or "perfect knowledge." It is a word Paul frequently uses for spiritual knowledge from God rather than just academic learning. The sense then is that as we allow the supernatural flow of God's grace and love to go through us, we receive supernatural increase of knowledge and revelation in return.

B. The Christian Emphasis on Duty, vv. 12-14

1. Binding in obligation, vv. 13, 14. Paul would very much like to have retained Onesimus. He is now a true Christian and a helpful person whom Paul could have trained in the faith. But over and against this strong desire and need stands Christian duty, and it easily prevails over every other consideration. Paul would do what is right, no matter what other considerations entered the case! His own comfort and personal desire counted for nothing when duty was clear!

   It is obvious that not only Paul's duty but Onesimus' as well is involved. It would be risky for Onesimus to return to

Philemon, since death was a possibility. However, there was a restitution to make. The master had been wronged, and regardless of how wrong the institution of slavery may have been, duty required that the man face the person he had wronged and make the necessary adjustment. It is plain that Onesimus was poor, and so Paul signs a personal pledge to assist this new Christian in meeting whatever claim was against him. What an example of love and kindness! What an example also of faithfulness to the claims of Christian duty!

2. Gracious in application, v. 21. Duty is not rigidly applied but rather infused with a spirit of grace and love. Note in v. 21 how Paul approaches Philemon with faith and full confidence. So much more can be achieved by expressing confidence in our learners than by approaching them with mistrust, accusation or rebuke, even before they have had a chance to feel love. The Pharisees failed at this point. They were always looking with a hard, critical spirit at those who might violate one of the little details of law. They paid tithes of mint and anise and cummin but forgot the weightier matters of the law, judgment, mercy and faith (Matt 23:23). Jesus showed them their error and entreated them to correct it, but they refused. Duty must be penetrated with love and grace to be true to Christ.

This letter is a good study in the proper approach to others in securing their approval of our requests. Paul did not make a demand but a request. It was made not from a position of authority but from a place of lowliness. It was made not with a spirit of doubt or accusation but in fully expressed confidence in the other person. It was made not selfishly but with a magnanimous offer to pay the servant's obligation. We can easily believe that the request was gladly granted and that the servant was fully forgiven.

C. Divine Providence, v. 15

Paul believed that God's providence runs through all events that affect the believer. He can see the possibility that God's purpose is working in all of these events relative to Onesimus in order to make him a better man and a better servant.

At the same time, Paul is not dogmatic; he uses the word "perhaps." There are some things about God's plans that we do not need to see clearly in advance. We may have confidence that God is working, but not until afterward (and maybe a long time afterward) do we see the end which God had in view. God's ways are higher than ours, and He works slowly at times. He does not have to tell us all of His ways, but we trust Him to work in all situations which affect us (Rom. 8:28).

D. The Changing Power of Grace, vv. 11-17

1. A change of character, vv. 11-14. The man Onesimus was an unprofitable man, dishonest, untrustworthy, sinful and lost. But he has been changed until his name is appropriate. He is now a useful man. He has formerly ministered in physical duties; now he is capable of ministering to Paul in the bonds of the Gospel. He has been merely a servant; now he is a brother beloved. The servant had definitely been converted (v. 10), and the change in his life showed in his character. Away with any kind of religious profession that does not produce such a change; it is false and dangerous! Grace does not just change our standing with God, it changes our character and makes us Christlike before men. If any religion does not do so, it is false.

2. A change of relationship, vv. 16, 17. Onesimus had been a servant before, but now he is to be considered as a brother. He may still serve, but by the grace of God he is no longer merely an instrument in the hands of his master.

    Many people have thought that Paul sanctioned the institution of slavery in this letter. Such a conclusion is surely not derived logically from the information we have here. While he did not recommend an uprising against the institution (Paul was no revolutionary in the popular modern sense), he taught new relationships in the bonds of the Gospel which were destined finally to throw off the galling yoke of slavery. When two men see each other as brothers in Christ, neither one will exploit the other or degrade him! This is still the answer to questions of race and class in the world. In Christ, men are brothers.

III. Spiritual Applications from the Epistle

This story is a kind of parable of our spiritual history if we are servants of God. As Martin Luther said, "We are all Onesimi."

A. We Have All Been Runaways From Our True and Rightful Master, Jesus Christ

    We were all rightfully His by right of creation and then by redemption. See Ps. 100:3 and I Cor. 6:19, 20. We have all turned away and gone our own way, as we read in Is. 53:6. Some have been more reckless than others, but all have gone their own way. This is the basic sin of mankind.

This runaway wandering life has left us disappointed, poor, and helpless to escape our misery. The prodigal son is a fitting example of such. Until a person comes to such a recognition of emptiness and meaninglessness, he will not be moved to seek salvation. It may be that a person has wealth, beauty, and pleasures of the flesh, but these will never satisfy the soul of man. They may blind him for awhile to the true need of his heart and to the beauty of the Savior, but they will not meet that need.

B. At the Point of Despair, Help is Available

Paul was ready to help Onesimus when he "came to himself" in Rome. Paul is like the Holy Spirit, who is always identified with our human situation. Jesus Christ is exalted at the throne, but the Spirit is with us "until the end of the age." Yet Jesus and the Spirit are one, working together for the recovery of the lost. Likewise, Paul and Philemon were one. Paul addresses him as a "fellowlaborer." In v. 14 he says, "without thy mind would I do nothing." This is the relation of the Spirit to Christ; He does not speak of Himself, but honors Christ in all things (John 16: 13, 14).

The Spirit through Paul so worked on Onesimus that he was ready and willing, with no external restraint, to return and be reconciled to his master. There was no army sent to keep Onesimus from running away again. His return was voluntary. But it was Paul who prepared for the return by bringing Onesimus to a place of willingness and by his entreaty to Philemon that he receive back the servant as a brother. So also the Spirit is the divine Intercessor. No man can come to the Father unless the Spirit draw him (see John 6:44).

C. There is a Willing Return to the Master

Like the prodigal, the runaway is on his way home. he deserves to die, according to the law and the custom of the day. But he goes with no claims of his own except the letter of Paul and his own readiness to confess and seek a new relationship.

The sinner who has had the Spirit working true penitence within him now humbly goes to Christ in full confession. He seeks forgiveness of the past. He has a claim that another has offered to pay his debt. In this case, it is Jesus Himself who has paid the debt, but it is the Spirit who lays this hope on our heart and encourages us to claim it of the Master.

Not only is there hope of forgiveness but also hope of a new relationship. The servant will not run away in the future. He now enters a new relationship, a service of love. He gladly submits to the ownership and mastery of the same one whom before he dreaded and from whom he fled.

Here is the beauty and gladness of the sanctified life. It is to have Christ not only as Savior but as Lord and Master as well. It is service not of self but of him who forgave and claimed us as His own. Always in future service there will be a penetration of love. The Master is the one who provides best, loves most, and rewards most fully. Service is not a drudgery to be loathed; it is fulfillment to be enjoyed and anticipated forever.

Review Questions
PHILEMON

1. What similarity is there between this epistle and Colossians?
2. What was the occasion of the letter?
3. For what reasons is it thought this may be the letter to Laodicea mentioned in Col. 4:16?
4. What reasons are there for this book being included in the New Testament canon?
5. What was the relation of Onesimus to Philemon?
6. It appears that there were at least three members in Philemon's family. Who were they?
7. What is the meaning of the name "Onesimus?"
8. Trace the story of Philemon as it is given us.
9. Where was Onesimus converted?
10. For what reason was Onesimus being returned to Philemon?
12. For what reason did Paul want Onesimus to return?
13. What punishment might Onesimus have received from Philemon?
14. What do we learn about Philemon's Christian character?
15. What kind of approach does Paul make in his requests to Philemon?
16. How does Paul seek to save Onesimus from any severe punishment?
17. In what way does Paul express the change in Onesimus' character since he has been converted to Christ?
18. What men were with Paul in prison at this time?
19. What spiritual applications can be made from this little epistle?
20. How have we all been like Onesimus?

The Epistle to the
HEBREWS

Introduction

I. The Author
This is a much-debated subject, and there is no settled answer. Even the early church debated the subject, with indecision.

A. It appears that Paul was not the author.
   The style is different from his in many places. Also, in 2:3 it is strongly suggested that the writer was not an apostle.

B. It may be that Apollos wrote it.
   The description of Apollos in Acts 18:24 fits with this style of writing. In Alexandria they used allegory, which is employed in Hebrews. It is a book "mighty in the Scriptures," frequently applying Old Testament Scriptures. In fact, it is almost a commentary on Leviticus.

C. It may be that Luke or another wrote it for Paul.

II. The Time of Writing.
Heb. 10:34 speaks of the "spoiling of their goods." This seems to refer to the persecution under Ananias the high priest in A.D. 63. However, it seems the temple sacrifices were still being offered (8:4; 10:1,11).

The sacrifices ended in July, A.D. 70, and the fall of Jerusalem came in August of the same year. The best date for this writing seems A.D. 66, or close to that.

III. Recipients of the Letter
It appears clearly to have been written to Christian Jews. Probably they were Jews in Palestine, who were under great pressure to go back to Judaism.

IV. Background

The Jews were under severe persecution. They had been banned from temple sacrifices under Ananias and the Sadducees, as well as having their goods confiscated. Cut off from the familiar ceremonies, they were derided as having an inferior religion, with no altar, no sacrifices, no incense or priests with beautiful vestments, and no temple. Under such persecution, many of the Christians were near to fainting and going back. Some were remaining in spiritual childhood; others were slothful. They needed to see that in Christ they had the fulfillment of what all of the ceremonies were only types. They needed encouragement to go on with Christ.

V. Purpose

To fortify the Hebrew Christians against the temptation to go back into Judaism.

VI. Some Key Words

There are a number of important expressions in the epistle, which are repeated frequently. The students should study them carefully to find their meaning and application. We mention only a few of them here.

A. *Better*

This we have chosen to use as the basis of our outline of the Epistle. It is used 13 times. The Christian dispensation is better than the Jewish dispensation.

B. *Lest*

This word is used in warning against something and is used 7 times.

1. Heb. 2:1, a warning against drifting.
2. Heb. 3:12, a warning against unbelief and apostasy.
3. Heb. 3:13, a warning against the deceitfulness of sin.
4. Heb. 4:1, a warning against coming short of God's rest.
5. Heb. 12:15, a warning against failing of the grace of God.
6. Heb. 12:15, a warning against the root of bitterness.
7. Heb. 12:16, a warning against profanity.

C. *Let Us*

This is a word of encouragement, whereas the former was one of warning. We need both.

1. Encouragements in our relationship to Christ, the Son: 4:1; 4:11; 4:14; 4:16; 6:1.
2. Encouragements as to our saintship: 10:22; 10:23; 10:24.
3. Encouragements in our service: 12:1; 12:28; 13:13; 13:15.

D. *Partakers*

There is a strong emphasis on fellowship in the epistle, and this key word is related. 2:14; 3:1; 3:14; 6:4; 10:33; 12:8; 12:10.

E. *We Have*

The enemies stressed the absence of altars and other visible elements of religion. The writer stresses what we do have that is better. See 4:14; 8:1; 10:21; 6:18; 6:19; 10:34; 13:10.

F. Note such other words as *Perfect* (perfection), *Blood, Covenant, Testament, Hold Fast, Sacrifice, Great* (greater), *Heavens* (heavenly); *Without, Eternal.*

The Study of the Epistle to the Hebrews

I. The Superiority of Christianity, 1:1-10

This is the doctrinal portion of the epistle, and is followed by a practical portion. There is an intermingling, with practical exhortations in the first part, and some doctrinal emphasis in the second part, but this gives the general emphasis.

A. The Better Revelation, 1-3

The book starts with grandeur and boldness, somewhat like Genesis and I John. It makes two assumptions: the existence of God, and the fact that He reveals Himself to mankind.

1. The earlier revelation, by the prophets

    a. It was given in fragments "sundry times." This refers not to the ages involved, but to the portions or fragments into which the revelation was broken. There was never a time under the prophets when there was a full revelation of God. Partial views were received and communicated by the different prophets. They did not fully understand the revelation they were giving, because it was not complete (I Pet. 1:10-12).

    It was somewhat like putting together a jigsaw puzzle. Each part is vital, but we can put many pieces into their places without a good idea of the picture we are making. God had been speaking for 4000 years and more, but the full revelation was still concealed.

    b. It was given in "divers manners." There were visions, dreams, promises, types and symbols, human examples, predictions, hymns, messages delivered, history written. All of them pointed toward the reality of Christ, but could not fully reveal Him or the Father.

2. The later revelation, by the Son

    a. It is the consummation of time— "these last days." Jesus brought the final dispensation. He will be replaced by no higher revelation. He is the fullness of divine revelation. In the last day of revelation, it will be the very same Christ who shall be revealed. Paul called it the "fullness of time" (Gal. 4:4).

b. He is the Son of God. The prophets were human; He is divine. They were fallible; He is infallible; they were servants; He is a Son. The writer gives seven eloquent, glorious facts about the superiority of Christ. May we appreciate them!

1) He is appointed heir of all things. God has many sons, but this one is so superior to all others (angels and men) that the entire inheritance is given to Him. In Bible times the eldest son got a double portion of the share in the inheritance, but Jesus gets all of it. The only way the others sons can share in the inheritance is to share in Christ Himself; and God has made this possible. See Rom. 8:17; John 16:15.

Christ's heirship must be revealed to us. His poverty when on earth did not suggest to those who saw Him that He owned all things. His Person and possessions are revealed by the Spirit.

2) By Him God made the worlds. The word "worlds" here includes not only material things but the ages of time as well. Time, space, and matter are of His creation. There could not be one speck of dust without Him.

3) He is the brightness of God's glory. He is equal with the Father in His divinity, though He descended to the level of humble humanity to redeem us. The nature of heaven is bright glory; it was seen in Christ on the Mt. of Transfiguration. He laid it aside to come to earth.

4) He is the express image of God's person. The word "express image" really means "character." All that God is in His moral nature is revealed in Christ; particularly all that God gives of Himself to us is given through Christ.

5) He upholdeth all things by the word of His power. We now know that the elements of this universe are in constant activity, with forces balancing inside the atom, and throughout the universe. For example, the force of gravity is sufficient to require a steel cable 8500 km (5,000 miles) in diameter to replace gravity and hold

the earth on its course. That is more than half as wide as the earth itself. Yet there is no cable at all, not even a spider web—just gravity!

It is the word of Christ that holds the universe together. He is everywhere present, upholding, governing, and energizing His creation.

6) By Himself He purged our sins. When the High Priest went into the most holy place in the temple, he went with the blood of bulls and goats; but Jesus with His own blood, once-for-all, put away our sins— accomplished the means of purification from all sin! His cleansing power is adequate; He alone accomplished it fully! We can thank God for His sufficiency!

7) He sat down at the right hand of the Majesty on high. When God finished the work of creation, He rested. So when Christ finished redemption, He rested. Not a rest from weariness, but of a perfectly finished work. The high priest had no place to sit in the temple; there was no completed work.

The right hand denotes the place of power and authority. The highest place in the universe is the "Majesty on high." There at the right hand—the place of designated authority—is our Savior, having finished the work of our redemption. How exalted He is, in His Person, and in His work!

B. The Better Messenger, 1:4-2:18

1. The importance of angels

   a. They are numerous. Many passages in the Bible express their great numbers. See, for example, Dan. 7:9,10; Heb. 12:22; Rev. 5:11.

   b. They are mighty (II Thes. 1:7-9). They sang at creation, guarded the gate of Eden, smote 185,000 Assyrians at Jerusalem in one night (Is. 37:36), delivered Peter from prison, guarded the tomb of Christ, and will deliver the dead in the great resurrection day.

   The great work of angels, to which the Jews paid most respect, was their mediation in the giving of the law (Acts 7:53). As related in Deut 33:2, there were ten thousands of holy angels accompanying the giving of the "fiery law." See also Gal. 3:19. The Jews felt there could never be any higher revelation than this one on Sinai, with the smoke, fire, shaking mountain, and the myriads of angels. So the Hebrew writer is showing that Christ is far higher as a messenger from God.

    c.   They are holy. See Deut. 33:2; Luke 9:26, for example.

2. The superior importance of Christ. There are seven scriptures quoted, which are used abundantly to prove the point of Christ's superiority.

    a.   He has a more excellent name than the angels, v. 4. This is the key to the passage. He has the name of "The Son of God." Psa. 2:7, II Sam. 7:14. Angels are sometimes called sons, as Christians are. But Christ is The Son, My Son, above all others.

    b.   He is to be worshiped by angels, Psa. 97:7. The greater is to be worshiped by the lesser, so He is greater than angels.

    c.   Angels are specifically called ministers, or servants, Psa. 104:4. This is a wonderful contemplation—the ministry of angels to the saints. (Peter was delivered from prison; Christ was strengthened in temptation; Paul was guarded in a storm at sea; our children have guardian angels, etc.) But Christ is far above the level of a servant.

    d.   Christ is God, the King eternal, Psa. 45:6,7. The righteous throne of God is His throne. So He is absolutely righteous and eternal. He is God. For these reasons, the Psalmist said that Christ was anointed above His fellows. He is above the angels!

    e.   Christ is the Creator of all things. All of creation shall wax old, but He, the Creator, is unaging, unchanging. See Psa. 102:25-27. The angels are created beings, and thus are lower than the Creator.

    f.   All of Christ's enemies shall be put under his feet. This is taken from Psa. 110:1, and is often used in the New Testament to show the deity of Christ, and His superiority to David. See Mt. 22:44; Acts 2:34,35.

    g.   The angels are ministering spirits—our ministers from God. Thus they are lower than Christ.

3. First admonition, 2:1-4. There are seven series of admonitions in this epistle, and this is the first of them. Here are great doctrinal truths, but the writer always had in mind the application of the truth. Note, doctrine is not something just for abstract mental contemplation. It is to produce action and shape character!

This is a mighty passage, and one which each of us should contemplate prayerfully. It has been the basis for mighty messages from God's prophets and preachers.

The argument is that, if those who disobeyed the law given by angels received just punishment, how can we expect to escape if we neglect the salvation spoken by Him who is so much higher than the angels, and was confirmed by signs, wonder, miracles, and gifts of the Spirit.

a. This salvation is great

1) In its scope, to "whosoever will."

2) In its cost, the blood of God's only Son.

3) In its eternal destiny, the shared glory of Christ forever.

4) In its deliverance, from all sin.

5) In its penalty if rejected, Heb. 10:28, 29.

Salvation is an important word in this epistle. See 1:14, 2:3, 2:10; 6:9; 7:25; 9:28.

b. It is possible to drift away from it.

1) We can forget by neglect. The words, "let them slip," mean to "run out" as in a leaky vessel. We gradually forget the impact of the message of salvation, if we do not stir our minds with its importance! Remember this: our human minds are leaky vessels! Don't let vital truth get away from you. Stir up yourself, and help to stir up others.

2) We can drift away from the truth. The words are translated that way also. When we forget the importance of truth, then we soon begin to drift ourselves. This was the great danger of the Hebrew Christians. At all times we must give careful attention to the truth. Never be careless in our regard for it! Eternal destiny depends on it!

Right here let us note the impact of this epistle: it is possible for Christian people to drift away from the truth and be lost. We want to observe how often and strongly the writer warns against this real danger. Still many people today refuse to admit the danger at all.

4. Why He became lower than the angels, 2:5-18. During His earthly life Christ had a position lower than the angels in glory. He was still God, but He was also man, on a genuinely human level. He was subject to death, which the angels are not.

   a. Man was made lower than the angels, 6-8. In this passage we have the fact and results of the fall of man. The terms "man" and the "son of man" refer to fallen man (Enoch and Adam). As one looks at the glory of the heavens he is drawn to think of the littleness of man. Why does God think of him, and visit him? This is the wonder of redemption, that God does visit man. In the working of His Spirit, His providences, and through Christ, He still visits man.

   Originally man was made to have dominion over all the physical creation, as it is clearly indicated in Psalm 8 and Gen. 1:26. This control was intended to be complete, that man by his word and authority should control the beasts, birds, and the earth itself. He was crowned with glory and honor. Glory is the superiority of the spiritual over the physical. Though made of the dust, man was closer to God than to the physical earth. He was crowned with honor, which is his authority over lower orders of beings.

   We see not yet all things subject to him. This is the result of the fall.

   b. "But we see Jesus." He became what man was intended to be, in His holiness, His authority over creation, His earthly glory. That is, He realized the constant presence of the Father, as man was intended to. He could command the fish of the sea, the waves of the sea, and the other elements of nature.

   c. He came to taste death for all men. His death was intended; it was not an accidental tragedy, but the purpose for which He came. Now we find why. We must recognize that "death" is more than physical; it is eternal, spiritual and physical. Christ died physically, and He also "tasted" spiritual and eternal death, so that we would never have to.

He came not only to die, but to destroy him that has the power of death, the devil, and deliver those who are in bondage from fear of death. All men have some fear of death, because of its mystery, and because after death comes the judgment. What an awful enemy death is!

In order to give victory over death, He died and rose again. He gained the keys to death and hell (Rev. 1:18), and now He gives us freedom from fear of these enemies.

d. He brings many sons to glory. Truly He is the first begotten of the Father, but through Him there are now many sons, who can share with Him the benefits of sonship. All things were by Him and for Him, but He has deliberately chosen to share His honors and gifts with us.

It was not sufficient to deliver us from death; we must also be brought to glory. It is well to remember that salvation is not only deliverance from sin and death, but also strength through trials, temptations, and strong oppositions, to His eternal glory, which we may share with Him! The Hebrew Christians had been delivered from sin, but they were about to faint from the arduous journey to glory. They needed to realize that Christ was there as their Leader to share the journey with them.

1) Christ delights to be with His brethren, in the midst of His church (12). Here is a quotation from Psa. 22:22. The next is from Isa. 8:17,18.

2) To be fully identified with them, as a brother and leader, He took their nature fully, including their flesh and blood.

3) We come back to our major argument in v. 16. Though He is better than angels, He became lower than the angels in order to lay hold of, and save, the seed of Abraham. It "behooved Him"—was expedient for Him—to become like mankind in every point. He became fully human, enduring all that we endure, except becoming a sinner. He was tempted in every point—though not in every detail—like we are tempted, that He might give proper help to us when we are tempted.

To summarize, He suffered to make reconciliation for our sins (v. 17), and He suffered to become a perfect captain, or leader, for us (v. 10). Now whatever we may endure on our journey, we can look to Him and know He understands. He has suffered it before us, and He has overcome. With Him we too can overcome. What a glorious encouragement this is!

5. There are seven points of Christ's identification with mankind in Chapter 2.

   a. He descended to man's level, vs. 7,9.

   b. He took man's nature, v. 16.

   c. He endured man's temptations, v. 18.

   d. He died in man's place, v. 14.

   e. He conquered man's foe, v. 14.

   f. He achieved man's victory, vs. 10,15.

   g. He secured man's salvation, v. 17.
   (From Chadwick, *Humanity and God*, p. 65).

C. The Better Leader, 3:1-19

   1. Moses was a very great leader. In fact, he was a type of Christ: in his sufferings, in his separation and rejection by his own brethren, in his zeal and sacrifice for his people, in his willingness to die for his people, and in his intimate fellowship with God.

      He was faithful in all his house. The term 'house' probably means the people of God. He gave the law, and faithfully applied it while he lived. The Jews revered him most highly.

   2. Christ was worthy of more glory, for several reasons.

      a. Moses was in the house, as a member of the family; Christ built the house. God built all things (v. 4). The repetition of this idea in these two ways shows that Christ is God, and that Christ has established the Church of God as well as the nation of Israel.

      b. Moses was a servant. He was a very faithful one, as we are shown in Num. 12:7. Yet he was just a servant (v. 5). His ministry was not ultimate, for He was a type and a witness of things to come.

Christ is a Son, over the house, of which Moses was a part.

3. Second admonition, 3:7-4:1. In v. 6 it is stated that we are the "house of Christ," "if we hold fast the confidence and rejoicing of hope firm unto the end." It is suggested, and reinforced elsewhere, that if we do not hold fast, and keep our hope firmly to the end, we may lose our place in the house. This is strengthened by reference to those under Moses' leadership who failed to enter into rest.

   a. Even under the leadership of one so faithful as Moses, there were those who, because of their evil hearts of unbelief, were rejected and refused entrance into the land of promise and rest.

   We may recall from Numbers 14 how the people refused to enter the land at Kadesh Barnea. Hence God sentenced them to 40 years of wandering in the wilderness until the adults should die. Then the people determined to enter the land, but they were defeated, because God would not lead them after their rebellion. Their unbelief in their hearts grieved God repeatedly. They provoked Him by the hardness and unbelief of their hearts, until He rejected them and let them die in the wilderness.

   b. In exactly the same way, the writer declared, it is possible now for believers to "depart from the living God," by yielding to unbelief. (12). It was the unbelief of some of them that kept them out of the land, while others who believed were able to enter. Hence it is a personal matter of faith, which determines whether or not we shall enter the promise.

   Let us repeat the argument: if under a leader like Moses people were sentenced to die because of their unbelief, it is certain that with a much better leader like Christ, we also may be rejected and lost if we give ourselves to unbelief.

   If we would be partakers of Christ, and His eternal glory, we must hold "the beginning of our confidence stedfast unto the end" (v. 14). A good beginning is not enough, just as a wonderful deliverance through the Red Sea did not suffice to bring them into Canaan.

We should exhort one another, knowing that we can be hardened by the "deceitfulness of sin." Let us not presume, as some do, that just because they were once believers they are eternally secure. The teaching of this epistle is strongly to the contrary. We need to encourage one another to press on and not to fail! The writer was addressing believers, and telling them that they could be hardened through the deceitfulness of sin. They could come short of the promised rest (4:1), and they should seriously fear this possibility!

D. The Better Rest, 4:1-16

This is a very important consideration. There are four different rests spoken of in chapter 4, each showing an advance in thought beyond the preceding one.

1. The creation rest, v. 4. In the physical creation we have an analogy to God's spiritual recreation. There was chaos, darkness and death. But God's Spirit moved on the chaos, bringing, light, order, separation, life and beauty. All was accomplished by the Word of God. God saw that it was good; He was satisfied, for His will was perfectly done. There was nothing in all of the creation that resisted His will. So He rested, for His will was accomplished, and there was no strife.

    This establishes an important principle: there is rest where God's will is fully accomplished without resistance.

    When sin entered, a discordant element entered creation. Nature and the heart of man had discord, strife, and conflict. There could be no rest in such disharmony. Isa. 57:21. The holiness of God does not rest in the presence of sin. The Spirit strives to bring the heart of man into subjection to the will of God (Gen. 6:3).

2. The sabbath rest, vv. 4, 9. The sabbath for man was instituted along with the law, and as a sign of the covenant between God and His people (Ex. 31:13-17). There was a negative aspect, refraining from work. But there was a positive aspect also, declared in Isa. 58:13,14, "If thou turn away thy foot from the Sabbath, from doing thy pleasure on my holy day; and call the Sabbath a delight, and the holy of the Lord, honourable and shalt honor him, not doing thine own ways, nor finding thine own pleasure, nor speaking thine own works: then thou shalt delight thyself in the Lord; and I will make thee to ride upon the high places of the earth; and I will feed thee with the

heritage of Jacob thy father: for the mouth of the Lord hath spoken it." It may be noticed here that the requirement includes a heart condition purified from selfishness, and filled with the love of God. As J.G. Mantle has said, "There can be no Sabbath where two wills are struggling, for God cannot rest save where His will is done. When one life rules man—his own self-will having been hated, renounced and crucified—the true Sabbath begins . . . ." Then he can delight himself in God, and God is satisfied with him, as He was with His first creation.

3. The Canaan rest, v. 8. It was a wonderful rest that was promised. Deut. 7, for example, shows it.

At Kadesh Barnea, they refused because of their unbelief. They even spoke of stoning Caleb and Joshua. Hence for forty years they were left to wander and die in the wilderness.

Even after they entered the land under Joshua, they did not fully appropriate the promises of God, but allowed some of the enemy to remain, who became snares to them, as God had warned. Eventually Israel was taken to Babylon because of the snare of the enemies which they allowed to remain. This illustrates the danger of allowing sinful traits to remain in the heart. There is to be total destruction of sin in the heart! There can be no true spiritual rest until this happens.

4. Divine rest, vs. 1, 3, 10, 11

   a. This is a better rest than the others.

      1) Jesus is a more capable leader than Joshua was, v. 8. In v. 8 it is undoubtedly Joshua who is meant. His name is the same in meaning as Jesus. Joshua did not give them that true rest. Under his leadership there were victories, but he did not give them complete victory in the land.

      2) Canaan rest is not the "rest of God." It was rest in the land; divine rest is in the heart. God called this "My rest." It is a sharing of His own restfulness in victory, and freedom from conflict.

         It is a rest from self-labor, v. 10. All spiritual labor must be wrought in the strength of God if it is to be effective. Jesus said, "The words that I speak unto you, I speak not of myself, but the Father that dwelleth in me, he doeth the works" (John 14:10). This is the rest in the midst of labor.

b. It is a rest through faith in His finished work. We may labor to draw nigh, but then we rest in His finished work, 4:3. As God rested from a perfect work of creation, so we can rest in the new creation which He has perfected for us. Moment by moment we can trust Him for victory over every foe, as the Israelites should have done to enter and to abide in the land. There is not only a crisis victory of entering, but a continuous abiding.

c. There is perfect victory over all sin, 12-16.

1) The Word of God is able to discover and reveal inward sin, 12:13. The figure here is of the ancient priest, who took the sacrificial victim, slew him, cut him open, and even opened the bones, displaying the marrow. Before a person can be cleansed from sin, that sin must be exposed to his own view as it is to God's view. But the heart is deceitful; who will admit his own sin? How can a person ever be brought to see his own inner sin, and confess it? The writer declares that the Word of God is able to do this. It is alive and powerful, and sharper than the sword. Even the sword must be in the hand of the priest; it has no power of itself. So the Word of God must be in the hand of an anointed messenger, empowered by the Spirit. The Word of God reveals the inner secrets of men's hearts.

What we could never know of our own unaided intelligence, God will reveal through His Word and the searching of the Spirit. We must all have this if we are to be made holy and acceptable to God.

In v. 13 it is stated that God sees perfectly all the inner life of man. He "looketh upon the heart." He sees the thoughts and intention. Man may look upon our actions; He sees the motives behind them. And He judges them in the light of His Word. May we pray with the Psalmist, "Search me, O God and know my heart . . ." (Psa. 139:23).

It is as hard to get men to face their own sin honestly as it is to cut through the joint and bone and expose the marrow. There is an inner hardness stronger than concrete in the bones of our bodies. Just so, it is a very hard thing to get people to admit their true spiritual condition. Inward sin is evasive, treacherous, deceitful. But God's Word can expose it and bring the person to humble, contrite acknowledgement of his sin.

2) The Great High Priest is able to take away the sin, 4:14-5:1. A new section is entered here, which we will develop more fully later. Let it be said at this point that the priest is installed to deal with sin. It is sin which separated between God and man, and requires the priestly office of mediation. It is He who offers the sacrifice for sin. Jesus is the great, able, perfect High Priest.

He was without sin, and He knows our frame perfectly. He knows our infirmities and our sin.

We can come boldly to Him, and find grace and mercy in the right time. When we see our sin and feel we can not endure for another hour with its deceit and pollution, we can cry to Him, and find help. He will deliver.

This rest from inward sin and strife is God's perfect rest!

d. Third admonition, 4:11-13. Since God sees our sin and provides a perfect remedy, just as He provided and promised a victorious entrance into the Holy Land, we should be sure that we enter that rest. The words "let us labour" mean to be hasty, diligent, earnest. It means to apply every possible effort as soon as possible to reach the goal. This matter of entering perfect rest of spirit, and being cleansed from sin is not an optional matter, to be treated casually. There is strong admonition against neglecting and refusing this rest.

E. The Better High Priest, 5:1-7:28, and other small portions.

The High Priest was the most revered person under the Old Testament economy. His identification with the people, his beautiful garments, his impressive ceremonies, his access to God on their behalf, and their names on his breastplate, made them respect him very highly. Before the coming of Christ, however, the priesthood had degenerated and become corrupt. Nevertheless, the Judaizers could taunt the Christians, who had been excommunicated from the temple, and say that they had no temple, no altar, no priest, and no sacrifices. In fact, the Christians really had no religion at all—only a despised Galilean! So the writer takes the greatest part of this epistle to show that they did have a High Priest—and One who was far superior to Aaron.

There are seven characteristics of Christ's priesthood by virtue of which He is a better High Priest. The first three of these characteristics were possessed by Aaron, though not to the same degree as Christ in some cases. The last four were not possessed by Aaron, though they were by Christ.

1. He was human, 2:17; 4:15. Hebrews 2:16 says that "He taketh hold of the seed of Abraham." God's purpose in Christ was to reach down and grasp fallen man, so that he can be lifted up again to fellowship with God. In order for this to be, Christ had to become man. Angels could not enter with us into our sufferings, temptations, and sorrows. Because He became a man, Christ could.

    a. Now He is a merciful High Priest. Because He knows fully what man endures in his manhood, Jesus can be merciful to us in our sorrows. Because He suffered for our sins, He can provide forgiveness for them. This is the great wonder of the atonement.

    b. He is a faithful High Priest, 2:17. This probably refers to His relation to God: He is always true to the will of God. He never came under condemnation for Himself, so He can always be our faithful representative before God. He is always before God as our Advocate, our Intercessor. We can always find in Him the help that we need. There is never a time when He leaves His office—when He is unavailable. He is always effective in His office.

2. He is great, 4:14. The old high priests ministered on earth, going into the Most Holy Place. Our Great High Priest has entered the heavens, into the very presence of the eternal God. He is there in our behalf, speaking for us, interceding for us, and offering the benefits of His atonement for us.

    He is the Son of God, and always is heard by the Father. Great officials may be too busy to hear the petitions of their subjects, but their sons always have access. Through Christ the Son we can always have access to God.

    There is not a problem or need of ours, but He is great enough to handle it. He never turns us away, saying, "I am sorry; I can't handle that problem."

3. He is compassionate, 5:2, 8. This is a marvelous addition to the preceding thought of His greatness. It is very common that when men ascend to high office, they tend to forget the common man and his needs. But although Jesus is ascended to the heavens, He is perfectly compassionate toward us. He feels what we feel (2:18, 4:15). There is not a child, youth, or old man—not a poor man, sick man, tempted man, or lonely man—but that Jesus can say, "I understand how you feel!" He knows our needs. He learned obedience, the writer says (5:8). This does not mean that He has been disobedient, but that He learned in experience what it means for a human person to obey God under all kinds of circumstances. He is fully touched with the feeling of our infirmities and temptations, so that He compassionately represents us before the Father, and He brings just the right help at just the right time.

4. He is called, after the order of Melchizedek, 5:5,10. The Judaizers would claim that they had the true priest, after the order of Aaron, who was specially called of God to that ministry. Here is the answer to their argument: Christ was called after an order that is superior to that of Aaron and the Levitical priesthood.

   The major argument of this epistle centers about the priesthood, and this is the primary emphasis concerning the priesthood: Christ is a priest of a better order than Aaron. Let us follow the argument.

   a. Psalm 110:4 states, "The Lord hath sworn, and will not repent, Thou art a priest forever after the order of Melchizedek." This is plainly a Psalm concerning Christ, as is elsewhere shown.

   b Melchizedek was a greater priest than Aaron, or others of the Levitical order.

      1) Abraham paid tithes to Melchizedek, showing that Melchizedek was greater than Abraham. Melchizedek blessed Abraham and the less is blessed of the greater, 7:7.

      2) In Abraham, Levi actually paid tithes to Melchizedek, for Levi was "in Abraham" when Abraham did so. Therefore Levi is lower than Melchizedek.

3) It is said of Melchizedek that he lived rather than died. Also it is said that he has "neither beginning of days or end of life." Commentators do not agree on the meaning. It may mean that there is no genealogy for him. Or it may mean that this was actually a preincarnate appearance of Christ Himself. The point here is that he is greater than Levi and the Levitical priesthood.

4) Levi came according to the law, vs. 5, 11, 12. The Levitical tribe was appointed as the priests (Ex. 40:15) of Israel. Melchizedek came not by the law, but by an oath of God Himself (7:21). The oath of God has precedence over the law (vv. 21, 22). It is therefore demonstrated that the law of the priesthood is disannulled (v. 18). The law could not bring perfection, so it must give way to God's means of perfection.

5) "The law made nothing perfect, but the bringing in of a better hope did, by which we draw nigh to God." Under the old priesthood men had to keep their distance from God. Only the high priest could go into the immediate presence of God. Now the way into the holiest is opened and we can all draw nigh to God (10:19-22).

5. He has an eternal priesthood, 7:16, 17. The law of Levitical priesthood has been shown to be weak and unprofitable (7:18). It is a carnal commandment, says the writer. That is, it was suited to the weakness and carnality of man—his frailty and mortality. Christ's priesthood is everlasting. He is not frail, nor mortal, and shall never pass away. The old priests were often lazy, sinful, and ineffective, so that the people declined in spiritual life. Now there is no such changing priesthood. He is eternal in His position. Therefore, we can be saved eternally. Here and now we can be brought up to the mark of purity and holy service.

The priesthood of Christ fully replaces the former order, which is therefore no more valid. It was the Judaizers who had no valid priest. Christ's priesthood is unchanging.

6. He is an able priest, 7:25. Here is a wonderful, and exalted statement of what is ours through Christ: "Wherefore he is able to save them to the uttermost that come unto God by him,

seeing he ever liveth to make intercession for them." The old priests were not able to make anybody perfect. They could only administer a temporary expedient—a kind of spiritual first aid—a stop-gap measure until more permanent help could be received. His salvation is thorough, final and eternal. The primary meaning of the term "uttermost" refers to measure rather than time. In other words, He can save to the greatest degree as well as to all time and eternity. This is related to His continuous intercession. His salvation is not a fixed and static relationship. It is related to His intercession and our coming to God by Him.

This ability of Christ comes from two facts, one of which has already been given, and one of which follows: His eternal unchangeableness, and His own perfect sinlessness. Here is a wonderful description of Christ's perfect holiness (v. 26). The old priests had to offer for their own sins before they could offer for the people. This had to be repeated often, since they were sinful and sinned often. But Christ offered once, and He is eternally perfect, so His full time and attention can be given to us. He is there forever, perfect, in our place before the Father. Through Him we can be saved fully, eternally!

7. He is seated at the right hand of God, 10:11-15. The old priests always stood, for they always had to be busy about the offerings and their work was never done. Salvation is completed in Christ. He has finished His work of redemption. Complete victory over all His foes is now a foregone conclusion. He is awaiting the day of His final revelation in triumph over all His foes. But the price is already paid, and the ultimate victory assured.

We are partakers in a wonderful, completed salvation, effected by the work of our wonderful High Priest!

F. Fourth Admonition, 5:11-6:20

This admonition begins suddenly, but it grows into one of the most solemn admonitions in all the Word of God.

1. Symptoms

    a. Prolonged spiritual babyhood, 5:12-14. Apparently some of these Christians had been so for an extended period of time. But they were remaining in spiritual babyhood, when they should have been bringing others to Christ and teaching them in the advanced truths of the faith.

b. Dullness of hearing, 5:11. They were unable to apprehend deep spiritual truth. This was the same condition as the disciples of Christ before Pentecost (John 16:12, 13). These Christians had not gone on to the fullness of the Spirit, so they did not have the spiritual insight they needed.

c. Slothfulness, 6:12. Some of the believers were inclined to settle down and make no progress, when there was so much opposition.

2. The danger: apostasy (vv. 4-8). It is not simple backsliding that is considered here, but the repudiation of Christ as the means of salvation. The teaching is plainly that it is possible for these believers to be eternally lost after they have received the salvation of Christ. It is an awesome and serious warning.

The question arises as to whether or not it is possible for one who has apostatized ever to be saved again. Verse 6 should read, "while they are crucifying to themselves the Son of God afresh . . ." It is impossible to be restored while they reject Christ. If any backslider should repent and return to Christ, he can be restored. See I John 5:16; Jas. 5: 19, 20.

3. The remedy: going on to perfection (6:1); diligence unto the end (6:11); faith and patience to inherit the promises of God (6:12).

a. "Let us go on unto perfection" is, in the original, "Let us be borne along to perfection." It refers, not to what we do by our own effort, but what God brings us to if we are totally yielded to Him. If men will follow the prompting of the Spirit of God without resistance, they will be carried on to perfection. That perfection is twofold: the crisis of deliverance from the disease of sin, which perpetuates childhood; and maturation to adulthood. Both are by the energizing grace of God. Full maturity cannot be achieved without deliverance from sin. That was why the Hebrew Christians were remaining in babyhood.

b. "Diligence to the full assurance of hope." We should compare this with the "full assurance of faith" (10:22). That is certainty of our acceptance with God, through forgiveness of sins, as witnessed to by the Holy Spirit, when we have fully trusted Christ.

The full assurance of hope relates to future glory. The same witnessing Spirit causes us to know that we are prepared for Heaven and its glory. If brought to the judgment seat of Christ we would be without any fear, as is stated in I John 4:17. Objectively this hope is based on two things: God's promise and His oath (17, 18). Subjectively it is also based on two things: faith and patience (v. 12).

The objective promise of God is absolutely sure, confirmed with His oath. So the hope is doubly immutable, and is like a strong anchor in a storm. (Abraham is given as a classic example of one who tried the anchor and found that it holds, in spite of all possible adversity.) The reasoning of the writer is that we can also prove the steadfastness of the anchor. The Christian Jews were exhorted to maintain the subjective aspects of the hope: faith and patience. They must show diligence unto the end. To run the race to the halfway point is not to succeed. We must run the race all the way to the finish. To carry out the anchor analogy, if one cuts the anchor line, hope is gone as sure as if the anchor did not hold.

The writer points out that these believers have earlier shown their love by their good works (v. 10), and they should continue to do so. It is strongly evident that even such believers, that have repented and believed in God (v. 1), could lose their hope and fall away. May God keep us from such a danger!

G. The Better Covenant, 8:1-13

The covenant concept was an extremely important one to the Jews. They could look back to the covenant which God made with Abraham, by which they had become God's special people (Gen. 12:2, 3). In giving the covenant of the law, God had set His people above all other people on the earth, if they should obey the law (Ex. 19: 5, 6). The covenant was the basis for the relationship between God and His people; so this concept of the covenant was supremely important.

1. The first covenant, v. 7. What is called the "first covenant" was the covenant of the law. It was not really the first which God gave. He had previously given the unconditional covenant of grace to Abraham, by which the people were promised the land of Canaan for their inheritance.

   a. It was a conditional covenant of works, Ex.19: 4, 5. The people were commanded to keep the whole law as the basis for the blessings of God. They should be a peculiar treasure unto God, a holy nation, and a kingdom of priests, if they should obey all of the commandments. In repeating the law for them, Moses strongly showed that they would be blessed if they obeyed the law, but would be cursed if they disobeyed. See Deut. 28:1, 2, 58, 59.

   b. It was a defective covenant relationship, v. 7.

      1) It was a temporary expedient, introduced 430 years after the covenant of grace (Gal. 3:17).

      2) It was introduced because of the sins of the people, to remind them of their sins, and to show them how terrible sin really is, Gal. 3:19. It was to be a schoolmaster, to bring the people to Christ, Gal. 3:24.

      3) It was an indirect communication, coming through the mediation of angels, Gal. 3:19. The covenant of grace was direct from God to Abraham.

      4) There was no power in it to bring righteousness. Rather, it brought condemnation. Those who should obey all but one point, and fail in that point, were still under condemnation, Heb. 7:19; James 2:10.

      5) In spite of all of this, the law itself was not at fault. It was introduced as a temporary expedient, to show the people their sinfulness, and to provide a temporary basis of atonement. For this purpose the tabernacle was set up as a pattern of heavenly, spiritual things. In its services there was a temporary arrangement for the people to be pardoned from their sins. The whole tabernacle service was only a shadow or type of heavenly things, 8:5. Christ could not be a priest in that tabernacle, because the law limited the priesthood to the tribe of Levi. So we have a better tabernacle for the service of a better priest.

2. The second covenant, 10-14. The people totally failed under the first covenant. They disobeyed, and brought the penalties of a broken law upon themselves, even the whole nation.

We should pause to see the love of God, which He displayed through His covenant relations. Even the covenant of law was one of love. Jer. 31:31-34 states the promise of the new covenant. Verse 32 says, "Not according to the covenant that I made with their fathers in the day that I took them by the hand to bring them out of the land of Egypt; which my covenant they brake, although I was an husband unto them." Even under the old covenant God was a "husband to His people," seeking to lead them by the hand, to make provisions for their sins, and to teach them His ways.

a. There is purification from sin in the heart, Heb. 8:10. The law is written in the heart. This is what God has always desired, as is stated in Psa 51:6, "behold, thou desirest truth in the inward parts." Under the law the motivation was external. Under the new covenant it is internal. Desire is placed in the heart, and energy is provided from within, as Christ dwells in us by His Spirit. Rom. 8:3, 4 says, "For what the law could not do, in that it was weak through the flesh, God sending his own Son in the likeness of sinful flesh, and for sin, condemned sin in the flesh, that the righteousness of the law might be fulfilled in us, who walk not after the flesh, but after the Spirit."

In Gal. 2:20 Paul says the life which he now lives comes from Christ dwelling within him. In Rom. 7:17 he stated that his former misconduct was because of sin dwelling within him. This change of inward condition and motivation is promised under the new covenant, and comes in the grace of entire sanctification.

b. There is illumination of the Person of God in Christ, v. 11. Under the old covenant relationship, the teachers were trying to get the people to know God. But under the new covenant, there is a revelation of God in the heart. This knowledge does not come by teaching, but by the work of the Spirit. Much emphasis is placed on this in the New Testament. Especially I Cor. 2 and I John dwell on the element of certain spiritual knowledge which is ours as we live the life in the Spirit. Psa. 51:6 states "In the hidden parts thou shalt make me to know wisdom." God imparts knowledge. We have insight into truth that the man of this world can never grasp. This is one of the rich blessings of the sanctified soul. This is what John also refers to in I John 2:20, 26, 27.

c. There is unity and fellowship with God, 8:10. Under the Old Testament economy, God seemed remote. He would come no closer than the Holy of Holies, and the people could not enter there. But under the new covenant God enters the very inner life of His people, strengthening them where they are weak, illuminating them where they can not understand, bringing peace where there was strife and love where there was loneliness! There is assurance of present blessing and hope of future glory!

Once sin reigned in the heart. Paul said, "Not I, but sin" (Rom. 7:17). After this wondrous experience of a new covenant relationship, he could say, "Not I, but Christ."

 d. There is a wondrous surety under this covenant, 7:22. Jesus Himself is the surety of this covenant, on both sides. He is God's guarantor toward us, and ours toward God. He has been our Mediator, offering the sacrifice, and providing grace to enable us to keep our part of the covenant obligation. He represents God and perfectly keeps God's promises to us.

 e. This covenant will never pass away. It is everlasting, as David said of that which was given him (II Sam. 23:5).

H. The Better Sacrifice, Chapters 9, 10.

 1. The key passage is 9:13, 14, which refers to two special offerings in Old Testament times. Let us study them, to see their special meaning.

  a. The Great Day of Atonement, v. 7, 12, 13. This is originally explained in Lev. 16. The offerings of atonement involved a bullock, and two goats, one of which was the scapegoat. The bullock was offered in the Most Holy place of the people. The blood of both bullock and goat were then used to sprinkle the mercy seat, the incense altar and the tabernacle, because of the sinfulness of the people. When the scapegoat had the sins of the people pronounced upon its head, it was sent into the wilderness to die. All of this was symbolic of Christ's death and His bearing our sins away, as He suffered without the gate. It is His blood that is the basis for the remission of sin. By all of this the people learned, a) the costliness of sin, and b) the necessity of bloodshed to purge the guilt and uncleanness of sin.

   The day of atonement came only once per year. The calf mentioned in v. 12 is the same as the young bullock of Lev. 16:3, 11.

  b. The sprinkling with the water of separation, v. 13. This is originally explained in Num. 19:2-22.

The heifer was red, which is symbolic of the blood sacrifice. It was without blemish, which signifies the perfect sinlessness of Christ. There was no moral defect in Him for which He needed to offer for Himself. It must not have borne a yoke, signifying that Christ was not compelled to suffer, but He did it freely without constraint.

The ashes of the heifer were to be saved to make a water of separation. There is doubtless a physical, sanitary element involved here in addition to the moral symbolism. Ashes have power to destroy germs, and this was God's germicidal prescription to prevent deadly epidemics from spreading. Morally there is deep significance also. The ashes were for "purification for sin" (Num. 19:9, 17). The dead bodies signify the inherited sin, or the body of death referred to by Paul, Rom. 7:24. The purification was complete on the seventh day, which is a type of perfection. If a person refused the water of separation, he should be cut off from among his people. So, if one refuses the cleansing of the blood of Christ, he can not hope for acceptance with God.

c. The lesson to be learned, 9:22. There were many rituals involving blood-shed, sprinkling, offerings, etc. Not all have been recited here. They were to teach the important lesson that "without the shedding of blood there is no remission of sin." Sin is costly. It was costly to those who committed the sin. They had to supply the beast for the sacrifice. When Jesus came as the Lamb of God, it demonstrated how much it cost God to put away our sin.

Another lesson to be learned is the necessity of the constant cleansing of the blood of Christ. In Num. 19:15 it is known that open vessels could be contaminated from the atmosphere. They must be kept covered or be treated as unclean. The very atmosphere in which we live is pervaded by the virus of sin, and we need the cleansing of the blood always to maintain purity in the sight of God. Satan is the "prince of the power of the air," and the whole world is pervaded by his power and influence (I John 5:19). Only the blood of Christ will suffice to keep us clean (I John 1:7).

2. Contrasts between the two sacrifices.

    a. Jesus offered Himself (9:14), whereas the Old Testament sacrifices were bound with cords and forced to give up their lives (Psa. 118:27). He did this through the impulse of the Holy Spirit—the eternal Spirit (v. 14). A self-sacrifice is the highest type of sacrifice there is, and this is the kind the Spirit of God desires. When the Son of God gave Himself, it was the highest possible sacrifice in the universe.

b. The offering of Jesus was morally perfect, holy and incorruptible (9:14; 10:29; I Pet. 1:18, 19), whereas the bodies of bulls and goats were only physically perfect. Their physical perfection was a symbol of the spiritual and moral perfection God was seeking for. The blood of bulls and goats had no worth in themselves, but the sacrifice of Jesus did. There was no sin or fault in Him, so He could make a morally meritorious sacrifice! Animals were morally neutral, though physically perfect. He was not only physically, but morally, perfect, and could make moral atonement.

c. The sacrifice of Jesus could take away sins (10:12), whereas the blood of bulls and goats could not (10:11). So effectively did the blood of Jesus provide for sins, that when they are removed they will never be remembered again (10:17). The animal sacrifices were only temporary expedients, like the taking of insulin shots to prevent death from sugar diabetes. They maintain life, but they do not cure the disease. The blood of Jesus provides a perfect cure.

d. The blood of Jesus can purify the conscience from dead works, to serve the living God (9:14; 10:22), whereas the blood of animals could not do so. In the old sacrifices there was respite from the penalty of sin, because of God's mercy, but it provided no relief from the conscience of sin (10:2, 3). While the animal sacrifices permitted God to withhold penalty, they did not stop the process of sin or the accusations of conscience when sin was committed. We may look in Lev. 5 for an example of the cost of repeated sinning. Not only was there a general day of atonement (Heb. 10:3), but there was also a necessary offering for sin every time sin was committed (Lev. 5:17-19). The value of the offense must be paid with one-fifth added in restitution, and an animal was to be slain unless the sinner was too poor, in which case he could offer fine flour. But there must be an offering. They were constantly reminded of the guilt of sin and the costliness of sin! The disease was never cured!

Through the blood of Jesus there is a halt to the process of sin! The conscience can be free from guilt of sins committed! (10:2). The process of sin is to be stopped through the power of Christ.

There is an important doctrinal truth at stake here. Many people—notably Calvinists—teach that men can never cease from sinning. The Bible, however, teaches that our consciences can be relieved from the conscience of sin. Then, either sinning must cease, or sin ceases to produce guilt. It is then a question of whether the sinner is transformed so that he no longer commits sin, or sin is transformed so that it no longer produces guilt. In effect the Calvinists take the latter position, whereas the Wesleyans take the former, which is surely the Biblical position.

e. The sacrifice of Christ is able to make the worshipers perfect in heart (10:14), whereas the animal sacrifices could not do so (10:1). The offering of Christ not only could give perfect pardon for sin and regeneration of the conscience from the guilt of sins committed (this has been already discussed); it could also purify the heart from the root principle of sin. Jesus came not only to remove the guilt, but the power of sin as well. It is when the root of sin is removed that the stream of life can be pure. This truth is enforced in the new covenant (10:16). The law is implanted in the heart, so that it can be kept by the power of God in us.

The high priest, to prepare himself for the feast of atonement, (according to Jewish writers) was to prepare himself by remaining at the tabernacle quite alone for a week before the feast. He was to refrain from anything that would make him ceremonially unclean, or disturb his devotions. On the evening before the feast he ate lightly, and maintained a vigil all night. In the morning he bathed and dressed himself in the holy white linen garment of a humble penitent, instead of his beautiful garments (Lev. 116:4).

For himself and his sons he was to have a bullock and a ram, for a sin offering, and a burnt offering, respectively. For the people he was to have two goats and a ram, the latter for the burnt offering, and the others for a sin offering.

It seems that the first trip into the Holy of Holies (Lev 16:12) was after the slaughter of the bull, when he carried a censer of coals and a container of incense. Inside the Holiest of all he was to place the incense over the coals so a cloud would cover the mercy seat. This was so "that he die not" (Lev. 16:13). Even though he could go into the Holy of Holies, the presence of God was to be covered with a cloud of incense. How great was the emphasis on the unapproachable holiness of God.

The Talmud says that the High Priest was to step backward out of the Holy of Holies, so as not to turn his back upon God, and return to the outer court. Then he took the basin of blood within the Holiest again, this time to sprinkle the blood on the mercy seat and seven times before it. Emphasis is thus on access to God.

Back in the court, the High Priest sacrificed the goat, and took its blood into the Holy of Holies, the third trip. The sprinkling was repeated, this time for the people.

After pronouncing the sins of the people on the scapegoat, the High Priest bathed and reclothed himself in his beautiful garments. He then offered the burnt offering (ram) for himself and his sons, and then for the people. The remains of the animals were to be burned outside the camp (Lev. 16:27; Heb. 13:11-13). Then the blessings of the priest were pronounced on the people.

Chapter 9 of Hebrews is the first place where blood is mentioned in the book, and here it is mentioned 12 times (an exception is human blood mentioned in 2:14).

The offering of blood on this day was specifically for the errors of the people. The word "errors" means "offenses in ignorance". It was to bring complete cleansing before God, summing up all that had been done before, and purging the entire record of the people (see Heb. 9:7). This day showed that it was unto God that the blood was offered.

Just so, Christ offered His blood in the true Holy of Holies. On his day the cleansing power of blood was shown, also (see Heb. 9:13). It is the first reference in Leviticus to cleansing from sin. There are numerous references to forgiveness before this (e.g., 4:20, 31, 35; 5:10,

13, 18). Here the emphasis is cleansing, Lev. 16:16, 19, 30. There is no mention of forgiveness.

The sacrifice of Jesus dealt with sins; it also dealt with sin, the root and principle back of the actions of sin (9:26). This is the deepest need of mankind, to have a purification of the fountain of the inner being. The purpose of the blood is purging, or cleansing. It is the inward part of man which is purged, as opposed to the outward part under the Old Testament sacrifices.

The work of sanctification is cleansing from sin—sin in action and sin in its unclean essence. We are sanctified through the offering of Christ (10:10). As we shall see, the entering into the Most Holy place is symbolic of entering into the life of holiness.

    f. The sacrifice of Christ, offered once, is efficacious for all who shall appropriate it, even to all eternity (9:26; 10:10; 10:14), whereas the animals had to be offered repeatedly (9:25, 26; 10:1.3.11). Sin, death, and hell are matters of eternal consequence, and the remedy must be as far-reaching in its effects. The offering of Christ has eternal merits. His offering was made by the "eternal Spirit," (9:14) and has eternal worth. The blood avails for sin forever! There will never be a time when sin or death or hell or the devil can rise and claim victory over the sacrifice of Christ. It purchases eternal salvation! (9:12, 15).

    g. The sacrifice of Christ avails for all men everywhere and in any age (9:28), whereas the offering of animals was limited in scope to the Jewish nation in the services of an earthly tabernacle (9:1).

3. The end of the old sacrificial system, 10:8, 9.

    a. The old was only a type or shadow of the new, 9:9; 9:23; 10:1. As a shadow has somewhat of the likeness of the substance, but is not itself substance, so the old sacrifices only had a pattern or figure of the real, and were not themselves of lasting value.

    b. The sacrifice of Christ itself gave value to the sacrifices under the Old Testament (9:15). They had no value whatsoever in themselves. It was the blood of Christ that undergirded even the Old Testament system.

c. Since the blood of Christ has been shed, the old system is invalid and has no more use, 10:9. In Gal. 5:4 Paul showed that any person who should now go back under the old system for his justification would be fallen from the grace of Christ.

I. The Better Tabernacle, 8:2, 5; chapters 9, 10. Key verses 9:11, 12.

The tabernacle, and the temple which replaced it, were rich with typology. The Judaizers loved the ceremonies of the temple, as in the early history of Israel they had clung to the tabernacle ceremonies. Here the writer shows that the entire system of the tabernacle and the temple was only typical—as shadow and not a reality.

1. The worldly sanctuary, 9:1. The meaning is that the old tabernacle consisted of material things, taken from this world.

   a. The structure, fixtures, and services are described, vv. 1-10. The conclusion is given that these things were good only until the time of reformation (v. 10), and could not make even the priest himself perfect, and certainly not the ones for whom he ministered (10:1).

   b. They were all pointers toward the heavenly things that were to come, 9:23, 24; 10:19-22.

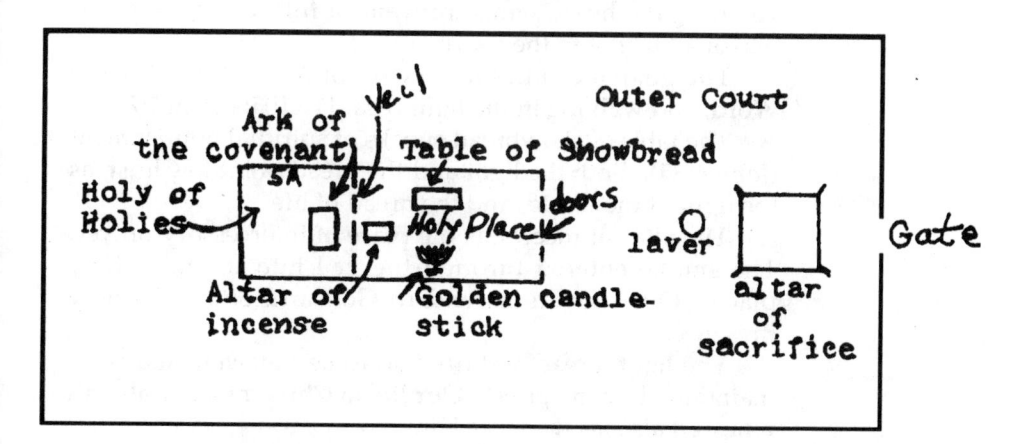

[Diagram of the tabernacle layout showing: Holy of Holies containing Ark of the covenant, veil, Holy Place containing Table of Showbread, Altar of incense, Golden candlestick, doors, laver, Outer Court with altar of sacrifice, and Gate]

2. The heavenly sanctuary, 9:23; 8:5. The term "heavenly" and "heavens" refers to spiritual reality, whether on the earth or in the heavens. The earthly tabernacle, as we have seen, was only a type or

a type or shadow of the spiritual or heavenly realities. Let us examine the features of the earthly to gain insights into their application.

a. The Outer Court. This was open as far as the altar of sacrifice to all Israelites who were clean. They were not to go beyond it. This court was the place of sacrifice for sin and represents the place of conviction and repentance for sin. There was the bloodshed. There the people brought their multitudes of animals to be offered. There they felt the cost of sin. There they met the priest, who could offer an offering for our sin. It represents the place where men see their sins and see the sacrifice made for their sins.

Only the priests washed at the laver, Ex. 30:17-21. But in the New Testament plan of salvation we are all made priests (Rev. 1:6), and we all need to be washed. There is the washing of regeneration (Titus 3:5) which is essential for every man if he would be reconciled to God.

b. The First Tabernacle, or Holy Place, 9:2. It is a place of service, which represents the regenerated life (9:6). There is service, but with only a limited fellowship. It is a holy place, but not the most holy place; it is the house of God, but not the revealed, immediate presence of God. That is the way with the regenerated life, in which there is still a veil over the heart, which prevents a full revelation of the person of Christ to the heart.

The golden candlestick speaks of instruction of God's Word, and walking in the light (Psa. 119:105; I John 1:7).

The table of showbread speaks of spiritual nourishment (John 6:35). Both the light and the bread point to Christ, as the light of the world, and the bread of life.

The altar of incense is the place of intercessory prayer. The smoke entered through the veil into the most holy place. Our prayers ascend to God and enter His holy presence.

The light, bread and fire had to be renewed, and were maintained by the priest. Our life in Christ must be always renewed also, as we serve Him.

c. The Most Holy Place, 9:3-10. It is the place of revealed presence and fellowship, and signifies the life of holiness. There was an awesome desire by the best men in Old Testament times to enter into the holiest of all. The

Psalmist spoke of it in 27:4. In Psa. 24:3-5 the requirement is given: there must be clean hands and a pure heart.

The priest was to wear linen garments into the holy place (Lev. 16:4). This is symbolic of purity. He always entered with blood, which he offered first for his own sins. So it is by the blood of cleansing that we can enter the most holy place. It was a place of fellowship with God. We are reminded of this in I John 1:7. Following the course of furnishings of the tabernacle led right into the holiest of all, where fellowship was complete.

God dwelt above the mercy seat, upon which the blood was sprinkled. It is by God's mercy that He receives the offering of Christ's blood and purges our hearts by faith in the efficacy of that blood.

The ark is a wonderful type of Christ: His manhood and deity signified by the shittim wood overlaid with gold; His perfect keeping of the law and enabling us to fulfill it, and the sustained freshness of the manna. In this life of holiness Christ is food to us, and righteousness to us. Moreover the rod of Aaron that budded was there. This speaks of perpetual and supernatural fruitfulness. God wants us to bear much fruit. This is done by the life of Christ within us.

The cherubims signify redeemed humanity in perfect fellowship, based on their being in Christ, and having Christ in the midst. (Matt. 18:20).

The same elements which are found in the first tabernacle are found in the second: light, bread, and the presence of God. But they are more spiritual here, marked by the revealed brightness and supernatural glory of God. What a privilege to dwell in the holy of holiness.

Many people know only the Holy Place where they "accomplish service" (9:6), but they are still separated by a veil from the intimate and full fellowship with God, which He desires. They have a veil "on their hearts," as Paul states in II Cor. 3: 15, 16. They need to enter the Most Holy Place and enjoy the fulness of God!

8. Fifth Admonition, 10:19-39

   a. The exhortation to enter the Holy of Holies, vv. 19-25

      1) A four-fold reason, vv. 19-21

a) The way into the Holy of Holies is opened to us. As long as the first tabernacle stood with its veil and its once-a-year entrance by the priest, God was signifying that men could not yet enter the Most Holy place (9:8). When Jesus died, the veil was rent in twain (Matt. 27:51) from the top to the bottom. God was thus showing that the way was now open, as it had never been before.

The veil was heavy, taking six men to carry it. It was about 20 meters high and very thick. Being torn from the top, it was evident that God, and not man, tore it open. It now demonstrated that a full reconciliation was prepared between God and men.

Every man now has the priestly privilege of going in and meeting God.

b) We have boldness to enter, by the blood of Christ. The old priests went in with extreme carefulness. If they did not meet the exact conditions of God, they could be smitten dead in the sanctuary. We do not enter carelessly, but boldly, because the blood of Christ is the basis. There is full cleansing from sin, so we can have fellowship. See I John 1:7. While we walk where we are directed to walk, and while the blood Cleanseth from all sin, we have perfect fellowship with God! There is no slavish fear of drawing nigh to God.

Why should any hesitate to respond to such an entreaty, when God wants us in His presence, to worship Him in the beauty of holiness?

c) Christ has provided a new and living way, through His flesh. The word "new and living" means "ever fresh and perfect." This means that we never have to leave this most Holy Place. There are many who feel that a life of holiness is totally impossible over a long period of time. No, the way is *ever living*.

The reason is that Christ provided a way through the flesh. His human flesh stood as a veil keeping Him from returning to the Holy of Holies in the Heavens, just as the sinful flesh of unsanctified men keeps them from entering into the beauty of holiness. But Christ provided victory over sinful flesh by the rending of His human flesh. As He died *for* sin, we can die *to* sin and enter the holiest of all.

The term "flesh" represents the entity of sin. When Christ died, it was placed under the sentence of death. By His cross we have perfect freedom and access to God's holiness!

There is constant renewing in this way, just as the manna never spoiled, the law was never broken, and the rod ever budded.

d) We have a great high priest over the house of God. There is a unity between the Holiest in our spiritual experience, and the Holiest in Heaven, where Christ has entered (9:24). Holiness and Heaven are virtually connected now, since Christ is our Great High Priest. We are there with Him in the Spirit, just as He is here with us in the Spirit. The priest is there with us, His sacrifice being a perfect offering for sin. If there should be an act of sin, as stated in I John 2:1, He is our Advocate, providing instant cleansing as we appeal to Him.

2) A four-fold attitude, v. 22.

a) A true heart. This, as we have shown before, is the essence of purity and holiness. It is truth in the inward parts which God seeks for in man. The blood of Christ provides the way, and thus imparts truth to the heart. A heart without any doublemindedness or hypocrisy is what is meant.

b) Full assurance of faith. A true heart, from which all deception has been removed, and which is fully yielded to God, is of perfect faith. It is disobedience which destroys faith. An obedient heart is a believing heart. Faith in its fullness involves mental acceptance of fact, volitional action and restful trust.

When the heart is purified, all of these elements are at their best, and full assurance results.

3) The fourfold privilege, 22-24.

    a) Draw near in faith. In the Old Testament the message of God is "Draw not nigh hither," Ex. 3:5. The Gospel message is "Come," and "Let us draw nigh." This is the result of the work of Christ, our great High Priest.

    b) Hold fast the profession of our faith without wavering. The accent is on "profession." The fullness of the cleansing work of God enables a man to witness. The work of the Spirit is to enable an effective witness. Whenever people are satisfied to remain silent concerning their witness, the life will soon be gone out of their religion. Never is the witness to cease, no matter how dark the night or oppressive the opposition. To speak of our faith strengthens it.

    c) Consider one another to provoke unto love. There is a strong element of fellowship, not only with God, but with fellow Christians, which is enhanced by the cleansing of Christ, and walking in the light. There were two cherubim above the mercy seat, which testified to the communion expected when sanctified people should enter there. "Where two or three are gathered in my name, there am I in the midst of them," said Jesus. Sanctified people have an unselfish interest in other people, and want to help them. How different from carnal self-seeking!

    d) Not forsaking the assembling of ourselves together. The need becomes greater as pressures increase. This has been found true again and again. Under Communism, or Roman tyranny, or other persecutions, the church has needed its times of assembly for mutual exhortation and fellowship. When the religion of Israel had sunk to a very low ebb, the few saints of God still exhorted one another and God took special notice of it, as we find in Mal. 3:16, 17.

b. The warning against going backward, vv. 26-39.

1) The danger of willful sin. The particular case envisioned here was the sin of rejecting Christ. The sacrifices of the Old Testament are no longer of any worth whatever. Now if they should reject Jesus Christ and His better sacrifice, there is no other sacrifice. This is then a warning against that total apostasy which would come with the rejection of Christ.

We might give this a more common application, though it was not intended in the immediate context. When a person willfully sins against the light of God, the sacrifice of Christ no longer covers his sins. He is guilty and he must bear that guilt, until he repents and turns again to obey God. In brief, the blood of Christ provides for no man while he willfully sins against God.

The severity of Moses' law refers to Numbers 15:30, where sins done willfully as opposed to sins done in ignorance are referred to; and to Deut. 17:6, where such extreme sins as idolatry are referred to. In the latter case two or three witnesses were necessary to put the man to death.

The most serious consequences are coming to such a person, for he so grossly belittles God, the blood, and the tender Spirit of grace. It will be a fearful thing for a person to meet God's vengeance in such a case. May we who have come to know Christ's love be ever careful that we not slip into carelessness and apostasy.

2) The appeal to past blessings. The argument may be summarized thus: "If in the past the blessings you received made the afflictions worthwhile, how much more should the reward before you, help you to endure the present hardships." The past blessings were the illumination by the Spirit, and inward assurance that they are children of God, and heir of God (v. 34). It is with this illumination that there begins the awareness of spiritual reality, and through it one enters into the life of the Spirit. The past sufferings were apparently severe. They included imprisonment, confiscation of property; and other persecutions. The reward before them now was the continued assurance of God's favor,

and the eternal inheritance and glory before them. The present sufferings are the excommunication from the synagogue and the strong appeal of the Judaizers for them to return to the Old Testament system.

3) The danger of drawing back to perdition, vv. 38,39. Here is one of the strongest evidences that one who has been justified by faith, could, by drawing back from following after God, be lost in perdition. But it is not necessary even in the most severe trouble if they continue to believe. (Faith is a continuing requirement, which becomes impossible when there is disobedience. There can not be pulling back and belief at the same time.)

II. The Christian Way of Life, 11:1-13:25

A. The Better Country, Chapter 11

In this chapter the writer shows that it was by faith, and not religious ceremony, that so many of the Old Testament heroes pleased God. The tabernacle with its furnishings and ceremonies was designed of God as object lessons to impart spiritual truth. But faith reaches beyond the things that are seen to those that are not seen. The definition of v. 1 makes this distinction, which must have greatly helped the Hebrew Christians to see the importance of looking beyond visible forms by faith.

The people who are listed in the chapter rested on the Word of God, in spite of the apparent impossibility of God's promises. Visible things were often in sharp opposition to what God promised, but they believed and received.

1. The series from Genesis, vv. 4-22. There are series here, as we shall classify them, and each gives some valuable types and illustrations of faith.

    a. Abel, the Faith that Saves, v. 4. Abel recognized his sin and the need of atonement, so he brought an offering of blood. By this he looked forward to Christ. Cain in contrast refused to acknowledge sin or need of blood sacrifice. He is like those today who preserve self esteem and have a works-centered religious program.

    Abel was justified by faith, and had God's witness to the same. So he illustrates saving faith, which still speaks to us today.

b. Enoch, the Faith that Sanctifies, vv. 5, 6. Here is progress beyond justification to full fellowship that walks in the light of God (I John 1:7). God witnessed that Enoch pleased Him. Enoch became a type of the church that is actively looking for the rapture (Jude 14), and God took him by translation. It is the pure in heart who are looking without fear, and are prepared to meet God as well as to walk in close fellowship here.

c. Noah, the Faith that Separates, v. 7. He lived for the future, believing God that all the present world was under sentence of death. There was a detachment from the world which none around him could embrace. He condemned the world, which is always a painful relationship. We must do the same if we would walk with God by faith. If we are conformed to this world, we are surely not separated unto God, and not watching eagerly for the coming of Christ.

d. Abraham, the Obedience of Faith, vv. 8-19. This is the longest biography in the group, for Abraham was the head of the Jewish nation. They looked back to him with admiration so it was good to show his faith. His life seems to comprehend all that is in the others.

   1) Faith separating, v. 8. He was called to leave his homeland, his kindred, and his father's house. But God had become so real to Abram that he willingly left all to follow God. He obeyed, not because he knew and understood the future, but because he believed God. Really, there is not any true faith if it does not obey God's Word.

   2) Faith sojourning, vv. 9, 10; vv. 13-16. Abraham was promised the land he should enter. Perhaps at first he thought possession would come quickly. But one of the vital lessons of faith is that of waiting. He waited 25 years for a son, and much longer than that for the land. In fact, not all of the promised land is possessed by Abraham's seed to this day. All Abram actually owned was the burial spot for Sarah, and that was bought with money. After much waiting Abram embraced the idea of a "better country" (See v. 16). Abraham and his sons were willing to live in tents, with no fixed dwelling, for they began to look for a

heavenly country. That would be the spiritual seed as "the stars of heaven."

God was not ashamed to take a man's name, and be called "the God of Abraham," because of such faith that waits and looks to the future.

3) Faith receiving seed, vv. 11-12. Note here that the whole process of that seed was supernatural. There could be no conception for Sarah after the course of nature. The conception and delivery were of miracle by faith. She reckoned on the faithfulness of God, against all symptoms and suggestions to the contrary.

Their natural, physical seed are like the sand of the sea. The spiritual seed are like the stars of heaven. It is true today that the new birth of a soul is entirely a supernatural process, by faith, and not by clever human programing.

Abraham let his name be changed to "Abraham" (Father of a multitude) before he had a son. He would be mocked at because of it, but he was willing, because he believed God.

4) Faith sacrificing, vv. 17-19. Here was the strongest test of faith. But Abraham knew God well enough to obey even when he could not understand. He declared his faith by asserting that he and Isaac would return from the mount of sacrifice. He reckoned that God would give a resurrection, which was granted "in a figure." He thus became an illustration of the death and resurrection of our Lord. On that same mountain the temple was later erected.

e. Isaac, the Faith that Suffers and is Patient, v. 20. It was a long process by which God brought this grasping, scheming, deceiver to a place where his name stood at the head of the nation, and the tribes were of his family. Not all of Abraham's sons were accepted, but all of Jacob's became heads of tribes, and their names will be on the gates of the New Jerusalem. It was faith that sustained Jacob through the loss of Joseph, and enabled him finally to see the two sons of Joseph. He learned by the things he suffered, and he became a prince with God. If Jacob could be so changed, there is hope for the fallen today!

- f. Joseph, the Faith that Turns Problems into Blessings, v. 22. He became a wondrous type of Christ, in his sufferings, not for his own sins, but for the sins of others. He looked to God in all of the fiery trial, and expected God to bring good from it, which He did! "Ye meant it for evil," he said to his brothers, "But God meant it for good" (Gen. 50:20).

2. The series from Egypt to Canaan, vv. 23-31.

   a. Faith for the family, Moses' parents, v. 23. Their son was under decree of death, but the parents believed God and planned to save the boy. They put him in an ark on the sea, trusting in God's mercy alone. God vindicated their faith. We should also claim our children for God, against all the plotting of the devil to destroy them. Pharaoh is a type of Satan, and he plans for the destruction of all our children in sin.

   b. Faith for personal choice, Moses', vv. 24-26. He had begun life with the force of a mother's prayers, but he had to make a personal choice whether to follow God or not. There was the way of affliction and the way of sinful pleasures: the reproach of Christ or the riches of Egypt. He chose the former, because he preferred eternal joys to momentary pleasures.

   c. Faith separating from the world, Moses', v. 27. This refers to the time when Moses was to lead the Children of Israel out of Egypt. There were delays, efforts at compromises, and reverses in apparent outcome. But Moses did not give up the cause to which God had called him. He did not agree to any of Pharaoh's subtle compromises, but demanded total separation of God's people from Egypt.

   We need men today who are strong to resist political pressure and the appeal of ease, money, and applause and stand strong for truth. They must be willing to receive anger, misrepresentation, and suffering for the sake of truth. This is the life of faith.

   d. Faith appropriating the blood of Christ, Moses', v. 28. The passover at the command of Christ was a clear type of the blood of Christ, shed on Calvary.

   e. Faith finding deliverance by the Word of God, Moses', v. 29. God brought them to the Red Sea and gave the command to go forward, and when they did so, there was a miraculous deliverance. This is a type of deliverance from sin, as we know.

    f. Faith claiming the inheritance, Joshua's (not mentioned), v. 30. We may notice that there is no reference to faith in the 40 years in the wilderness. For indeed those years were not years of faith, but of wandering and dying because of unbelief and disobedience. They illustrate the people who refuse to go on to holiness at Kadesh Barnea, and thus who backslide and die. Jericho is a type of the Holy Spirit, which is received by faith and obedience. Canaan is a type of the rest of faith in Christ.

    g. Faith that transforms the lowest sinner into a saint of God, Rahab, v. 31. It is very symbolic that after Jericho was taken, a Gentile person should be saved from death and enter into a life of faith in God. It is like the outreach of the church after Pentecost. When we are filled with the Spirit, we are expected to seek the lost and bring them to Jesus.

3. The summary of the great multitude of faithfulness, vv. 13, 39, 40.

    a. They had not yet received the promise. Abraham did not receive the Promised Land; he waited long for a son, and never did see the multitude of descendants. So we have not yet received our heavenly country.

    b. They saw afar off with the eye of faith, and were persuaded of the promises.

    c. They embraced the promises. This means the promises became very dear to them—the dearest treasures, which determined their attitude toward other things. They were willing to endure affliction, death, ridicule, and much more rather than relinquish the promises. This came as a powerful appeal to the Hebrew Christians, not to depend on the visible ceremonies of religion, but to hold to the invisible realities.

    d. They confessed that they were pilgrims. True faith leads to confession. Doubt leads to silence in many cases. "We having the same spirit of faith, according as it is written, I believed, and therefore have spoken; we also believe, and therefore speak" (II Cor. 4:13).

Let us maintain the profession of our faith, 10:23.

B. The Better Discipline, 12:1-17

With the great faith chapter as a background, the writer now shows the value of discipline in producing a mature faith. There is faith of assurance and there is faith of endurance. It is the latter which is particularly under consideration in this chapter. The word "chastening," which occurs several times, means "child-training" or "discipline."

1. The Example of Jesus, vv. 2-4. He passed over the same pathway of faith which we are called upon to traverse. He finished the course, showing that it is possible to do so by faith. He did so by faith, the same kind as ours.

    a. The joy before Him, v. 2. Impelling Him on was the hope of His eternal Kingship in Heaven, and the relation to the victorious church, as well as the approval of His Father who sent Him.

    b. The pain he endured—the cross, the shame, the darkness, the forsaking by the Father, the bloodshed, death and hell. There was the mockery of vile sinners, the forsaking by His disciples, and the turning away of God's face. How great was His sorrow, more than any others!

2. Sixth Admonition, to finish the race of faith, vv. 1-17. Here is the argument drawn from the case of Christ. Let us also run the race.

    a. The crisis of preparation, v. 1. There is to be a removal of weights, or hindrances, then there is to be a removal of sin which clings tightly to us. This is an apt description of the carnal mind. All worldliness, selfishness, materialism, and carnality oppose the race of faith, and must be removed.

    b. The continuance of endurance. The word "patience" in v. 1 means "endurance." This is a continuous process in which discipline comes to us from God.

        1) Their temptations during the race.

            a) To despise chastening or discipline, v. 5. They were in real danger of refusing to endure this discipline. Once they had joyfully endured, but they were now in danger of despising the training, maturing process.

b) To faint under chastening, vv. 3, 5. What God designs to bring us closer to Himself, some allow to take them father away. They will not endure.

2) The purposes of discipline.

a) The discovery of remaining sin in the heart, v.5. The word "rebuke" means to locate and condemn sin. It is the same word used of the Spirit in John 16:8. It is God's purpose to bring us into situations where we recognize sin and appeal for a remedy. The Psalmist welcomed such testing in 139:23, 24.

b) It is essential to the education of sons. We are under a great weight of ignorance, which is infirmity rather than sin. A person may be delivered from sin, but still be very ignorant. God wants to teach us, and this requires discipline.

c) That we may receive the impartation of His holiness, v. 10.

He who reveals our sin desires to remove the sin and give us His own holiness. Discipline alone will not accomplish this; however, it is designed to bring us to the place where we will receive His grace by faith.

d) That we may produce the peaceable fruits of righteousness, v. 11.

Here it is plainly stated that the discipline itself does not do the work of grace. It is designed to exercise us to faith; and to receive the grace of God.

3) The exercise to be induced by discipline, vv. 12-17.

a) They are to stir up themselves to diligence in faith. Isa. 35:3 is referred to. It is evident that the grace of God is not something unilaterally imposed on an elect number. God wants to impart grace, but we must stir ourselves to take hold of His help.

b) They are to walk straight themselves, so that they do not influence others to depart from the way. We have responsibility for ourselves, but we also have responsibility for those we may influence.

- c) They are to follow after peace and holiness, v. 14. There is a constant diligence necessary in this matter. Holiness is not only a grace received, but a life to be lived. If we would see the Lord, we must under-go the necessary life of discipline.

- d) They are to guard against apostasy, v. 15. Here again is a strong statement about falling from grace. It is such a danger that a person must watch diligently against it, not resting on a false doctrine of unconditional security.

- e) They are to guard against false teachers who shall draw away people into apostasy. This seems to be the meaning of the root of bitterness.

- f) Holiness is to be pursued as the safety against temptation or profanity, such as that of Esau. He bartered away his blessing for a temporary pleasure. The Christians are warned that they are in danger of doing the same. If they follow holiness carefully they will be strong against sin and backsliding.

  Just as Esau found no way to recover his birthright, there is an apostasy from which men can never recover. They were to take warning and avoid that at all costs!

C. The Better Fellowship, 12:18-24.

The Hebrew Christians had been cut off from the fellowship of the temple services. The writer is showing them how much superior the fellowship is which they now may enjoy. The section brings forth the contrast between the two Pentecosts, old and new. The Jews regarded the feast of Pentecost as being commemorative of the giving of the law on Sinai. As the law on Sinai gave to Israel national unity and purpose, so the outpouring of the Spirit gives spiritual unity and purpose to the Church. It is imperative that we know and experience the fellowship of this new dispensation.

There are seven earthly things under the old and seven heavenly things under the new which are brought into contrast.

1. The Old Dispensation, vv.18-21

   a. A mountain that could not be touched. That told of the distance between a holy God and sinful men.

b. A burning fire. This symbolized the holiness and majesty of God.

   c. A heavy cloud covering. God was hidden from view from the people.

   d. Intense darkness. There was fearfulness about that manifestation.

   e. A strong tempest, or thunderstorm. This added to the suggestion that the law was to inspire awe and reverence for the might and power of God.

   f. The sound of a trumpet. The trumpet called the attention of the people. All were to be impressed with this awesome revelation of the law of God.

   g. A terrifying voice of words. At this the people were most fearful, and even Moses "exceedingly feared and quaked." God was displaying His holiness and majesty, with which the people could not have any immediate communion whatever. The law produced no fellowship; it rather emphasized distance.

2. The New Dispensation, vv. 22-24

   a. The Heavenly Jerusalem. This is the city where God dwelled, and we are of this spiritual Mount Zion. It is free, whereas the former was a source of bondage. In coming direct to God's dwelling in the power of Pentecost we are made free from fear, sin, legalistic bondage, distance. This Jerusalem also is a mother; there is a fruitfulness when people enter into this liberty and immediacy of fellowship!

   b. To innumerable hosts of angels. While Satan and his hosts infect this world and would always delight to injure and defeat God's people, we know God's holy angels are here also, defending God's people, and ministering to them. There is a fellowship here, which will be understood better when we get to Heaven; but even now it is beneficial to us.

   c. The General Assembly and Church of the Firstborn. Their names are enrolled in Heaven, as Jesus said in Luke 10:20. The names of the oldest sons of Israel were enrolled in registers (Num. 3:42, 43), and here is the spiritual counterpart. In God's family all are firstborn, being in Christ, and they share with Him the rights of His inheritance. All are one in Him, since there is nothing of natural birth, position, ability, or family lineage which affect this inheritance.

d. To God the Judge of all. The Judge is our Father; we love Him and are in His Beloved Son. The Son has taken our sins on Himself, and we are justified in Him. What a loving relationship this produces!

e. To the spirits of just men made perfect. This seems to refer to those who have achieved that final, resurrection perfection. We are already one with them, and very possibly they watch with eagerness our progress in the race. We have loved ones who are there; let us press on to join them!

f. To Jesus the Mediator of the new covenant. We are in Him, the bridge between God and man. Our security and hope are in Him.

g. The blood of sprinkling. This is the ground of all the rest. While the blood cleanseth, we have fellowship (I John 1:7). This is the basis of the new covenant. Abel's blood cried for vengeance. Jesus' blood cries for reconciliation. He purchased us with His own blood. It speaks for us, assuring us of our acceptance in the Beloved, and that we are received and loved for Christ's sake. He died for us and we are in Him!

What a wonderful fellowship this is, with God, with angels, with the living church here, and in Heaven, and with Christ our Mediator! Let us treasure, preserve, and enlarge it!

D. The Better Service, 12:25-29; 13:20-21

1. The shaking of the temporary, v.27. The Hebrew Christians were burdened by the changes that were occurring; the persecutions, the excommunication, the loss of property. They were tempted to feel that God was forsaking them. The writer assures them that God is bringing them to that which is eternally true and permanent.

In every age there are changes which Christians are called to face: the destruction of the temple, removal of home, the scourge of warfare, the failure of friends, the loss of health, betrayal by those whom we have trusted. What do these things mean about God's faithfulness? The writer assures us, as He assured those Christians, that God intends for every shakeable thing to be shaken, that we may be brought to an unshakeable foundation.

God, our "consuming fire," is burning away from our lives everything that is fleshly, worldly, and chaffy.

Paul was one who had experienced the shaking process until he could face anything confidently. See his words of confidence in Phil. 4:11-13 and Romans 8:38, 39.

2. Grace for Acceptable Service, v. 28

    a. The attitude involved, "reverence and godly fear." Reverence involved a high regard for God's worthiness, of our very best service. Godly fear is not terror, but the greatest carefulness to please Him in all things.

    b. The God who perfects us, 13:20

        1) The God of peace. Peace is the putting in harmony of all disturbing, discordant elements. This term guarantees to us that God will put into perfect harmony all the elements of our nature, and bring all into harmony with Himself.

        2) The God of power. He brought from the dead our Lord Jesus, and this is the assurance of His power to deliver us from the clutches of sin. This is elaborated in Eph.1 and 2.

        3) The God of promise. The "everlasting covenant" is the new covenant we have already studied, which promises inward truthfulness, and an eternal inheritance among the sanctified.

    c. The perfection produced, v. 21

        1) It is positive as well as negative. Not only is there a removal of sin; there is a production of good works. This is God's purpose in saving us, as Paul declares in Phil. 2:13 and Eph. 2:10.

        2) It is perfection in God's sight. It is perfection to do His will, not necessarily without mistake, but without rebellion or resentment. God knows our frame, our natural limitations. He sees the attitude that is reverent and fearful, desiring supremely to please Him.

3) It is an inwrought perfection. God works in us to produce the desires, the strength, the motivation, and the peace.

E. The Seventh Admonition, and Final Exhortations, 12:25-13:25

1. Refuse not Him that speaketh from Heaven. Jesus now speaks through the Gospel system. If there was punishment for disobeying and scorning the law, how much more certain shall be the punishment of those who refuse the love and mercy shown to us through the Gospel. There was fear produced under the law. There is also a careful, godly fear to be produced under the gospel, not a casual sense of security that we will be eternally saved regardless of our conduct.

2. Maintain Christian human relationships, 13:1-7.

    a. Hospitality toward brethren, v. 1, 2. In those days there were few suitable inns or hotels for those who traveled. So it was often needful for Christians to open their homes and entertain strangers. They are urged to help one another, and so to express the love of Christ. There may be great blessings for the one entertaining, as there was for Abraham and Sarah.

    b. Sympathy for the afflicted ones, v. 3. Christians are to be sympathetic, doing for those oppressed as we would like to be treated in such a case. Christians often did send gifts, as Paul testified to the Philippians.

    c. Respect for the marriage bond, v. 4. There were people then, as now, who taught that marriage should not be allowed for those who wanted to be eminently holy. The writer contradicts such a notion, approving marriage in all. However, he also places limits of relations between persons of the opposite sex, limiting such to the marriage bond. Marriage is God's ordinance, and those who violate it, either by prohibiting it or by allowing sex relations outside its bounds, are condemned of God.

    d. Contentment, vv. 5, 6.

        1) The avoidance of covetousness. The Bible places strong condemnation on this sin, ranking it as idolatry. Covetousness involves the craving for things—a desire

to have more and more—until there is no satisfaction without them.

    2) The pledge of God's provision. Here is a jewel of assurance from God. There are five negatives in the original. It might be translated, "No, I will never leave thee; not I: I will never, never cast thee off." This must have come as a gracious assurance to those Christians who had been cut off from temple worship, and had been deprived of their goods.

    3) The affirmation we can make as a consequence. The word which God spoke to Joshua, David and Solomon, "The Lord is my helper; I will not fear what man can do unto me." This is God's cure for worry. Our God will never leave us, or forget to provide what is best for us, as we trust in Him. Let us always remember this!

  e. Remembrance of teachers and guides, vv. 7, 17.

    1) Those who have departed, v. 7. We are to consider the end of their life, how they died, giving up their lives for Christ. The enduring faith of the martyrs should be an encouragement and stimulus to the faith of those who follow behind them.

    2) Those who still live, v. 17. God has placed spiritual rulers in the Church; and so long as they rule in the fear of God, they are to be respected. They are to teach the "word of God" (v. 7) and not their own ideas. Their purpose is not to advance their own ends, but to watch for the souls of those under their care. They are acting so as to be ready to give account of their stewardship. If any do not follow these principles, they are not worthy of rule. Teachers are to be obeyed, not from their own merits, but as they fulfill these requirements.

3. Attachment to the Unchanging Christ, 8-14. He is eternal, divine, and immutable. He is the anchor for faith, and the encouragement for perseverance. He was the true "Lamb of God" undergirding the old sacrifices. He is the Mediator now, and will be in the throne of God eternally, as the "Lamb slain from the foundation of the world" (Rev. 5:6).

  a. We should not be moved by novel and changeable doctrines. This warns against a fickle, vacillating spirit, taking whatever doctrine offers the greatest novelty or hope of personal gain. Some people use doctrine as a convenience, following whatever teaching offers them personal gain.

The grace of Christ is unchanging, and it meets the needs of the heart. It has been shown that beasts—their blood and their flesh when eaten—did not profit the comers in their hearts, where the lasting need is. From now on the emphasis is the satisfaction of the needs of the heart. Christ has provided that through His grace.

   b. We must go unto Him, "without the camp." The Hebrew Christians had been urged to come back to the Jewish ceremonies and the altar sacrifices. So the writer shows that our true altar is without the camp of Jewish ceremony. The cross of Jesus (our true altar) was outside the gate, in order to sanctify His people. Therefore we should be willing to leave the camp (the ceremonies of the established religion) and join Jesus in His reproach and sanctifying purpose.

If these Christians should be driven from Jerusalem, from all temple privileges, and even all property rights, they are only giving up what is temporary. The permanent values abide in Christ, and we have them in Him. "Here we have no continuing city. . . ."

4. The offering of spiritual sacrifices, vv. 15, 16. Following out the comparison, the writer shows that we have sacrifices to offer, as well as an altar.

   a. The sacrifice of praise, the fruit of our lips. As there were continual offerings under the old dispensation, so there is a continual offering of praise to God under the new. They offered the fruit of the land or of the block; now we offer the "fruit of our lips." Praise form the heart is acceptable unto God.

   b. Communication to others. We are to be benevolent, helping those who are needy, and sharing what we have in the name of Christ. This pleases God, for it shows Christlikeness. Christ gave Himself, and if we share His love, we will give of ourselves to help others.

5. Appeal for prayer, v. 18, 19. This sounds like such an appeal as Paul might make, and is one argument for his authorship. He gives as his reason for making such an appeal that his conscience is pure before God, and that he wants to be removed from the present hindrance (perhaps prison) and be brought to them the sooner. If the writer always needed prayer, surely we do also—at all times.

III. Conclusion

A. Summary of the epistle: "A word of exhortation." The final appeal is that they permit and receive it.

B. The reference to Timothy. It seems that Timothy was sent away on some errand, and that when he returned, the writer, with Timothy, would visit the Hebrew Christians.

C. Final salute, showing that the writer was in Italy, and that there were saints there. Probably he was in Rome, and in prison.

This epistle is ever so important to show the true and proper relation between the Old Testament and New Testament system. We could never have a full view of the subject without this book.

Review Questions
HEBREWS

1. State three persons who have been suggested as authors of Hebrews and give reasons for each.
2. Give one good reason why Paul is often believed not to be the author.
3. Give two facts within the epistle which help us locate the probable date when the epistle was written.
4. What is the probable date of writing?
5. To whom was the epistle probably written?
6. What was the historical background of the epistle?
7. Why was the epistle written?
8. What key word have we used to divide the outline of our study?
9. In addition to the primary "key word," what are some other important words used often in the book?
11. The author gives seven great facts about the superiority of Christ and His revelation. What are they?
12. What is signified by the statement that Jesus "sat down at the right hand" of God?
13. Give five reasons why Christ is to be considered greater than the angels. What means does the author use to prove this superiority?
14. How many great admonitions are given in Hebrews?
15. State five ways in which our salvation is considered to be great in this epistle?
16. Against what are the readers warned in the first admonition?
17. What is meant by the fact that man, in the beginning, was crowned with "glory and honor?"
18. Why did Jesus become lower than the angels? (Chapter 2 suggests at least two outstanding reasons.)
19. In the subject "The Better Leader," with whom is Christ compared?
20. In what ways is Christ considered to be greater than Moses?
21. Show how that from each of the first two admonitions it is possible for a person to depart from Christ and thus be in danger of losing his salvation.
22. What four rests are discussed in Chapters 3 and 4?
23. In what way is each of the four rests related to sin in the heart?
24. What is involved in keeping the Sabbath holy unto the Lord, according to Isaiah 58?
25. How do the wicked tribes of Canaan represent sin in the heart?
26. Did Joshua give the people rest when they entered Canaan? Explain your answer.

27. Why were the people of Israel not willing to enter Canaan at Kadesh Barnea?
28. How does the author use Ps. 9:7-11 to show that there is still a rest for the people of God?
29. Describe the "Divine rest" which remains for the people of God.
30. How is the ministry of the Word (Heb. 4:12-13) related to the divine rest?
31. Explain the figure of speech used in Heb. 4:13-14.
32. Give the seven outstanding characteristics of Christ's priesthood.
33. Give three evidences that Melchizedek was greater than Aaron.
34. What important fact does the author bring forth from his reference to Melchizedek?
35. Since Christ has come, what has happened to the old order of Priesthood?
36. For what reason is Jesus able to save us to the uttermost (7:25)?
37. The thought of perfection in Hebrews contains two main ideas. What are they?
38. What is the difference between the "full assurance of faith" and the "full assurance of hope?"
39. In the fourth admonition, what were the symptoms which revealed the danger of apostasy?
40. Explain what is meant by a covenant.
41. What does the writer mean by the "First Covenant?"
42. Show four ways in which the First Covenant was defective.
43. From what Old Testament writer does the Hebrew author take the New Covenant?
44. State the four great facts about the New Covenant.
45. Show how the New Covenant requires cleansing from sin in the heart.
46. In discussing "The Better Sacrifice," what two Old Testament offerings are considered?
47. For what two reasons did the priest go into the Holy of Holies?
48. What was the function of the two goats?
49. What was the significance of the ashes of the heifer?
50. What reason does the author give for making an appeal for prayer?